The Comeback Kid

THE COMEBACK KID

The Life and Career of Bill Clinton

by Charles F. Allen
and Jonathan Portis

A Birch Lane Press Book
Published by Carol Publishing Group

A Birch Lane Press Book
Published by Carol Publishing Group
Birch Lane Press is a registered trademark of Carol Communications, Inc.
Editorial Offices: 600 Madison Avenue, New York, N.Y. 10022
Sales & Distribution Offices: 120 Enterprise Avenue, Secaucus, N.J. 07094
In Canada: Canadian Manda Group, P.O. Box 920 Station U, Toronto, Ontario M8Z 5P9
Queries regarding rights and permissions should be addressed to Carol Publishing Group,
600 Madison Avenue, New York, N.Y. 10022

Carol Publishing Group books are available at special discounts for bulk purchases, for
sales promotions, fund raising, or educational purposes. Special editions can be created
to specifications. For details contact: Special Sales Department, Carol Publishing Group,
120 Enterprise Avenue, Secaucus, N.J. 07094

Manufactured in the United States of America
10   9   8   7   6   5   4   3   2   1

Library of Congress Cataloging-in-Publication Data

Allen, Charles F. (Charles Flynn)
    The comeback kid : the life and career of Bill Clinton / by
Charles F. Allen and Jonathan Portis.
        p.   cm.
    Cover title: The life and career of Bill Clinton.
    Includes bibliographical references.
    ISBN 1-55972-154-5
    1. Clinton, Bill, 1946–   . 2. Presidential candidates—United
States—Biography.   3. Governors—Arkansas—Biography.
4. Presidents—United States—Election—1992.   I. Portis, Jonathan.
II. Title.   III. Title: Life and career of Bill Clinton.
E840.8.C57A44   1992
973.928'092—dc20
    [B]   92-19745
                                                                CIP

Contents

Foreword

THIS BOOK HAD ITS GENESIS IN A GRADUATE SEMINAR I CONDUCTED at the University of Mississippi in the spring of 1988. The principal purpose of the seminar was to stimulate the doctoral candidates to generate ideas about possible topics for dissertations. Remembering my own experience in the 1950s as a student, faculty member and assistant provost at Teachers College, Columbia University, I concluded that the best approach was simply to engage the seminar group in brainstorming sessions, during which the candidates were encouraged to draw upon their own experiences to think up ideas that reflected their interests and their familiarity with education problems and with people who had demonstrated unusual leadership in dealing with these complex problems. Examples of this kind of educational leadership I remember citing were those of ex-Governor William Winter of Mississippi, who pioneered in educational reform from 1980 to 1984, and Governor Bill Clinton of Arkansas, who also launched massive improvement strategies for the educational program of Arkansas in the 1980s.

One of the participants in my seminar was Charles Flynn Allen, a seasoned educator who had served as teacher, high school principal, school superintendent, county supervisor and educational administrative supervisor for the Arkansas Department of Education. He had led and conducted numerous studies of high schools that were seeking accreditation by the North Central Association. Allen picked up on my suggestion that Governor Clinton would be an excellent subject for biographical study in a dissertation, with special focus on his work in improving the public schools of Arkansas.

My interest in Clinton's biography is also grounded in my association with the Center for the Study of Southern Culture, a research organization with which I have been involved since its inception. No aspect of Southern culture is beyond the concern of the center, which is headquartered on the campus of the University of Mississippi. It is impossible to enhance the cultural aspirations of a people without improving their educational opportunities. Basic to the sustenance and uplifting of a democracy is the quality of education and its availability to all. Governor Clinton's experience and leadership in improving Arkansas education was bold and extensive, contributing to his recognition as one of the foremost educational leaders in the United States.

There have been a half-dozen or so mileposts of U.S. education in the twentieth century, and one of the most recent is the placement of public education high on the agenda of governors across the country. Few other governors, if any, have sustained effective interest and attention in educational matters over as long a period of time as Governor Clinton.

Among those who know what good education is all about, Governor Clinton ranks near the top. Perhaps no presidential candidate since Woodrow Wilson has been as well versed in educational issues as Bill Clinton. His undergraduate education at Georgetown University was a virtual laboratory for the observation and study of government and public service. His experience as a Rhodes scholar at Oxford University gave him the intensive international perspective so vital for leaders in the world of today and tomorrow. Subsequent education at the Yale Law School introduced Bill Clinton to the legal system of the United States with a comprehensiveness few other law schools could have matched.

Governor Clinton's rapid rise through the Arkansas political system, capped by his reelection several times as governor, demonstrates the trust that the people of his home state have in him and helps to explain why he is worthy of a biographical study. His accomplishments, the same accomplishments that led to his becoming a presidential candidate, merit being recorded at mid-life; thus the monumental undertaking of Charles Allen to illuminate and synthesize Governor Clinton's life, with particular reference to his effective efforts in school reform.

The research of Charles Allen was a meticulous undertaking, well suited to the qualities and experience Allen brought with him to the writing table. Penning a biography while the subject is alive tends to make complete objectivity impossible. The advantage is in being able to get at contemporary sources that would otherwise be difficult, if not impossible, the get hold of. Charles Allen was conscious of these problems and made the most of the opportunity to record for posterity the life of a person still active in public life. Like most doctoral candidates, Allen did not have the luxury of unlimited time. But he managed his research and writing skillfully, with determination and vigor.

Allen's coauthor, Jonathan Portis, is a native Arkansan and an experienced editor at both the *Arkansas Gazette* in Little Rock and Memphis's *Commercial Appeal*. His newspaper career has paralleled the political career of Bill Clinton, offering him the chance to observe the sweep of the governor's lifework. He has helped transform the dissertation's narrative from an intellectual treatise into a dynamic and moving story of Bill Clinton the man, whose contributions to his state may soon be extended to a national and global perspective.

> Franklin E. Moak
> Professor of Higher Education
> and Adjunct Professor
> of Southern Studies
> University of Mississippi
> Oxford, Mississippi
> April 1992

Preface

A COMPREHENSIVE BIOGRAPHY OF ARKANSAS GOVERNOR WILLIAM Jefferson Clinton would require volumes, if only to cover his years of work with the Arkansas General Assembly.

This biography is a thorough examination of a man who dreamed of being president of the United States from his earliest days. The constraints of time and space compel us to compress, or even eliminate, much of his dealings with the state legislature. We shall leave that to future writers with a more specific focus.

The centerpiece of this biography is Governor Bill Clinton's education program, specifically his reforms of 1983 and the methods by which they were accomplished. While we believe them to be his most significant achievements to date, we think they also provide insight into the complex inner workings of a shrewd and determined politician. The education battle was one of the furnaces in which Clinton's political mettle was tempered.

The authors are grateful to the *Arkansas Democrat-Gazette* for allowing us to quote liberally from the news columns of that newspaper and its predecessors, the *Arkansas Democrat* and the *Arkansas Gazette*. John Robert Starr was most kind to allow us to quote from his book *Yellow Dogs and Dark Horses*, as was David Osborne, whose book *Laboratories of Democracy* provided invaluable insight into newly emerging theories of politics. We are also indebted to the following people for allowing us to conduct interviews: U.S. Senator Dale Bumpers, U.S. Senator David Pryor, former U.S. Senator J. William Fulbright, Patty Howe Criner, state Senator Lu Hardin, state Senator Morril Harriman Jr., Sid Johnson, Cora McHenry, Virginia Kelley, Governor Ray Mabus of Mississippi, Sheffield Nelson, Dr. Paul Root, Billy Simpson, Virgil M. Spurlin, Carolyn Staley, Strobe Talbott, Lieutenant Governor Jim Guy Tucker, Dr. Tommy Venters, Betsey Wright and, of course, Governor Bill Clinton and Hillary Rodham Clinton. Immeasurable assistance was provided by Jack Bass, Virginia Anne Allen, Sherry Kinyon Portis, Dr. Franklin E. Moak, Dr. Kathy Van Laningham and Judy Gaddy.

The Comeback Kid

1

A Sense of Mortality

THERE IS A DIGNIFIED OLD BUILDING IN DOWNTOWN LITTLE ROCK known as the Old State House. It was Arkansas's first capitol, remaining in use from 1836 to 1914, when a larger one was built.

The Old State House sits on a rise above the Arkansas River and faces the financial district of downtown Little Rock. Primarily a museum now, it is sometimes used for ceremonial functions. With its gleaming white columns, crowning oak trees and iron fence, it looks more like an old Southern mansion than a government building. In fact, it vaguely resembles the White House.

At noon on October 3, 1991, Governor Bill Clinton of Arkansas would announce his candidacy for president while standing on the steps of the Old State House.

Shortly before 9 A.M. on that day, a bright, warm Thursday, Bill Clinton jogged alone down the sidewalk in front of the Old State House. A few reporters and photographers were standing nearby when Clinton came running down Markham Street and turned up Spring Street. The reporters approached him, but he waved them away, shouting on the run that he wanted to finish his three-mile jaunt.

"I don't know how many more mornings I'll have like this, and I wanted to spend this one like I normally do," he said. The photographers snapped pictures of Clinton in his T-shirt ("The

3

Jacksons Tour," it said) and ill-fitting gym shorts as he chugged by. A well-wisher who had reached out to shake the governor's hand suddenly lost his balance and fell backward. The governor stopped, helped the man to his feet and made sure the man was not hurt. Clinton then headed further downtown, dodging the cars and eventually vanishing. Few people took notice. It was a common sight to see the governor running alone on the sidewalks and streets of downtown Little Rock.

A three-miler was quite a distance for an overweight forty-five-year-old governor, but it was nothing for Bill Clinton. He had been running after one thing or another all of his life.

* * *

In 1946, fate conspired against William Jefferson Blythe III and his young wife, Virginia Cassidy Blythe. Like all young couples, they were planning a storybook existence—family, togetherness, enough money to live comfortably and quietly.

Their romance had begun in the early 1940s, when Virginia was a nurse in training at Tri-State Hospital in Shreveport, Louisiana, just south of the Arkansas border. Blythe, at twenty-seven, was a tall, handsome man from Sherman, Texas, with a promising career in automobile sales in Shreveport. The couple met at the hospital, where Blythe had come for a visit with a friend. Virginia later described it as love at first sight.

William Blythe and Virginia Cassidy were soon married, but World War II separated the couple for three years when Blythe went into the service. The storybook dreams were put on hold.

When the war ended, Blythe found himself in the same position as millions of other veterans—with little money and no work. After a search, he landed a job in Chicago selling heavy construction equipment. Chicago was thousands of miles away from Shreveport and required him to travel around the midsection of America.

"He'd be maybe two or three hundred miles away and drive in every night to keep me from being alone," Virginia said in a later interview.

William Blythe's responsibilities soon increased: His wife was pregnant. Blythe spent most of his time on the road and could not be with her. They agreed that she should move in with her parents in Hope, Arkansas, until he could set up a permanent residence for them. Blythe knew he had to do something fast to keep his family intact. So he bought a house in Chicago and made plans to move Virginia there.

Virginia was six months pregnant when Blythe climbed into his car to drive from Chicago to Arkansas to pick her up and start a new life with his new family.

He never made it. The dream ended on Highway 61 in the town of Sikeston, Missouri, when Blythe's car left the highway and crashed into a ditch. He was knocked unconscious and drowned in only a few inches of water.

Three months later, on August 19, 1946, William Jefferson Blythe IV was born in Hope, a farming town in an area called the Ark-La-Tex, where the borders of the states of Arkansas, Louisiana and Texas meet. This area was a historic crossroads for frontier travelers.

It wasn't long before family members were calling the boy "Bill" and "Billy," the names his father had also carried. Virginia said her son's physical appearance—his hands, the way he sometimes gestured with his head—reminded her of his father.

The economic conditions of the 1940s made it impossible for a woman to support a child alone. Virginia left Billy at Hope with her parents, the Cassidys, while she pursued further training as a nurse-anesthetist at Charity Hospital in New Orleans. She planned to advance her career to a point where she could be self-sufficient and raise her child.

Billy remained with his grandparents in Hope for more than two years in a lower-middle-class environment. The boy's grandfather, who owned a small grocery store in the black section of town, believed in education and was a strong influence on his grandson. His grandmother instilled a strict sense of discipline in the young boy.

Bill remembers that his grandparents "had a lot to do with my early commitment to learning." He said they taught him "to count and read. I was reading little books when I was three. They didn't have much formal education, but they really helped imbed in me a real sense of educational achievement, which was reinforced at home." Family members remember young Billy Blythe reading the newspaper in the first grade.

The grandparents also instilled in him the potent fervor of the

Southern brand of Christianity and gave him early training in Bible study. The boy's other grandparents, his father's parents, were no longer alive when he was born.

While in Hope, Bill became friends with Thomas F. "Mack" McLarty, who would come back into his life later and who would become an influential Arkansan and chairman of Arkla, Inc., a huge natural gas conglomerate. Virginia says the two have never lost touch and always introduce each other as "my oldest friend." Even in his first years of life, Bill had an uncanny ability to bond with people who would become powerful and influential.

*   *   *

After finishing her training in New Orleans, Virginia returned to Hope. When Bill was four, Virginia married Roger Clinton, a car dealer. After Bill's seventh birthday, the family moved to Hot Springs, where Roger Clinton worked at a Buick dealership and Virginia took a job as a nurse-anesthetist at a hospital. Virginia Kelley (her name by marriage today) says she and her parents recognized Bill's special talents early in his life. Even the house-keeper who took care of Bill when he was in the second grade recognized in him the ability to lead. "She prayed that he'd be a minister, because she could see his leadership qualities," Kelley said. "She'd say, 'Have you ever thought about it?'—how he could lead people to Christ."

Although he and his family were devout Southern Baptists, Bill attended a Catholic school, St. John's, in the second grade at Hot Springs. His mother decided this school would provide a smoother transition from the smaller Hope public schools to the much larger Hot Springs public school system.

Kelley recalls a problem Bill had at the Catholic school. One day he came home with a perfect report card except for a *D* in conduct. When Kelley went to St. John's to see the teacher, she was told, "Why, there's no real problem; it's just that...he is so sharp and he's so alert...he knows the answer immediately and will not give the others a chance....I have to get his attention one way or the other. And this is the only way I know to do it, because he is so competitive he will not be able to stand this *D*." "And," Kelley adds, "it worked." She noted that her son was always fiercely competitive. Two years later, at age nine, Bill switched to Ramble Elementary, a public school.

Through his early school days, he was known as Bill Clinton or Billy Clinton, although he did not legally change his name until he was fifteen. He later said he took his stepfather's name because he wanted to bring solidarity to a troubled family. When Bill was ten, Virginia and Roger had a son, whom they named Roger Clinton Jr.

Hot Springs was both famous and infamous when Bill Clinton was growing up. On the surface it appeared to be a quiet, Southern resort city surrounded by lakes and mountains. It was known for the restorative effects of its natural hot springs, and people came from all over the world to take the baths.

But Hot Springs was really a gambling mecca stuck in the middle of the Bible Belt. Gambling was, and is, illegal in Arkansas. But since the turn of the century, state and local officials had looked the other way while clubs in Hot Springs operated wide-open casinos and slot machines throughout the town. It was an exciting and dangerous town that attracted glamorous figures from Hollywood and notorious mobsters from Chicago and New York. The city's nightclubs offered top-name entertainment. Few other small towns in America could match it for its cosmopolitan mixture.

Bill Clinton, steeped in stern Baptist discipline, had little contact with this exotic world, although his parents frequented the casinos. (The open gambling came to an abrupt halt in 1967 when a new governor, Winthrop Rockefeller, ordered illegal gambling shut down.)

The town retained a first-rate thoroughbred horse track, Oaklawn Park, where pari-mutuel betting is legal. Bill Clinton's mother still plays the two-dollar windows. She is, however, an outspoken opponent of legalizing other forms of gambling in Hot Springs, a topic that is much discussed in the town.

Although Bill Clinton lived outside the heady swirl and danger of the casinos, he had to wrestle with increasing violence within his own household. He was forced to come to grips with the stormy relationship between his mother and stepfather. Roger Clinton Sr. was a heavy drinker with a mean streak. He and Virginia had a volatile relationship, frequently separating. Today, Kelley admits openly that Roger Clinton was an alcoholic—"a wonderful man, but alcoholic," she says.

Because of his stepfather's troubles, young Bill Clinton experienced plenty of ugly incidents in his home when he was a young man. Once, Roger Clinton Sr. even fired a gun inside the house.

Such violence was intermittent, but it began to wear on the young Bill Clinton. It finally came to a point of confrontation when he was fourteen. His stepfather had been fighting with his mother and his younger brother. It was more than Bill Clinton could bear. He grabbed his mother and his brother and placed himself between them and the angry, drunken stepfather.

"You will never hit either of them again," he shouted. "If you want them, you'll have to go through me."

Roger Clinton Sr.'s violence at home stopped, although the drinking never did. Bill Clinton's mother and stepfather separated many times, but always reconciled.

Virginia Kelley emphasizes that Bill loved his stepfather, but hated the demons that controlled the man. She feels Bill's memory of his stepfather is a continuing influence as far as alcohol is concerned. "I don't guess I've ever seen Bill take a drink of hard liquor," Virginia Kelley said. "I've seen him take a beer at a social gathering or in the hot summertime when we're out on the lake."

Virginia was an adoring mother whose relationship with her boys was especially close. However, her job as a nurse-anesthetist took her away from the home at odd hours. She often was on twenty-four-hour call for surgery.

When Bill was seven, Roger Clinton Sr. bought a farm outside of town and Virginia found a housekeeper to care for the boys while she and her husband worked. When he was older, Bill Clinton and his friends would find themselves in the role of baby-sitter for Roger Jr., who was ten years younger than Bill. Clinton's mother says he took care of his younger brother because he wanted to, not because he had to. Even though the family had a housekeeper to watch the boys, young Bill "just took the responsibility," Kelley said.

* * *

The family bought its first television set in 1956, when Bill Clinton was nine years old. The glowing machine was to have an immeasurable effect on the impressionable boy. He immediately became fascinated while watching the 1956 political conventions.

"I think it sort of came home to me in a way on television that it wouldn't have otherwise," Clinton has said. Already an avid reader, he had been poring over the newspapers for years. But television was different. It brought a sense of immediacy and participation to Bill Clinton. He watched in awe as John F. Kennedy and Estes Kefauver fought for the vice presidential nomination during the Democratic convention.

In 1963, the summer that Bill Clinton turned seventeen, he again was exposed to politics, this time at Boys State, a camp where high school boys and girls learned the electoral process by joining fictitious parties and running for office. It was the perfect laboratory for Bill Clinton. His old friend, Mack McLarty, was elected governor of the fictitious state. But Bill Clinton was shooting higher. He wanted to be elected a delegate to Boys Nation, which meant a trip to Washington and a chance to participate in the real thing. He won the election.

The delegates to Boys Nation made the rounds of Washington, D.C., visiting politicians' offices and the historic sites. Clinton dined in the Senate dining room with Senator J. William Fulbright, a Democrat from Arkansas who was chairman of the powerful Senate Foreign Relations Committee.

The boys also went to the White House. When President John F. Kennedy walked outside to greet the boys, Bill Clinton was ecstatic. Here was his idol, standing only a few feet away. Clinton walked up to the president and shook hands with him. That hot July day in 1963 was a turning point for Bill Clinton. He had entertained thoughts of becoming a Baptist minister, or possibly a musician or teacher. Now he knew he would become a politician.

Four months later, President John F. Kennedy was assassinated in Dallas.

"Shaking hands with John Kennedy and sitting in the Senate dining room with Senator Fulbright, whom he admired, that touched him," said Patty Howe Criner, a Little Rock real estate agent who grew up in Hot Springs with Clinton and later worked on his staff in the governor's office.

Clinton's mother said her son told her when he returned from Washington that he was determined to enter politics.

"When he came back from Washington, holding this picture of himself with Jack Kennedy, and the expression on his face, I knew right then that politics was the answer for him," Kelley said.

Clinton believes the experience of Boys State and Boys Nation changed his life. Just being elected a delegate was an accomplishment, he said.

"I didn't know if I could win a race like that," Clinton said, "because when I was a student politician [in high school], I was about as controversial as I have been in my later life. I was not one of these guys who won all of his races. And I wasn't always universally popular."

Though he had been president of his junior class, Clinton got an early taste of political defeat when he became a senior at Hot Springs High School. He was running for senior class secretary against his good friend Carolyn Staley. Staley recalls that the future governor said to her outside the auditorium where the balloting was going on, "If you beat me, I'll never forgive you." She did beat him, but the two remain friends today.

Staley remembers that Clinton was always competitive in high school. "He had to be the class leader. He had to be the best in the band. He had to be the best in his class, in grades. And he wanted to be in the top in anything that put him at the forefront of any course."

One example of his aggressiveness concerns an incident Staley says Clinton's mother related to her. "He ran in and he was holding his paper and he was just screaming, 'I beat Jim McDougal on a math test!'" McDougal, Staley said, was "a math-science genius in our class. And we were blessed with a lot of those, so that the competition in our high school was fierce."

Bill had another major interest in his early life—music. He was a leader in the Hot Springs High School Band. In his high school senior yearbook, Bill Clinton is pictured blowing his saxophone in a jazz combo with two classmates, Joe Newman and Randy Goodrum, all wearing dark glasses. Classmates later remembered the group, Three Blind Mice, as "not bad." Of the three, only Goodrum went on to a music career, becoming a highly regarded songwriter in Nashville and Los Angeles.

Criner said Clinton had a fine tenor voice and that he loved to cruise around town doing Elvis Presley imitations. His rendition of "Love Me Tender" was especially good, she recalled. "Bill wanted to be a musician long before he wanted to be a politician," Criner added.

When Clinton was in high school, he participated in other activities. He worked at Levi Hospital, a nonprofit treatment and research center. He also was active in DeMolay, a civic organization that develops leadership in young people. He was initiated into the Hot Springs chapter in 1961 and went on to win its most prestigious awards. In 1988, DeMolay International inducted Clinton into its Hall of Fame.

Clinton was also president of the high school version of the Kiwanis civic club called the Key Club and the scholastic honor group known as the Beta Club. He was a member of the National Honor Society, composed of top scholars across the country. Clinton was regarded as a standout student, friendly and brainy. He was a National Merit Scholarship semifinalist, putting him among the nation's academic elite. Out of a class of 323, Clinton finished fourth.

Criner remembers that Bill's teachers were among his best friends in high school. "You know how students who are really active in clubs and organizations and still have good grades maintain close relationships with their teachers," Criner said. "These are the people who have an interest in education and who love learning. His closest friends were his schoolteachers. I mean in every campaign I have ever worked in with Bill, teachers who are older now have sent him their money every time. They've written him letters of support. He went back and visited with— during the attorney general's race—several of the teachers who taught him at Hot Springs High School to say, 'Here's what I'm doing. What do you think I need to say?' and talk about issues because he was so involved in the school program then."

Clinton had an early jump on impressing his teachers. In a political campaign years later, a Clinton worker canvassing for votes telephoned a nun who had taught Clinton at the Catholic elementary school. The nun told the Clinton campaign worker that Clinton could be "anything he wants to be; and if he wants to be president, then he's going to be president." The campaign worker then asked the nun for her support for Clinton, and the nun replied: "My goodness, you've had my support since he was in the second grade."

One of Clinton's former high school teachers, Dr. Paul Root, now dean of the College of Education at Ouachita Baptist University at Arkadelphia, Arkansas, recalls Clinton as a bright student in his tenth-grade world history class. At that time, students were grouped by ability, and the class contained about eighteen to twenty "extremely bright" students. "While he was an excellent student," Root said, "he was not the only one in the class." But Root recalls one trait that did single Clinton out from the other students. Clinton "was a serious student, but he was playful in terms of dealing with the subject matter. He had fun with the class. It wasn't just 'I've got to do this because it's required.' He enjoyed what we were doing."

Root also remembers that Clinton, even in high school, "knew what he wanted to do" and was involved in school politics. "He had a direction already set, it appeared."

Criner remembers that fellow students, as well as teachers, liked Clinton. "People really looked up to Bill as a leader," she said. Criner also said Clinton's mother told her that "he always had the girls carrying his books home for him after school, and he'd be giving lectures and talking to them about things they'd learned at school."

The governor's closest high school friends, bonded by music, were Carolyn Staley, a talented classical singer today; Paul David Leopoulos, now in the computer business at Little Rock; and Joe Newman, one of the Three Blind Mice, who now works for an insurance agency. Clinton also enjoyed playing backyard basketball and football, going to movies and playing folk music. About his athletic ability, McLarty recalled that Clinton was "not quite as coordinated as perhaps he would like to remember."

Staley lived next door to the Clinton family during high school. They rode to school together, with Clinton driving his car and she and the others paying him a total of two dollars a week for gas. She was his accompanist on the piano when he played saxophone in band competitions.

"Our friendship included our love for music and the fact that we both had younger brothers and sisters and that they were friends and we took care of them some," Staley said. "We were both Baptist kids. We both had in common our love for government and sense of leadership. We were both achievers."

Staley recalls that Clinton's relationship with his brother Roger was almost parental. Because his mother often left for her hospital job before the boys were awake, Bill had to get his younger brother out of bed, dressed and off to school. "Bill was forced into an independence early, which I think has bearing on his leadership," Staley said.

Criner also remembers Bill as being independent from an early age. "I can remember Bill Clinton's mother taking him to the hospital in the middle of the night when she'd have to go do a case, and she'd wrap him up asleep...take him in the hospital, and he'd sleep there. I can remember Bill as a kid going to Park Place Baptist Church, and he'd walk down the street every Sunday morning going to church by himself."

Clinton took care to include his brother in many of his activities. Toward Roger Clinton Jr., Staley recalls, he had a "sense of love, of concern for this young man, the sense of 'I want the best for you.' Roger would go with Bill and me lots of places...and it was a sense of fatherly love, brotherly love...I'm going to put you under my wing. I'm going to make sure that you have the very best in life, and I'm not going to leave you home alone." Staley later added, "You go back to what motivates a person to take risks in leadership, and I think a lot of it is love.

"Bill has always cared so much about people," Criner said. She remembered the time one Thanksgiving when Clinton's mother sent him down to a little corner grocery store to pick up some items. "There was a kid sitting on a bench in front of the grocery store," Criner recalled, "and the kid—I don't know whether Bill knew him—but he sat down to visit with him, and the kid didn't have anyplace to go for Thanksgiving. Bill brings the kid home."

Concern for close friends also was evident. An evening spent talking with a friend became more important to the young Clinton than going out on a date. As a child and teenager, Clinton was overweight and didn't slim down and become known as "good-looking" until his late teens and early twenties, although his friends say he did date.

Clinton remains close to childhood friends today; and Staley,

Leopoulos, Newman and Clinton try to get together for lunch or dinner once a month when Clinton is not campaigning. They say it is a time to laugh and joke and remember old times, and add that they do not discuss politics. They might play the board game Trivial Pursuit or gather around the piano.

As a governor and presidential candidate working long hours, Clinton says he misses having time to be with friends:

> When I was a kid, I thought I was busier than anybody else I knew. But there still seemed to be worlds of time to just kind of be with people. I don't get to do that much anymore. It's [time with friends] a very important part of my life. A person in public life, you know, they just see you sort of in snippets on television or in the newspaper or something. And you can—if you're not careful—you come across like a machine, and if you're not careful, you wind up being one, if all you do, if there's nothing to you but your work.

Though it was a tough call for a teenager in the rock 'n' roll sixties, Clinton chose politics over music. Upon graduation from high school, Clinton had a few opportunities for college scholarships to study music. Instead he chose to attend Georgetown University and pursue an undergraduate degree in international studies.

In later years, Arkansas political columnist John Brummett commented on Clinton's career choice: "One can only wonder what might have happened if young Billy had not been elected at Arkansas Boys State to represent the state at Boys Nation, and if, just suppose, he had met Elvis Presley instead of JFK that summer."

Clinton's high school music teacher, Virgil Spurlin of Hot Springs, remembers him as "a very talented person." Clinton took band classes in elementary school, junior high and high school. "He made All-State, of course, in high school on tenor sax. And even in grade school he was just outstanding," Spurlin said. "As he went along, he not only developed his musical talents but all the other talents that he has as well. He was one of my top officers...I couldn't furnish him with enough sight-reading music to satisfy him. He just took all the classics and everything and just played them as if that saxophone were a violin, and it didn't matter what key or anything. And as far as his leadership ability…fantastic. He was a leader from the word go, and he set an example for others. He didn't just say 'Go to it,' but he said, 'Follow me.'"

Spurlin said he believed Clinton made his choice for public service over music because "I don't think the opportunities were as real for him in that field [music] as they are in politics—and education especially." Spurlin emphasized Clinton's high intellectual ability. "I just haven't seen anything quite like him in my teaching experience," he said. "There have been other bright people for sure, but Bill Clinton just has it easily head and shoulders above anybody in leadership ability."

Of Clinton's musical talent, Spurlin said:

> We had a pretty good music library in our school in our band program. In fact, I think that most symphony orchestras would do well to read some of the music; and I never did find a piece of music that he couldn't sight-read on that saxophone. I don't care if it was in six sharps or five flats, and how fast or how slow it went or what kind of expression. One time down in Camden [Arkansas], I believe he was in a stage band, kind of a jazz band, and he was a soloist, and he received the outstanding soloist for the state in this particular case. And it wasn't just the fact that he was an accomplished musician, but he had to read music of all kinds of moods and different kinds of music, from jazz to classical to everything in the book, and he just did a phenomenal job in that. He's the only one in my band who ever received such distinction.

Spurlin said that it didn't surprise him at all when Clinton played the saxophone "as well as he did" later in life as Johnny Carson's guest on *The Tonight Show*.

Today, Clinton considers his experiences in the Hot Springs band some of the most important of his youth. "All my musical competitions were great because it was so competitive, but, in a way, you were fighting against yourself. And music, to me, was—is—kind of representative of everything I like most in life. It's beautiful and fun but very rigorous. If you wanted to be good, you had to work like crazy. And it was a real relationship between effort and reward. My musical life experiences were just as important to me, in terms of forming my development, as my political experiences or my academic life."

*   *   *

Clinton's friends say that his mother probably was the most influential person in his life. They see much of his mother in his persona and character. They say his mother is "an intelligent and compassionate woman whose personal attributes are sometimes overshadowed by her physical appearance." Virginia Kelley's appearance is conspicuous. The things one notices first about her are the white stripe in her hair, her heavy makeup and her deep voice.

Perhaps because she has endured widowhood three times, Clinton's mother has been called a "strong and special person with a special personal friendship" with her son. Clinton's friends used to tease him because his mother kept so many pictures of him around the house.

Clinton's friend Leopoulos said that Kelley "was a very good friend to him [Bill], very supportive. She would sit and talk to him about social and moral issues, encourage him to think for himself, and as a result he was very independent." Kelley also helped her son develop a compassion for people and issues, Leopoulos said.

The young Clinton often argued that Arkansans, "though poor and disadvantaged, were as bright and talented as people anywhere," Leopoulos said. "He was always talking about ideas. You know, I know this sounds corny, or typical, but I always knew that he would be a leader. He is absolutely the most capable person I ever met."

Virginia Kelley remembered an incident when Clinton was only eight or nine years old. After reading an article in the newspaper about how poorly Arkansas ranked in national education surveys, he asked her, "Mom, aren't the kids in Arkansas born with the same brain as people [in other states]?"

Kelley, a die-hard Southerner, claimed that Bill Clinton "is the one who taught me civil rights. He was seeing black people mistreated in school. And he felt then it was just because of their color, and he just could hardly stand it."

Clinton himself has said that civil rights was one of the issues that drew him to a political career. The South was the civil rights battleground, and the fight was occurring all around him while he was in high school in the early 1960s. Many white Southerners at the time believed in the "separate but equal" position, in which blacks have equal facilities and opportunities but are physically separated from white society.

Clinton took the unpopular view that blacks were entitled to full participation in every facet of the American experience. He was keenly interested in the leadership qualities of Dr. Martin Luther King Jr., the civil rights leader. King was not nearly so popular with Clinton's white classmates, and Clinton found himself in frequent arguments on the topic.

Kelley said she felt a sense of destiny about her son early in his life. She remembered his drive to work and succeed, his independence and his desire to help others. Kelley said that Bill was "not a momma's boy. He was independent, without being arrogant."

Clinton's family life was marked by death, as he watched his mother lose two mates. Her first husband, William Blythe III, was killed in that auto crash in 1946 shortly before Bill was born. Roger Clinton Sr. died of cancer in 1967, when Bill Clinton was in college. Her third husband, Jeff Dwire, died of a heart ailment complicated by diabetes in 1974.

"We've had so many times that our closeness was a result of climbing so many hills," Kelley said. "Every time the boys would be stabilized, then we'd have the unfortunate loss in our family."

Virginia Kelley believes Roger Clinton Sr. was Bill's role model and that her third husband, Jeff Dwire, was more of a father to Roger Clinton Jr.

During the frequent years when there was no father in the house, Bill, Roger Jr. and Virginia would "put things to a vote that were really important to our family," Kelley said.

Clinton's mother retired in 1981 after thirty years as a nurse-anesthetist. In 1982 she married Dick Kelley, a top executive with Kelley Brokerage Company in Little Rock. They still maintain a lakeside home in Hot Springs.

Clinton acknowledges the great influence his mother has had on him:

> She was, I thought, a good role model in three ways. She always worked; did a good job as a parent; and we had a lot of adversity in our life when I was growing up, and she handled

it real well, and I think she gave me a high pain threshold, which, I think, is a very important thing to have in public life. You have to be able to take a lot of criticism—suffer defeats and get up tomorrow and fight again.

Clinton also believes an event that occurred before he was born—the death of his father—had a profound influence on his life as well:

It's a very difficult thing to be raised with a myth. All of my relatives attempted to make it a positive rather than a negative thing. But I think I always felt, in some sense, that I should be in a hurry in life, because it gave me a real sense of mortality. I mean, most kids never think about when they're going to have to run out of time, when they might die. I thought about it all the time because my father died at twenty-nine, before I was born. By the same token now, I feel as if I've had a very full life. I mean, whatever happens to me, I've already outlived him by years. So I've always had a different view than most people have. And I think it's one reason I was always in such a hurry to do things—which is both good and bad.

And I guess having my own child was probably one of the things that had ever enabled [me] to get off that kind of career track—like in 1987 when I decided I wouldn't run for president. I don't think there was any question that just being able to have a family life and have that whole set of experiences that I didn't even imagine when I was a child growing up—at least compared to my father who was already dead—had a big impact on me.

But, anyway, I think when I was younger, that's one of the reasons I was always in a hurry. And I also think I thought I had to live for myself and for him too. I sort of had to meet a very high standard of conduct and accomplishment, in part because of his absence. It's a funny thing, but the older I get the more I realize that sort of shaped my childhood—that great memory.

That childhood included the public schools. Clinton's early experiences in education in Arkansas sparked a desire—almost an obsession—to improve the state's education system. This became a theme that threads its way through all of Clinton's professional life.

Clinton attended public schools in Hot Springs, experiencing firsthand the Arkansas educational system. This was a system that had progressed dramatically since its beginnings but still had many shortcomings.

The schools Clinton attended had no kindergarten, no consistent standards, no program for gifted or disadvantaged students, no free textbooks for high school students, and poorly paid and sometimes poorly trained teachers. The schools were segregated until Clinton's high school years, when the federal government finally forced the state to observe the law of the land. Teachers were not required to have even a bachelor's degree to obtain teaching certificates until 1963.

Clinton did have the advantage of being educated in one of the larger city school districts. These districts had a historical advantage in their development simply because they had more money as a result of a larger industrial tax base.

Clinton speaks highly of his teachers in public school. "I thought most of them were genuinely not only dedicated, but gifted," he said. "I think I got an excellent background in English and math—not quite so good in some of the sciences. It was difficult then, as it is now, to recruit the experienced science teachers," he said.

Clinton remembers that the district lost its physics teacher and had to hire someone right out of college, whose major had not been physics. "It was just the best they could do. And we were a big high school in Hot Springs that paid fairly good wages."

Clinton said he felt that even though there were some problems, "by and large I thought the school system did an excellent job. And I didn't have much trouble competing with the kids from the big schools in the East, from the private academies, when I went to Georgetown."

He remembers several teachers who influenced him. "The teachers whom I really liked were, first of all, demanding," Clinton said. "They made us work hard, and they gave hard tests. I tended to do better, by the way, all my life in the hard courses than the easy courses."

Young Clinton had one problem in public school—"talking too

much." He said he had the highest academic grades in his elementary school class but was ranked third because of his citizenship. "I could never keep my mouth shut," he said. But he liked the teachers who made him "toe the line."

Clinton particularly liked teachers who not only were good disciplinarians, but who made learning fun, who "had a good sense of humor."

One teacher he remembers is Doyle Cole. "I was in his class when John Kennedy was assassinated. It was the first year we [were] taught trigonometry. We had seven people in the class. So I was able to take algebra one and two, geometry, calculus and trigonometry. And it was just an exhilarating experience. All the other students were real smart, and I loved that."

An English teacher whom Clinton still holds in high regard is Ruth Sweeney, "who had lived in Chicago and a lot of other places in the country, and I thought she was a sophisticated, neat person." For Sweeney, Clinton memorized one hundred lines of *Macbeth*. In 1990 he would recall those lines and recite them to a high school class in the small town of Vilonia, Arkansas.

"I hadn't [recited] it in twenty-something years," Clinton said, "and I started reeling it off, and these kids, their eyes got as big as dollars. I quoted this whole soliloquy. And it was all because of Ruth Sweeney."

Another teacher whom Clinton remembers fondly and communicated with until her death at age ninety was Kathleen Schaer, "a remarkable woman." She told him the day he was graduated from elementary school that he would end up either in jail or as governor. "She actually said that," Clinton recalled.

On graduation from Hot Springs High School in 1964, Clinton embarked on an ambitious higher education program. Dr. Paul Root describes the seventeen-year-old Clinton fresh out of high school: "I could see then that he was becoming...I don't know if we'd call it visionary or not, but he was really thinking long-range, and he knew where he was going, or knew where he wanted to go, and was finding ways to get there."

From Hot Springs High School, Clinton entered Georgetown University in September 1964, shortly after he turned eighteen. Georgetown, a Jesuit-founded school in Washington, D.C., was the only college to which Clinton had applied. He had asked his high school counselor which was the best school if one wanted to be a diplomat and she had answered, "Georgetown University."

"It was late in the year when he was accepted," Kelley said. "I went up with him for orientation, and we went into this Jesuit's office and he started questioning Bill, and he asked Bill about his foreign language, and Bill said, 'I haven't had any [modern] foreign language; I've had four years of Latin'...asked him about his religion, and Bill said he was Southern Baptist. All the wrong answers."

When the two walked out of that office, Clinton told his mother not to worry. "By the time I leave here, they'll know why they accepted me."

Today, Clinton says he selected Georgetown for three reasons. One, when he went to Boys Nation, he "fell in love with Washington" and wanted to go back there to college. Two, he wanted to "go to the place that was the most rigorous academically." And three, he wanted to attend a school "where I could get a good background in foreign affairs." His interest in foreign affairs, he says, was because "I thought America would become more involved in the rest of the world in my adult lifetime."

If he had not been accepted by Georgetown, he would have gone to the University of Arkansas at Fayetteville. "They had the open admission policy if you were a good student," Clinton recalled.

Clinton said Georgetown was an opportunity for him "to try to get exposed to the rest of the world." But at the same time, he already knew that he "wanted to come back home to Arkansas and be in public life. And I knew that politically it would be advantageous for me to stay here [Arkansas] to go to school. But I felt that if I went away to school and exposed myself to the rest of the country and learned something about the rest of the world, then if I ever could get elected down here, I'd do a better job."

There was a magnetic pull in Washington, and Clinton could not resist it.

2

The Scholar Sees the World

BILL CLINTON ENROLLED IN GEORGETOWN IN 1964, INTERESTED IN international studies as preparation for a career in politics. His family could barely afford to pay for such an expensive school. Clinton had to work at part-time jobs to bring in extra money. During the summer he returned to Arkansas to work in the campaign of Frank Holt, a candidate for governor.

David Pryor, now a U.S. senator from Arkansas, also campaigned that summer as a candidate for Congress. Pryor was walking down Main Street in a south Arkansas town, carrying a bucketful of thimbles promoting his campaign, when he encountered Clinton.

The two men introduced themselves to each other and began talking politics.

"I was very impressed," Pryor said, "even though it was just a sidewalk chat."

While campaigning for Frank Holt, Clinton came to know Arkansas Supreme Court Justice Jack Holt, who was Frank Holt's nephew. Although Frank Holt was defeated for governor, the campaign paid off for Bill Clinton. When it was time for Clinton to return to Georgetown in the fall, he was desperately in need of money to continue his studies. He had always admired Senator J. William Fulbright, so he decided to seek a job in Fulbright's office. He asked Chief Justice Jack Holt for a recommendation.

Clinton won the job on Holt's recommendation to Lee Williams, Fulbright's administrative assistant. "Jack [Holt] and I had worked for his uncle Frank, in his campaign for governor, and I needed a job to go back to Georgetown," Clinton said. "I couldn't afford to pay for it anymore."

Clinton remembers the night Williams called him in Hot Springs to offer him the Washington job. "He said, 'Well, you can have a part-time job for $3,500 a year or a full-time job for $5,000.' And I said, 'How about two part-time jobs?' And this is a verbatim conversation—he said, 'You're just the guy I'm looking for.' He said, 'Be here Monday.' And that's a true story. It was Friday morning. I'd had no sleep. I got up, got all my bags packed and everything, and I was there Monday for work."

Pryor saw the student again in 1968 when Clinton came by the congressman's office in Washington and brought Pryor up to date on his educational career. "I saw in that meeting an intensity in this young man that truly impressed me," Pryor said. "I felt he was someone who not only was very gifted but, in addition, he has a tremendous commitment to causes and to ideals along that line."

Clinton majored in international government studies at Georgetown, pursuing a bachelor of arts degree, which he obtained in 1968. He was voted class president in both his freshman and sophomore years.

Clinton today considers Georgetown "an incredible experience" and describes his years there as "like a feast...I'd never been out of Arkansas really very much, and there I was with people from all over the country and all over the world...teachers from all over the world."

In 1967, at age twenty-one, Clinton was to enter into a second life-changing episode with his stepfather, Roger Clinton Sr.

The elder Clinton was dying of cancer. He had been admitted to Duke University Hospital in Durham, N.C., about 250 miles south of Washington and Georgetown. Bill Clinton realized that it was up to him to bring a final reconciliation to their turbulent relationship. For six weeks, Bill Clinton made the drive every weekend from Washington to Durham to visit his stepfather.

"I think he knew that I was coming down there just because I loved him," Clinton told the *New York Times* years later. "There was nothing else to fight over, nothing else to run from. It was a wonderful time in my life, and I think in his."

Virginia Kelley reacts with similar emotion when she recalls the final struggle of two strong-willed men to heal the scars of turmoil and find a way to express their love for each other.

"I'll never forget how wonderful Bill was to him before he died," Kelley said. "Roger had such pride...he was vain and, as much as he drank, he was one of the cleanest individuals you ever saw— well dressed. And when he got so that he was not able to go to the bathroom, for example, Bill would bodily pick him up and take him to the bathroom so that he could maintain his dignity."

But after only six weeks of this newfound closeness, Clinton had lost another father.

*   *   *

High school friend Carolyn Staley visited Clinton at Georgetown and remembers that he had a clear sense of vision and the determination to right injustice even as a college student. One visit that stands out in her memory occurred at the time of Martin Luther King's assassination in 1968. America's major cities were engulfed in race riots.

"I remember flying in and seeing the city [Washington] on fire," she said. Clinton and Staley served as volunteers in the riot zones, driving Red Cross emergency vehicles that weekend. Staley said they pulled hats and scarves over their faces, as they had been instructed, to hide the color of their skin.

"We got out and walked throughout the city and saw the burning, the looting...and were very much brought into face-to-face significance with what was going on," Staley said.

Staley also remembers that Clinton began to form his ideas about Arkansas's need for educational improvement during that time.

"I remember a conversation very distinctly one time about education, when Bill was speaking about his concern that Arkansas children were not getting what he believed to be the best education they ought to be able to receive." A consensus was reached in the conversation that "there must be something about education that we could make a difference about," Staley said, "something that needs to be done, and that kids in Arkansas need to have the best teachers possible—the best education possible, and the best resources possible.

"It was very clear, very clear then that there was already a pulse, a concern and a determination that when life gave him the opportunities that would put him in the driver's seat, that he fully intended to do something about it."

Staley recalls being with Clinton in Hot Springs when he was vacationing from college and seeing in him a sense of political destiny, one that was encouraged by his friends and his mother.

"He would call and say, 'Come over. I've got some orange juice made and bring your copy of the paper and we'll work the crossword puzzle,'" Staley continued. "We'd have a race to see who could finish the crossword puzzle first."

Staley said that on occasion Clinton's mother would come into the kitchen angry about some injustice she had witnessed. Kelley would say, "I'm so mad I could die. I'm just so mad." The three of them would then talk about the problem.

"There was a kitchen court," Staley said. "She would have something on her heart. She would share it with her son. She would know what she was doing. I feel sure that she did, giving him opportunities to hear something that was wrong and then discuss a solution—some possible options to fixing it."

Clinton's friends in Hot Springs and his new friends from college were always welcome in his mother's home.

One of Clinton's Georgetown roommates was Thomas Caplan, a writer who now lives in Baltimore. His first introduction to Clinton occurred when Clinton knocked on the door of his dormitory room and said, "Hello, I'm Bill Clinton. Will you help me run for president of the class?" Caplan, and others, said yes and Clinton won.

Clinton wanted to bring Caplan home for Easter. Caplan was from a wealthy family and had traveled extensively.

"He's been to Europe," Clinton told his mother over the phone, "but he's never been to Arkansas." She consented for him to come.

"He [Caplan] was so quiet I was afraid he wasn't having a good time," Kelley said. Clinton told her that his roommate wasn't a name-dropper, although he knew the Kennedy family and had spent time with them at Hyannis Port, Massachusetts.

"When [Caplan] started to loosen up, I had him reaching for the butter in the middle of the table just like everybody else," Kelley said.

Kelley visited Caplan again when she went to Georgetown for her son's graduation ceremonies. Caplan told her that he didn't know if they would be able to eat breakfast that morning because it was Clinton's turn to buy. Caplan told her: "I bought it the last time, and he won't eat until he can afford to buy it the next time."

Kelley recalled that Caplan told her he did not trust Clinton when they first met. "I'll just put it to you as plain as I know how, Virginia," Caplan said. "He [Clinton] just told me one day—Tom, you don't have a thing in this world I want."

Caplan explained to Virginia: "I just could not trust him. I just did not believe a human being could be this good."

* * *

Clinton's Georgetown classmates have clear memories of a young man who was going places.

In 1988, Clinton attended a reunion of the Georgetown Class of 1968. Classmates remembered him "just like what he is today," said Tom Measday of Livingston, New Jersey. "He was very well spoken, very dedicated to what he was doing, very hardworking and very political. He knew everybody."

Not all the classmates at the reunion knew who Clinton was or that he had contemplated running for president in 1987. One person made the classic mistake of confusing the state of Arkansas with Arizona, and had Clinton confused with Arizona Governor Evan Mecham, who had been impeached.

Most, however, did know him, and some knew him well. An example is Bob Hannan, a Veterans Administration employee and chairman of the Dover, New Hampshire, school board. "I fully expect him to be president someday. There's no question," Hannan said.

Another former classmate, Tom Campbell, a pilot for USAir in Orange County, California, had brought a scrapbook to the reunion. One page contained a campaign poster with Clinton's photo that read: "A Realistic Approach to Student Government. Bill Clinton. Candidate. President of the Student Council." Another page contained Clinton's freshman campaign platform. He had promised to distribute a newsletter and make improvements in social life "through work on the homecoming float and the Class of '68 dance." Clinton's statement had concluded, "The feasibility of every plank has been carefully examined."

Campbell said the poster was proof of Clinton's ambitions. "Bill never wondered where he was going to be when he grew up. He's always aimed at a political future."

The forty-one-year-old Clinton delivered a speech at that reunion. He spoke of developing trade and growth for the American economy, expanding educational opportunities, improving health care and fighting the drug war. Clinton received a standing ovation. Afterward there were several remarks about Clinton becoming president or, at least, a running mate for Michael Dukakis, the Democratic nominee for president at that time.

* * *

Old friend Patty Criner was in Arkansas when Clinton attended Georgetown. He wrote to her on a regular basis and told her school was "really hard."

He also told Criner, "You won't believe this, but the professors want me to apply for a Rhodes Scholarship." Although he told Criner he felt he didn't have "a chance in the world" to get the scholarship, he was "really studying and really working hard."

Criner remembers the day Clinton won the scholarship. She was with his mother in Hot Springs, awaiting the news. "It was the most exciting thing in the world for him," Criner said.

Kelley remembered sitting by the phone all day until her son called with the outcome of the interview. "I never refused to do an anesthetic [procedure] before in my life. But this was on a Saturday...and the doctor called me, and I said, 'I'm sorry. You'll just have to call somebody else.' I did not leave the phone all day long. I gave him a London Fog raincoat for good luck for him to take to New Orleans [where the Rhodes Scholarship interviews were conducted]. And it was around five o'clock in the afternoon, and he called and he said, 'Well, Mother, how do you think I'll look in English tweed?'"

Clinton's final interview followed a competitive selection process. Clinton told his mother that he had picked up a *Time* magazine at the airport and read an article about the first heart transplant. It turned out that one of his interview questions was on that subject. The excited Clinton told his mother that picking up the magazine had been "the luckiest thing in this world."

For Clinton, the opportunity to attend Oxford, to study and travel, was an education in itself. "He took every bit of it to heart and was so grateful for every bit of it," Criner said.

"He would write his mother how grateful he was." His mother was helping him financially while he attended Georgetown, but Clinton always worked at a part-time job to support himself.

Clinton's only break from the study-work routine would not come until his Oxford years, when he would be able to concentrate on school without having to work at one or more jobs.

* * *

Clinton would attend Oxford University at age twenty-two and would study for two years, from 1968 to 1970, as a Rhodes Scholar. Fulbright, who had provided the job that helped Clinton to afford to study at Georgetown, had been a Rhodes Scholar himself. Clinton has expressed the feeling that if it were not for Fulbright he might never have won the scholarship.

While Clinton was overseas, opposition to the Vietnam War began to grow in the United States. Clinton's position against the war and his draft deferment would come back to haunt him in the 1992 presidential campaign.

Clinton has given several answers to questions about the role he played in antiwar protests. In 1978, he told the *Arkansas Gazette* that he had only observed the demonstrations.

Yet in a letter that he wrote in 1969, and which surfaced in 1992, Clinton states: "I have written and spoken and marched against the war....After I left Arkansas last summer, I went to Washington to work in the national headquarters of the Moratorium, then to England to organize the Americans...for demonstrations October 15 and November 16."

Similar confusion surrounds his draft status. During the war, the federal government changed the conditions for a deferment from the draft several times. Clinton initially received a student deferment for his undergraduate studies.

The confusion arose when he graduated from Georgetown and

went to Oxford. At the time, some graduate students could receive deferments while others could not, depending on a set of complex rules created by the Defense Department and the Nixon administration. Clinton, apparently with no deferment, headed for England. After he arrived in England, he apparently received a notice of induction from his draft board. But the date for reporting to the authorities had passed. Clinton called the board to seek advice. The board granted him a deferment for the rest of the year.

When Clinton returned to Hot Springs in the summer of 1969, he realized he probably would not receive a deferment for a second year of graduate study at Oxford. He then committed to enroll in the University of Arkansas Law School and to join the Reserve Officers Training School at the university. Because he would essentially be training for the military while attending law school, he figured this maneuver would get him several more years of deferment, possibly until the end of the war.

But Clinton changed his mind, and decided to return to Oxford for a second year. He canceled his ROTC agreement and put himself up for the draft. While Clinton was in England, the Nixon administration created a draft lottery based on birth dates. Clinton received a high lottery number, which practically guaranteed that he would not be drafted, and he was not.

Friends say Clinton anguished over his position on the draft and on the war. At the time it was known as "the poor boys' war" because the draftees who went to the front lines were lower-income white men and black men who could not afford college for a deferment, or who had no political pull with the local draft boards.

Critics point to Clinton's contradictory statements on his anti-war involvement and his confused draft status as prime examples of the "Slick Willie" brand of politics—using maneuvers and doublespeak to get what he wants. Clinton denies that he used any "tricks" to avoid military service and points to the fact that for several weeks he was vulnerable to the draft, but was not chosen.

At Oxford, Clinton became acquainted with another Arkansan, Cliff Jackson, who was studying at the university as a Fulbright fellow. This was one friendship that would not pay off for Clinton.

In fact, Jackson would become one of Clinton's severest critics in later years and would cause him a great deal of trouble during his presidential campaign in 1992.

* * *

The academic atmosphere at Oxford was perfect for Bill Clinton. He was allowed to study anything and everything. Clinton was a voracious reader, eager to learn, quickly developing multiple interests. He tended toward lofty conversation about ideas and ideals.

His high school pal Paul David Leopoulos visited him in England. Clinton took Leopoulos to an art museum and explained each piece in minute detail and with great enthusiasm. Leopoulos was amazed at his fervor for the great works of art. He had never shown much curiosity about art before coming to Oxford.

"He is interested in everything, and he wants to consume everything," Leopoulos later told a reporter. "He is almost a fanatic about information. He gathers and retains it better than anyone I've ever known. He is fascinated with everything and knowledgeable about so many things. I get upset sometimes when people talk about him as nothing more than a politician."

Clinton's best friend at Oxford was Strobe Talbott, who later became a senior correspondent for *Time* magazine. Talbott said Clinton was "quite outstanding, even as a very young man, for the way in which he combined a very obvious and eloquent idealism—that is, a passionate interest in large issues that are involved in public policy—with a practical sense of politics....He was very interested in both the cosmic and the nitty-gritty."

Talbott also remembers that Clinton, in his Oxford years, was competitive. "Part of his success, I think, derives from his ability to be extremely competitive without turning people off," he said. "He doesn't come across as being vicious or mean and hungry; and, as a result, he doesn't frighten people or antagonize people. At least, that is my impression from Oxford days, and that squares with my impression of how he has conducted himself since then."

The former roommate recalls that Clinton "took full advantage of the fact that he was off on the other side of the Atlantic Ocean, far away from the distractions and preoccupations that had consumed him as a student leader at Georgetown....He really threw himself into the wonderful intellectual smorgasbord that Oxford had to offer. He read a great deal both curricularly and extracurricularly and audited all kinds of lectures, including ones outside of his area of study, and generally took full advantage of the educational opportunities that a great university presented, at a time in his life when he did not have a great deal of other commitments or pressures on him."

Clinton relished his years at Oxford. "Being in England was incredible," he said. "I got to travel a lot. I got to spend a lot of personal time—learn things, go see things. I read about three hundred books both years I was there.

"For a person like me who just likes to organize every minute of the day—I'm almost compulsively overactive—to have two years where you couldn't do that...it was a great deal," he said.

Clinton was offered a scholarship to attend Yale Law School. He chose to matriculate there, even though he could have had a third year on the Rhodes Scholarship.

"He hated to do that [turn down the third year], but he wanted a law degree," Kelley said. "It was something for them to offer to pay him to come to this school. He still had outside jobs to supplement the income. But he's always had scholarships."

Clinton looks back with mixed feelings about his decision to end his study at Oxford. "I kind of regret the fact that I never got a degree [from Oxford]," he said. "My class had the highest percentage of Rhodes Scholars that never earned a degree, because we were right there in the middle of that Vietnam War buildup." Clinton said the threat of being drafted into service in Vietnam practically dictated a student's curriculum.

"We were over there changing courses—three or four times— because we knew that...we'd get a year, and it'd be done. And so, ironically, at the end of my first year is when President Nixon started to wind the war down; so there were only a couple of us who were actually drafted."

It is now known that Clinton also smoked marijuana while attending Oxford. "When I was in England, I experimented with marijuana a time or two, and I didn't like it. I didn't inhale and never tried it again," Clinton said in a 1992 interview. He later added, "I was curious, other people were doing it and I tried it. I assumed it was against the law, but when we got there they told us that as long as we did it inside our apartments or whatever, nobody would hassle us. But I was not into that." Clinton's confession, especially the "didn't inhale" quote, would bring him much ridicule at a point in his 1992 presidential campaign when he least needed trouble.

* * *

Bill Clinton entered Yale Law School in 1971 as a twenty-five-year-old "long-haired young liberal who had just come back from Oxford." He says he was "not a traditional law student. I had to work my way through." Even with the scholarship and a loan, Clinton had to take on as many as three part-time jobs at once. "I taught in a little community college," he said. He also worked for a city councilman in Hartford and for a lawyer in downtown New Haven. Part of his job for the lawyer was investigating civil cases.

"I wound up going into tenements where people were shooting up heroin, doing stuff like that. I mean, I had some interesting jobs." Clinton also became involved in Democratic politics in Connecticut.

One of his teachers was the conservative constitutional law professor Robert H. Bork. Clinton said he used "to go round and round" with Bork in the classroom. The governor later told friends that by the end of the course, he was about the only member of the class who had not been beaten into submission.

Both men would come under scrutiny in 1987, when Clinton contemplated running for president and Bork was nominated by then-President Ronald Reagan to the United States Supreme Court.

Clinton submitted written testimony to the Senate Judiciary Committee opposing Bork's nomination. The testimony cited Bork's constitutional theories of individual and civil rights and his judicial activism. Clinton's testimony said Bork's views on civil rights could cause reactionary forces in the South to try to "reopen old wounds."

Clinton also cited two utility-case decisions, one involving Arkansas Power and Light Company. Clinton said that Bork's opinion in the case would cause AP&L customers to pay "rates so exploitative they would be ruinous to our people."

Bork did not become a member of the Supreme Court, and Clinton today feels he did the right thing concerning him:

> I liked him. I respected him. But I also believe that he meant what he said, and I thought that when he...basically

went up there for those confirmation hearings, and they tried to paper over all this stuff he'd said...I didn't find that persuasive, because I had been in his class many years ago. But, anyway, I like him fine. I think he was a good, challenging teacher, but I took him at his word. I think he did mean everything he said; and I think...the Senate should have made their decision based on the assumption that he did.

* * *

Yale was important to Clinton for reasons other than his education. It was during his first year there, in 1971, that he met Hillary Rodham. "I'd just broken up with another girl, and the last thing I wanted to do was get involved with anybody," Clinton said of their meeting.

"We were in a class together where—I'm embarrassed to say this; I don't want to set a bad example—but neither one of us attended this particular class very often, because the guy who taught the class had written the textbook. So the test was always the textbook, and it was one of those deals where the book was better than the movie. He was a great writer, not a particularly great lecturer."

Clinton spotted Hillary Rodham in class one day and followed her out, but didn't have enough courage to speak to her.

A couple of days later he saw Rodham again in the library:

This guy was trying to talk me into joining the *Yale Law Review* and telling me I could clerk for the U.S. Supreme Court if I were a member of the *Yale Law Review*, which is probably true. And then I could go on to New York and make a ton of money. And I kept telling him I didn't want to do all of that. I wanted to go home to Arkansas. It didn't matter to anybody [in Arkansas] whether I was on the *Yale Law Review* or not. And they were trying to get Southerners, they wanted geo-graphical balance on the *Law Review*....I just didn't much want to do it. And all this time I was talking to this guy about the *Law Review*, I was looking at Hillary at the other end of the library. And the Yale Law School Library is a real long, narrow [room]. She was down at the other end, and...I just was staring at her....And she closed this book, and she walked all the way down the library...and she came up to me and she said, "Look, if you're going to keep staring at me, and I'm going to keep staring back, I think we should at least know each other. I'm Hillary Rodham. What's your name?"

Clinton had a problem—he couldn't remember his name. "I was so embarrassed. But that's a true story," he said. "That's exactly how we met. It turned out she knew who I was. But I didn't know that at the time either. But I was real impressed that she did that. And we've been together, more or less, ever since."

Hillary Rodham, born in Chicago on October 26, 1947, was the daughter of Hugh and Dorothy Rodham. She grew up in Park Ridge, Illinois, along with two brothers. In 1969, Rodham graduated with high honors from Wellesley College in Wellesley, Massachusetts. From there she went to Yale.

The professors at Yale proved to be influential on both Clinton and Rodham. Several of them had been members of the John F. Kennedy administration, including Burke Marshall, who had been director of the Civil Rights Division for the Justice Department during Kennedy's administration and part of Lyndon Johnson's presidency. Marshall was responsible for the drafting of a civil rights agenda and the federal role in the South during the early 1960s.

"People like that helped symbolize the kind of public [and] private professional opportunities and obligations that I was interested in," Hillary Clinton remembers. "They went in and out of public service, and I really thought that was a good model and they might have had very different points of view, but they used their education and their professional training to be of public benefit."

Most of her classmates at Yale wanted to clerk for the Supreme Court after graduation, according to Hillary Clinton. But Bill Clinton was "always intent upon what he was going to do, which was to come home to Arkansas," she said. "Most of us, including me when I first met him, didn't really have any idea of what that meant. I mean, we'd never been to Arkansas. We didn't know very much about the state. Frankly, what we knew was colored by 1957 and Orval Faubus. And so we just didn't really have much of an idea at all."

In 1957, nine black students attempted to enter the all-white

Central High School in Little Rock. Governor Orval Faubus ordered the state's National Guard to prevent the students from entering. President Dwight D. Eisenhower then ordered the Army's 101st Airborne Division into Little Rock to protect the black students and to see that they were allowed to enter the school. The incident brought infamy to Little Rock and to Arkansas. Many Americans like Hillary Rodham had only heard of Arkansas in the context of this civil rights showdown.

* * *

In 1972, Clinton, then twenty-six, and Rodham, twenty-five, took time off from school to go to Texas to work in the presidential campaign of George McGovern. Although Clinton was a liberal who had supported McGovern long before he won the nomination, Clinton nevertheless realized that "the McGovernites" had lost touch with the American people. Years later he told David Broder, *Washington Post* columnist: "What was so disturbing to the average American voter was not that [McGovern] seemed so liberal on the war, but that the entire movement seemed unstable, irrational." He added that, to the average person, "This campaign and this man did not have a core, a center, that was common to the great majority of the country."

The trek to Texas did have one lasting benefit for Clinton. It was there that he met Betsey Wright, who would later become his chief aide and campaign manager. Wright already was an active Texas political operative in 1972. She later said she had been more impressed with Rodham's political potential than with Clinton's.

After graduating from Yale in 1973, both Rodham and Clinton were offered several positions in Washington. Rodham worked for the Children's Defense Fund in Boston for a few months before accepting a job as a member of the counsel staff for the House Judiciary Committee. The committee was conducting an inquiry into the possible impeachment of President Richard Nixon over the Watergate affair.

Clinton could have chosen to work for the committee too. He and Rodham were among five or six students whom Burke Marshall had recommended for the job. But Clinton chose to return to Arkansas.

"I certainly was not ready to move completely to Arkansas yet," Hillary Clinton said later. "I just didn't know whether that would be a decision that Bill would stick [with]..."

Clinton's mother was worried about the relationship between Bill Clinton and Hillary Rodham. "He loved Hillary so much at Yale," she said. "He was really concerned about whether she really would be happy in Arkansas, or would even come. But he told her going in, he said, 'I promised myself a long time ago, if the people of Arkansas will let me, I'll break my back to help my state.' And he said, 'That's my life. And that's the way it has to be for me.'"

3

An Experiment in Arkansas

WHEN BILL CLINTON LEFT YALE LAW SCHOOL, HE HAD A SIMPLE, immediate goal: return to Hot Springs, borrow money and set up a private law practice. That plan ran counter to the standard practice for young graduates with his credentials. Most headed for the big cities and big law firms. Most Arkansas law school graduates headed for Little Rock, the state's capital and largest city, with a population of nearly 170,000. Hot Springs had a population of about 36,000.

"I wasn't interested in coming to Little Rock—I mean, working for a law firm, much less teaching," Clinton said. "I had always been kind of on my own and independent and was very much self-reliant, and I...couldn't imagine working for a big unit. I just wanted to set up a law practice."

Clinton was preparing to leave Yale when Marvin Chirelstein, a professor, suggested he apply to the University of Arkansas Law School in Fayetteville because it had two vacancies for professors. Clinton thought about the teaching job while driving home from New Haven to Hot Springs. When he reached Arkansas, he pulled off the interstate highway to place a phone call to Wylie Davis, dean of the law school. He had changed his mind about the small law practice.

Clinton recalls that he said to Davis: "I don't have anything set to do; but I'm coming home to Arkansas, and you might want me to come teach up there a year because I'll teach anything, and I don't mind working, and I don't believe in tenure, so you can get rid of me anytime you want."

Clinton was told that, at age twenty-six, he was too young to teach in the law school.

"I've been too young to do everything I've ever done," Clinton countered. He wrangled an interview and soon found himself on the faculty.

Clinton's mother said he turned down positions with major law firms on the East Coast. Instead he took the University of Arkansas job, which paid $25,000 a year. Virginia Kelley remembers thinking at the time: "What is the deal?...We have struggled ten years to educate this man." But she realized that "money is not important to Bill." Kelley said her son once told her, "The only reason in this world that I would like to have a lot of money [is] I believe I know where to place it, a lot more than most [people]. I know where it's needed, and for that I would like to have a lot of money."

"Money means nothing to him," Kelley said.

Clinton's decision to seek opportunity in Arkansas was made in the face of some depressing statistics. In 1975, the per capita income was less than $4,510 a year, forty-ninth in the nation, just above Mississippi. There is an old saying in Arkansas, "Thank God for Mississippi," meaning Arkansas would rank dead last in practically every category if Mississippi did not exist. The national per capita income that year was $5,861. Arkansas has a population of about 2.3 million. In physical size, it covers about 53,000 square miles, about the same as New York State. Its black population is about 16 percent, and Hispanics number fewer than 19,000. Agriculture is the dominant industry, far outstripping manufacturing and retailing in number of employees and earnings.

Patty Criner recalled how much Clinton liked living in Fayetteville, Arkansas, and teaching there. "Fayetteville's a lot like New Haven, Connecticut," Criner said. "And it was relaxed."

Fayetteville is a university town in the Ozark Mountains near the Missouri border. With a population of about 36,000, it is similar in size to Clinton's hometown of Hot Springs.

Fall 1973 was Clinton's first semester teaching in Fayetteville.

Criner feels that Hillary, not Bill, is the better lawyer, but that Bill Clinton is the better teacher. "Bill got through law school, but Hillary helped him," Criner said. "They studied together, and she helped him a lot because she's really a bright, bright lawyer. But he enjoyed the academic environment, and some of his close friends now are people who taught at the law school [in Fayetteville]."

Among Clinton's students were young lawyers-to-be who would later end up in positions of power in Arkansas government. Two were Lu Hardin of Russellville, Arkansas, who would become a state senator, and David Matthews of Lowell, Arkansas, who would be elected state representative.

Both Hardin and Matthews have said Clinton was a good teacher. Other former students have been more critical, saying Clinton was not always well prepared and seemed preoccupied with his political debut.

"Bill Clinton was very enthusiastic and a very dedicated professor," Hardin said. "The characteristic that I remember in the spring of 1974 about Bill Clinton was an incredible sense of fairness in the classroom."

Hardin remembers Clinton as showing both sides of issues: "He allowed students freedom to express opinions and was very thought-provoking."

Clinton also took time to mingle with students. "He interacted with students well, and on a couple of different occasions we played half-court basketball together," Hardin said. "He really went the extra mile in getting to know students."

Hardin criticized Clinton for being late in posting his grades. Although this practice was not uncommon among the professors of law, Hardin said, Clinton's grades were posted later than any other professor's had ever been. For those students on probation, the grades were crucial. The wait could be grueling, and students tried to keep each other informed as to when Clinton posted grades.

Hardin gave an example: "I was playing in a golf tournament on Labor Day. Another law student hollered across the golf course that Bill Clinton had just posted his grades for the spring semester."

Another of Clinton's law students who would go on to become a leader in the state legislature was Morril Harriman Jr., state senator from Van Buren, Arkansas. Harriman's assessment of Clinton as a teacher is that he was "a good instructor" and "cared about the methods and the manner in which he gave the instructions."

The first time Harriman saw Clinton in class he thought Clinton was a fellow student because he was so young.

Harriman remembers that Clinton sometimes lectured off the subject, bringing up such issues as the Watergate scandal. "You could tell that he was very concerned over what had taken place in the Watergate situation," Harriman said. Clinton and his class discussed the legal issues and governmental philosophy behind Watergate.

*   *   *

In 1974, at the age of twenty-seven, Clinton decided to enter the race for the Democratic nomination for Congress in the heavily Republican Third District of Arkansas. He was still teaching at the University of Arkansas Law School.

In stepping into Arkansas politics, Clinton knew he was entering a maze of regional peculiarities. For instance, in the 1968 elections, when Clinton was at Oxford, the majority of Arkansans had voted for ultraconservative independent candidate George Wallace for president, over Republican Richard Nixon and Democrat Hubert Humphrey. At the same time, the state elected a liberal Democrat, Dale Bumpers, as governor, over a Republican incumbent, Winthrop Rockefeller. The voters also reelected to the U.S. Senate liberal Democrat J. William Fulbright, whose opposition to the Vietnam War made him one of the most controversial figures of his time. Political analysts are still scratching their heads over that election.

In 1974, Clinton took on John Paul Hammerschmidt, the Republican incumbent, who was considered unbeatable. In fact, Hammerschmidt had not experienced a tough race since he was elected in 1966. He was extremely popular throughout his district, a huge area that covered much of north and west Arkansas, including Clinton's hometown of Hot Springs.

Hammerschmidt, who was fifty-four at the time, was known for constituent service. Residents of his district who had trouble with the federal bureaucracy—a tangle with the Social Security Administration, for instance—could call Hammerschmidt's office and usually count on getting a satisfactory resolution. Hammerschmidt was a wealthy businessman from Harrison, Arkansas, who had a reputation for being able to take care of the district's influential business interests as well as "the regular folks."

Clinton had been teaching for three months when he decided to embark on his political career.

"The only reason I ran for Congress is they couldn't get anybody else to do it," Clinton said later. He had asked some friends if they were interested in running, but they all declined. "I didn't intend to get into politics that early," he said. "I was sort of easing into my life, and I loved Fayetteville."

Although Clinton did not leave his position at the University of Arkansas during the campaign, he arranged to be paid only for actual teaching time.

Looking back, Clinton said many of the decisions he has made that have shaped his later life were "based totally on instinct and the moment." He has said that he didn't even expect to win the race against Hammerschmidt.

He felt strongly enough about running, though, to turn down a job offer from John Doar, who had been an assistant head of the Civil Rights Division under President Kennedy. Doar was heading the congressional impeachment staff investigating Nixon and was looking for bright young lawyers to help him. He wanted Clinton to be his special assistant and to help with hiring other lawyers.

"I said, 'I don't want to do that,'" Clinton recalled. "He said, 'What do you mean?...Every person your age in America would cut off their arm for this opportunity.' And I said, 'Yeah, but there's lots of people as smart as I am in law,' and I said, 'Lots of people can do this job. I'm going to stay down here and run for Congress, because I can't find another living soul to do that.'"

Clinton did agree to help Doar find a top-notch staff. He recommended Hillary Rodham (calling her "the smartest person I've ever known") and several others—all of whom were hired.

The campaign proved vigorous. Clinton traveled the district in his little car, learning the basics of campaigning: what to say, what not to say, how to listen to voters.

Clinton would later characterize his campaign as "an experiment." He would say that he and a few friends from the Fayetteville academic circles wanted to have some fun, so they began a political campaign.

In 1992, Clinton would tell Peter Applebome of the *New York Times* that it was the "best campaign I ever ran."

Clinton said, "I just got in my little car and drove and had a hell of a time. I was still in my 1970 Gremlin, and later I had a little Chevelle truck with AstroTurf in the back."

Although Clinton said no one else was willing to run against Hammerschmidt, there were, in fact, three other Democratic candidates: Gene Rainwater, David Stewart and James Scanlon. Clinton, the least known of the four, won 44 percent of the vote in the primary and went into a runoff with Rainwater.

Clinton walked away with the runoff, taking 69 percent of the vote. He had spent $43,000 during the primary and runoff. Much of the money came from the Committee on Political Education, an arm of the AFL-CIO, and the Political Action Committee for Education, an arm of the Arkansas Education Association (AEA).

Despite the impressive showing in the runoff, few observers gave Clinton much of a chance of winning against Hammerschmidt. Clinton was young and unknown, wore his hair long and was treading on dangerous territory by criticizing Hammerschmidt's cozy relationship with Arkansas's industrial interests and his continuing support of President Richard Nixon during the Watergate scandal.

Clinton had one more major problem: the Vietnam War. But by August 1974, President Richard Nixon had resigned in the face of impeachment and the American effort in Vietnam was becoming embarrassing. Conservative Republicans such as Hammerschmidt were holding faithful to their belief that American military might could stop the Communist menace in Southeast Asia and bring peace to Vietnam.

Liberal Democrats such as Clinton believed America had no business interfering in what they characterized as a civil war within Vietnam. They blamed the "military-industrial complex" for prolonging and expanding the war in order to make "obscene profits."

The American people were emotionally exhausted by the war. It had gone on too long and had divided the nation. Most Americans were of the opinion that there only two options left: an all-out military effort to win it or withdrawal of all American troops, leaving the Vietnamese to fight their own war.

It was during this 1974 election that Clinton's draft record and his alleged participation in antiwar demonstrations became an issue. In April 1969, a war protester had climbed into a tree on the University of Arkansas campus and vowed not to come down until the war ended. The vigil had lasted for only a few days and was a minor incident at a time when the campus was wracked by serious demonstrations. But it had made for good newspaper copy and photographs.

After Clinton won the Democratic primary, a rumor emerged from the Hammerschmidt camp that Clinton had been the protester in the tree. It became a point of ridicule against the Clinton campaign.

Clinton argued that he could not have been the man in the tree because he was in England in April 1969. Despite repeated denials, and the fact that the real protester came forth to identify himself, the "man in the tree" myth clings to Clinton to this day in Arkansas, if not in national politics. It is a story that he cannot shake.

To gain attention during the campaign, Clinton sent a telegram to President Gerald Ford recommending measures for an economic address the president was to make to Congress. Clinton told the president that his own "economic advisers" had been "small farmers, small-business men, working people, retirees and almost anyone you can imagine." Throughout the primary and the campaign, he focused on the need for a more responsive congress.

Hammerschmidt remained in Washington for most of the campaign, but during the last three weeks his advisers finally convinced him that Clinton posed a real threat. He returned to Arkansas and accused Clinton of distorting his voting record. He called Clinton "immature" and said he had a "radical, left-wing philosophy." Hammerschmidt said the "main thrust of [Clinton's] campaign is trying to prey on the obvious frustrations of the economy." He also brought out Clinton's work in the 1972 run for the presidency by George McGovern and emphasized that Clinton had received "a great deal of labor money" for his campaign.

Of Hammerschmidt, Clinton said: "No man who has stood in

Congress and supported Nixon's policies, no man who has supported Nixon's vetoes, no man who tends to cover up the Watergate
affair, deserves to represent this district."

The Little Rock media began to take notice of the fight in
northwest Arkansas. The invincible Hammerschmidt actually appeared to be worried that this long-haired upstart could beat him.
Editors dispatched reporters to find out about this Clinton fellow.

The journalists, jaded by hot summer campaigns and endless,
soporific speeches, were jolted awake. Clinton was something new
and different: an articulate, liberal politician wading deep into
conservative waters. He appeared to be both fearless and friendly.

A writer for the Little Rock *Arkansas Democrat* reported at the
time, "The campaign styles of the two candidates contrast dramatically. Clinton runs—literally, physically runs—from place to
place as he strives to personally meet as many of the district's
eligible voters as possible."

The reporter described one such incident: "At one point, Clinton
had about twenty minutes to get from Fort Smith to Lavaca [about
twenty miles]. Stopped at a traffic light, he spotted some men
working on a sewer repair project. Clinton said, 'There's ten votes,'
and jumped out of the car to talk to them."

Another reporter who covered the campaign for a northwest
Arkansas newspaper recalled years later that "Clinton did not
arouse quite as much controversy as one would have thought—as
much as a long-haired, twenty-eight-year-old law professor should
have. He became a big media sensation everywhere. I remember
watching him going into a high school once and everybody was
falling all over him. He had this young-guy, baby-faced charisma.
Everybody loved it. It was going over with a lot of older folks too.
They were telling him, 'We've been for John Paul all these years,
but we think we like you this time.' Remember, though, that those
were the Watergate years. He rode that wave for quite a while."

Clinton got an easy ride from most of the media that summer. He
had no record on which to run, other than his education credentials, which impressed reporters and editors.

Clinton drew some criticism from an unexpected area. *The
Grapevine*, a Fayetteville countercultural newspaper with a definite neo-leftist philosophy, sent a reporter to cover Clinton on the

campaign trail. The reporter, Michael Gaspeny, caught up with Clinton in September 1974 in Clinton's hometown of Hot Springs. Under a headline that said "Hustling in Hot Springs with William Jefferson Clinton," Gaspeny wrote that he met "with the Clinton staff in an undistinguished suite at the Arlington [Hotel] in order to confirm an interview promised to this paper last spring. I had been assured of a half-hour audience previously, but after consultation with two lieutenants, the length of the meeting dwindles to ten minutes and then to five.

"I begin to wonder if I can do an accurate portrait of a figure in whose presence I spend five minutes scribbling notes. 'We hope it's a good article,' I am repeatedly told. 'Your paper can bring us a lot of votes. We need everything we can get from the university.' I decline, mentioning that I have not yet been hired as a promo-man for the Clinton campaign.

"I mingle with the staff for a while and discover that I am impressed by the hardihood and charm of the workers. They are young—mostly women—former campus politicians, joiners and gadflies who remind me of the volunteers who beat the bushes for Eugene McCarthy in 1968. These are the kind of people who stand in the rain at high school football games to distribute campaign leaflets.

"The workers are influenced by the Dexedrine-like effects of campaigning white-line fever; an inversion that naturally seizes the members of a cult. The volunteers are extremely reluctant to talk about themselves. They constantly mutter the aspirant's name in hushed tones: 'Bill thinks...,' 'Bill feels...,' 'Bill does...'

"I feel as if I am either in a confession box or am party to the recitation of a first-grade primer. There is a monotonous circularity to all the conversation."

Clinton said several times after the campaign that Gaspeny's account was one of the few unfavorable articles written about him.

Other politicians also took notice of Clinton's skills as a speaker. Now-Senator David Pryor recalled Clinton's short but impressive speech at a political rally during the campaign. All the statewide and district candidates were invited to speak that night for three minutes each. Among them was U.S. Senator Robert Byrd of West Virginia, speaking on behalf of Senator J. William Fulbright, who was being challenged by Dale Bumpers, then-governor of Arkansas. Byrd, however, did not invoke the most enthusiastic response from the audience that night. The most excitement was generated by the final speaker of the long evening—Bill Clinton.

"The crowd was restless, ready to go home," Pryor said. "It was ten o'clock. He got up in those three minutes and immediately mesmerized the audience of several hundred people in a very brilliant three-minute political presentation, brought the crowd to its feet."

* * *

In the midst of the campaign, Hillary Rodham joined the University of Arkansas Law School faculty. She had been working for the Watergate committee from January 1974 until August, when Nixon resigned. The work was "nonstop," Hillary Clinton remembers. "I was exhausted. We'd been working eighteen-to-twenty-hour days."

After Nixon's resignation, Rodham picked up the phone and called dean Wylie Davis and asked him for a job at the law school. Rodham arrived in Fayetteville that August and was soon on the faculty, as well as running a legal aid clinic and a project that sent students to work with prison inmates.

"Bill was at that time in the general election," Hillary Clinton said. "We had a very interesting first couple of months there, and I loved Fayetteville. I loved the university. I loved the law school. I loved my colleagues. I made some of the best friends I ever had in my life," she said. "It was an adjustment, in the sense that I'd never really lived in the South and I'd never lived in a small town, but I felt so immediately at home...."

Hillary Rodham also took on another task. She became the unofficial campaign manager for Bill Clinton. Friends say the "experiment" was a disorganized affair until Rodham came in and began putting things into order.

Clinton's experiment put a scare into Hammerschmidt, but it did not defeat him. Hammerschmidt won with 51.5 percent of the vote. No Democrat before or since has done better against Hammerschmidt.

It was then that Clinton first became known as the "boy wonder" of Arkansas politics, in the words of *Arkansas Gazette* writer Ernest Dumas.

"John Paul Hammerschmidt was considered unbeatable, and this guy almost did it," Dumas told writer David Osborne. "That's what we all wrote about: Bill Clinton—here's the man to watch, the rising star."

In March 1992, when Clinton was seeking the Democratic nomination for president, Hammerschmidt announced his retirement from Congress.

* * *

After a year of living in Fayetteville, Hillary Rodham traveled back home to Chicago to see her parents, then to the East Coast to visit her old friends. She was trying to make a decision about whether to stay in Arkansas.

She was still undecided when she returned in August 1975 to Fayetteville. She and Clinton had been maintaining separate quarters during this time. Fayetteville, for all its academic liberalism, still had a prevailing conservative social code forbidding such arrangements as living together.

Gail Sheehy, writing in *Vanity Fair* magazine, described Clinton's welcome for Hillary Rodham:

"When Bill picked her up at the midget airport, he was ebullient. 'You know that house you liked?' Hillary looked blank. 'What house?'

"As Bill tells the story, she'd made a passing comment about a pretty little glazed-brick house. He'd gone out and bought it, feathering the nest with an antique bed and flowered sheets from Wal-Mart. 'So you're gong to have to marry me,' he declared, winding up his pitch as he pulled into the driveway of the house. Two months later she did."

Hillary Rodham, who loved challenges, was unable to find a bigger one than a life with Bill Clinton. On Saturday, October 11, 1975, almost a year after the election, Bill Clinton, twenty-nine, and Hillary Rodham, twenty-seven, were married by a Methodist minister in the house Clinton had bought. Rodham retained her own name, a decision that later would be dragged into the political arena.

The wedding was a small, private ceremony at the groom's Fayetteville home. The couple exchanged family heirloom rings. Only immediate family and close friends attended. Roger Clinton Jr. served his brother as best man. Other family members attending were Clinton's mother, the bride's parents and her brothers, Hugh and Tony Rodham, both students at the University of Arkansas at the time.

The wedding reception, held the next day, attracted about two hundred friends and political supporters. Clinton told his friends that he would run again for office in 1976 but that he had not decided whether to seek the state attorney general post or to challenge Hammerschmidt again. He also said he had been promised considerable support should he face Hammerschmidt.

One of the guests was Jim Guy Tucker, then attorney general of the state of Arkansas. Tucker had met Clinton a few months earlier when Clinton had invited him to speak to one of his law classes. Clinton had flown to Little Rock with Tucker after the Fayetteville visit, and the topic of their conversation during the trip was the job of attorney general.

"I told him I thought attorney general was just an absolutely terrific job to have, and we talked about the duties of the office," Tucker said. It was Tucker's observation that Clinton had "an activist view of the law, in the sense of how the law can be used...as a tool of advocacy in accomplishing public policies and goals. He was obviously very bright and capable of understanding what you can and cannot do with the law."

Clinton would soon be able to use Tucker's insight into the role of attorney general, as he took the next step in his political journey.

4

The Born Politician

THE "EXPERIMENT" HAD IGNITED A FIRE. BILL CLINTON WOULD NOT lose his next competition for public office. Clinton was, in fact, headed down a clear, smooth path to the governor's office.

Clinton had discovered a love for campaigning. It is a grueling, nonstop job that many politicians hate. Bill Clinton thrived on it. Campaigning gave him the chance to connect with people.

Political writer David Osborne called this Clinton's greatest asset:

> He thrives on the handshaking and elbow-rubbing that are the backbone of politics in Arkansas, and people bask in his warmth. Rather than wearing him down, the personal contact seems to rev him up. He is as comfortable and natural telling jokes with the good ol' boys as discussing international economic problems with a group of professors. Among governors today, he is virtually unparalleled at either.

At the time, Little Rock had two independent newspapers, the *Arkansas Gazette* and the *Arkansas Democrat*. The *Gazette* had a liberal Democratic editorial policy, while the *Democrat* generally took the conservative line.

After the 1974 race, an *Arkansas Gazette* editorial page writer called Clinton "a brilliant young law professor" and remarked: "It is regrettable that Arkansas did not quite add its own extra momentum to the national Democratic landslide...In any event Bill Clinton very nearly made it to Congress and surely he will be back in 1976."

Clinton, only twenty-eight, also had been endorsed by the National Committee for an Effective Congress in Washington, D.C. A news release from that organization called Clinton's campaign the "most impressive grass-roots effort in the country today."

It was during this initial venture into Arkansas politics that Clinton first endorsed educational improvement, thus earning the support of the Arkansas Education Association. In its announcement of support, the AEA's Political Action Committee for education cited "Clinton's consistent stand on the issues affecting the quality of education in Arkansas."

The AEA also noted "Clinton's position that the right to decide how to spend federal aid to education in Arkansas must be the province of the local school districts and communities involved." The group said it was encouraged by Clinton's "advocacy for teacher improvement and training programs and other needed supplementary programs whose objectives are to contribute to the advancement of educational excellence throughout the state."

In an address to teachers, Clinton said he favored "a substantial increase in the federal contribution for education." He added that federal grants for education should not be restricted to particular purposes. He also called for federal legislation to protect the pensions of teachers who move from state to state.

In 1976, Clinton would win his first political victory, and in January 1977 he assumed the office of attorney general of the state of Arkansas. (Jim Guy Tucker had vacated the office to run for Congress, and Clinton had won an easy primary victory, garnering 60 percent of the vote against George T. Jernigan, who had served as an appointed secretary of state in the 1960s, and Clarence Cash, an assistant attorney general. No Republican even attempted to run against him.)

After his election, Clinton "cultivated a pro-consumer, antiutility image," in the words of John Robert Starr, columnist for the *Arkansas Democrat*.

Clinton appeared to be almost fearless, if not reckless, in taking on the Arkansas political and business establishment. The legislature had long been dominated by utility and business interests. Clinton, serving as the state's lawyer, worked to keep utilities from raising rates. He operated the office almost in the same way he had operated his first campaign in 1974—by walking into places where he was unpopular and speaking his mind.

The young attorney general hired a staff equally young and idealistic. One of Clinton's achievements in his first state-level office was to reduce overcrowding in the state's prisons by expanding the work-release program. This program allowed prisoners to have regular jobs by day, then be locked in special facilities at night. The idea was to prepare them for life outside of prison.

During his term as attorney general, newspapers around the state noted Clinton's "considerable amount of speech-making." The *Log Cabin Democrat* in Conway, stating in an editorial that Clinton had been called "one of the state's fast-rising political stars," went on to say that he was "an attractive, articulate political leader."

The newspaper also said that "his record as attorney general has been studded with examples of hard work, consumer concerns and a generally aggressive stance that has led him into a variety of situations with seeming zest." The newspaper also speculated on Clinton's political future: "He is young and popular, and certainly must be getting a considerable amount of rather flattering encouragement to seek higher office." Among the offices mentioned as those to which he might aspire were governor, congressman or senator.

In 1977, Clinton printed an "Attorney General's Report" that the *Arkansas Gazette* said described "in glowing terms the activities of his first year in office." The newspaper investigated whether state money had been used to publish what was essentially a public relations effort for a candidate for governor. But Clinton was in the clear: He had used campaign funds to pay for the printing and distribution of the report.

This was the first instance of intense press scrutiny of Clinton.

When Clinton wasn't fighting the utilities, he was watching how Governor David Pryor handled the legislature and such complex affairs as the state budget. Always a student, Clinton was doing his homework for his next job.

Attorney General Clinton rode to an easy victory in the gubernatorial primary of 1978. He carried seventy-one of seventy-five counties, collecting 60 percent of the vote and winning the Democratic nomination without a runoff. "The organization that carried him into office had been put together with painstaking care over four years," *Democrat* columnist Starr later observed. "It was without question the best organization ever put together in Arkansas without machine support."

During the campaign for governor in 1978, Clinton would face a barrage of criticism surrounding his personal life. Opponents accused him of having liberal views on gun control, marijuana laws, capital punishment and women's rights. Hillary Rodham's use of her last name would become a recurrent note, although she joined him on the campaign trail and worked enthusiastically on election strategy.

Clinton, however, managed to turn the opposition around by placing himself among the South's "compromise progressive candidates" and maintaining that these new Southerners reflected the region's rising aspirations and more flexible attitudes.

Clinton, thirty-one, defeated four opponents in the Democratic primary: Joe D. Woodward, Randall Mathis, Frank Lady and Monroe Schwarzlose. He grabbed 60 percent of the vote in the runoff with Woodward.

According to Starr, Clinton had had his organization ready for a statewide campaign two years earlier, in 1976, but had had nowhere to use it until Jim Guy Tucker gave up the attorney general's office to run for Congress. The organization served him well. Clinton defeated Republican Lynn Lowe in the general election, amassing 338,684 votes to Lowe's 195,550.

* * *

Taking office at age thirty-two, he was the youngest governor in the nation.

"The foundation was laid for the establishment of Camelot at the Capitol. No one, least of all Clinton himself, imagined that two years later he would be the nation's youngest former governor," Starr wrote.

Indeed, during that first gubernatorial campaign, Clinton told members of the high school press that his career interest was to serve as governor "as long as the people will have me." (Arkansas governors were, in 1978, elected to two-year terms, with no limits on the number of terms they could seek.)

Always abreast of national policies and politics, one of Clinton's first actions as governor-elect was to head for Washington for a meeting with President Jimmy Carter to discuss the state's executive budget and whether it would meet Carter's anti-inflation guidelines. Clinton was concerned that a proposed raise for teachers "might be considered inflationary." (Clinton already had a close relationship with the White House, having run Carter's campaign in Arkansas in 1976.)

Clinton also was visible on the national scene as governor-elect when he moderated a discussion on national health care during the Democratic Party's national midterm convention in Memphis. An Arkansas newspaper, the *Searcy Daily Citizen*, reported that Clinton received more than his share of the attention of the media during the convention. The paper said speculation circulated during the convention that Clinton could be a running mate for Senator Edward Kennedy in the next presidential race. Another rumor was that Carter had selected Clinton to chair the meeting because he had chosen him to be his running mate in a bid for reelection.

Clinton's response was that he had just been elected governor and was not ready to leap into the national spotlight. The editorial report in the *Citizen* continued:

> What interests us the most is the fact that these experienced newsmen were so impressed by Clinton that none of them stopped to consider that the qualifications for vice-president are the same as those of President because, in the event of the death of a President, the vice-president must take his place. Clinton is now 32. He can't be President until he is at least 35. Hence, he can't be a running-mate for a presidential candidate in 1980. The reason most of these newsmen overlooked that interesting fact is that Clinton is, far and away, the most attractive candidate material the Democratic Party has going right now; though tagged as a liberal, he is giving all the indications of being a fiscal conservative at a time when that's the mood of the country.

Perhaps more important, as far as Clinton's future is

concerned, is the fact that the Democratic Party that met in Memphis is not a collection of the wildies of former days but a new and more responsible breed. And Clinton, aside from being attractive, is also a Rhodes Scholar with a lot of political moxie.

Another Arkansas newspaper, the *Helena World*, predicted that Clinton would take over the governor's office with fresh efficiency. "Already we can see the new broom of Bill Clinton making a wide sweep."

The *Arkansas Gazette* heralded Clinton's election as the end of the era of "old-style political bosses, the sort who used political patronage to dominate constituents, most of whom were poor and uneducated." The writer went on to say, "The events of 1978 have ended a political revolution in the state that began twelve years ago...The old demon of [racial hatred] is nearly gone, and the political debate focuses on other issues: better education, more roads, higher-paying jobs."

* * *

Bill Clinton took his first oath of office as governor on January 10, 1979, in the packed House chamber of the Capitol. Hillary Rodham held the Bible while he took the oath. As a symbol of allegiance to Arkansas, she wore a necklace that contained the 4.25-carat Kahn diamond, valued at $20,000. The diamond had been mined at the Arkansas Crater of Diamonds State Park. This park contains the only diamond mine in North America and visitors who find diamonds are allowed to keep them. The diamond is one of Arkansas's symbols and is represented on its state flag.

Although the House was packed for the swearing-in, all but about two hundred people declined to attend Clinton's inaugural speech in the bitter cold on the steps of the Capitol.

In his speech, Clinton promised to move Arkansas toward "a new era of achievement and excellence" and "a life that will be the envy of the nation." A focal point of his inaugural speech was education. He began by saying that the state had lingered too long at the bottom on education spending and in teacher salaries. "We must try to reverse that," he said.

Clinton said money for education would be part of a plan that would include "better accountability and assessment of students and teachers, a fairer distribution of aid, more efficient organization of school districts and recognition of work still to be done in programs for kindergarten, special-education and gifted and talented children."

Other issues Clinton promised to tackle were economic development, equal opportunity, environmental protection, tax relief for the elderly, emotionally disturbed children, abuse of power by government officials and help for those who are "old and weak or needy." Clinton announced his plans to establish an Energy Department and to replace the Arkansas Industrial Development Commission with an Economic Development Department.

In 1978, the Arkansas per capita income was $6,183 a year, still in forty-ninth place, just above Mississippi. The national per capita income that year averaged $7,820 a year.

Clinton decided to hold his inaugural ball at Robinson Auditorium in downtown Little Rock. The theme was "Diamonds and Denim," the idea being to combine the new sophistication of the Clinton era with the down-home tradition that Arkansans were more familiar with. Guests were told to wear formal clothes or denim, or a combination of both. They were encouraged to be comfortable and natural. The party was a smash.

Clinton, who had depended on the black vote for his gubernatorial election and who was rapidly gaining more support from the black community, made a risky decision: He invited former Governor Orval Faubus to the inaugural ball.

Faubus was the governor who had tried to prevent the desegregation of Little Rock's Central High School in 1957 and, in the process, brought infamy to the state. In the minds of many Americans, Faubus's name was synonymous with racism.

Starr called Clinton's inaugural party "a triumph of public relations and political fence-mending." But of the invitation of Faubus, Starr later said:

> His decision to invite Faubus to the inauguration revealed a character trait that some could admire. He thought inviting Faubus was the right thing to do, so he did it, without regard to political consequences. He assumed that because he was

willing to absolve Faubus after so many years, others were equally as willing to forgive. He was wrong. Many times during the next two years, he would take what he believed to be the right course without asking for advice or accepting it when it was offered. He was guided only by his own conscience.

* * *

The challenge for Bill Clinton to reform education in Arkansas was not an easy one. Teachers were underpaid and school funding was skimpy. Arkansas student test scores were a disgrace when compared with the rest of the nation. The fight began almost immediately during his first term. His fifty-five-minute State of the State address to the General Assembly on January 15, 1979, outlined an education plan with two controversial proposals:

1. A bill providing fair dismissal procedures for teachers, tied to legislation requiring all new teachers to pass a standard competency examination before being certified to teach.
2. A bill calling for mandatory achievement tests for all students in three grades each year. The testing system, he said, would enable parents, educators and state officials to make decisions about education.

Clinton also proposed a bill to address the unpopular issue of school consolidation. At that time, the state had 382 school districts and spent about $6 million a year in special subsidies to small districts. The issue was controversial, because many of the small schools were in small towns and had developed their own sense of identity and community. Consolidation meant the schools would be combined with one or more surrounding school districts. Local residents believed school consolidation would destroy local identity and contribute to the decline of small towns.

Clinton decided the job of writing a proposal on consolidation would be done by a commission that would study the issue for the next two years. He said, "I'm not proposing that small rural schools be closed, but rather that duplicative and inefficient administrative structures should be eliminated." The commission would complete a plan for reorganizing schools by July 1, 1980.

The governor's bill was introduced by state Senator Clarence E. Bell of Parkin, chairman of the Senate Education Committee. The plan would have to be enacted by the legislature, presumably in 1981.

But a firestorm of opposition arose. Most of the legislators represented areas with small school districts. Their constituents were adamantly opposed to reorganizing or consolidating school districts. Clinton, seeing that he could never get it passed, was forced to withdraw the bill.

It was a major failure and one of the first tests of Clinton's idealism. Reality had slapped him hard.

The governor's bill to require all new teachers to take the National Teacher Examination successfully passed the legislature and became law. Arkansas was one of the last states to require teachers who had just graduated from college to take this national exam, which tested them on general knowledge and in their areas of expertise. Because it affected only new teachers, there was little controversy. The Arkansas Education Association did not oppose the law. Speaking to the Future Teachers of America and the Student National Education Association in Little Rock, Clinton defended the law, saying that even though that test might not reveal everything about a teacher's competence, "We want to have standards for everybody."

Clinton called a special session of the legislature in January 1980 when state revenues fell below projections, causing a crisis in funding critical state services.

The legislature approved Clinton's plan to provide quick money for education and other critical needs. Employers had been deducting state income taxes from employees and turning the tax over to the state on a quarterly basis. Clinton changed this. requiring employers to send the money to the state on a monthly basis. This brought money into the treasury at a faster rate and allowed it to be spent on projects immediately. About $21 million was allocated to the Public School Fund, and about half of that to teachers' salaries, making possible an average raise of $1,200 per year for two years.

Clinton did encounter opposition from the Arkansas Education Association, however, over his plan for distributing tax funds to public schools. The AEA was not happy with the amount of teachers' raises.

The issue worsened when tax collections dropped and it looked as though there would not be enough money to fund the $1,200 raise in the second year, but only about $900 for each teacher. Clinton, however, held to his commitment of $1,200 the first year, saying that what had been accomplished was "unprecedented" in Arkansas history.

Arkansas state law does not allow deficit spending. The state lives by the rule of the balanced budget. By law, the state can only spend as much money as it takes in. If a program goes over budget, the money stops. The stringency of the law requires state officials to move money around from program to program as the need arises, and such shifting of funds is always controversial and difficult.

Clinton pointed out to school administrators that Arkansas law would not allow deficit spending to meet the promised raises the second year if the revenues were not there. "I don't know what the economy of this state is going to do, and neither do you and neither does anyone else, so you've got to help me explain this to the schoolteachers," he said.

Teachers benefited in another way during the 1980 special session through legislation passed by the Clinton administration called the Fair Dismissal Bill (Act 766). The law protected Arkansas teachers from termination of their contracts for "arbitrary, capricious and unsubstantiated reasons." The bill also specified that teachers with three or more years of experience be evaluated in writing each year before contract renewal. The system for the evaluations had been set up by Act 400 of 1975.

Clinton had to call another special session in April to address a problem with utility property tax assessments that would cost the state $18 million and shortchange the $21 million public school fund allotment approved during the January session. The shortfall resulted when the Public Service Commission and the State Transportation Commission upheld appeals by three utilities and five railroads that had the effect of reducing those companies' tax assessments and, thus, the public school fund. The governor's plan was, in the words of the *Arkansas Gazette*, "amended to oblivion."

Clinton was unsuccessful in guaranteeing the schools they would get their money.

Clinton was butting heads with the legislature and the national economy, and losing in almost every area.

The year 1980 did bring some success for Clinton's educational reform efforts. The Governor's School for Gifted and Talented Students was established. About three hundred high school students participated in the five-week program held on a college campus. The cost of the school to the state was about $250,000. Students studied art, choral music, instrumental music, drama, language arts, mathematics and natural and social sciences. Each student was able to spend time with instructors learning theories, developments and practices in his or her chosen area of study. A special faculty was selected from among college and high school instructors.

The Governor's School would bring Clinton criticism, and accusations of liberalism. A student wrote in a newsletter that the school had shown a film featuring "sexual and moral degeneracy" and another film that "raised questions about God and religion and left the answer to the viewer." A fundamentalist Christian group accused the school of teaching "humanism, pessimism and feminism."

That year also brought a significant change to Clinton's personal life. His daughter, Chelsea Victoria Clinton, was born on February 27, 1980. The birth was expected around March 15. Clinton had just returned to Little Rock from a trip to Washington and had been in the Governor's Mansion only about fifteen minutes when his wife began to experience labor pains. Although the Clintons had taken a course in the Lamaze method of delivery, they were unable to use it when doctors at Little Rock's Baptist Medical Center delivered the baby by cesarean section because of its position in the womb. After the ordeal, a hospital worker told a newspaper that Clinton "walked all over the area last night holding the baby in his arms."

* * *

Another important move that Clinton made to improve education during his first term as governor was to bring Don Roberts, then superintendent of schools in Newport News, Virginia, back to his home state of Arkansas as director of the state Department of Education. With Roberts came his large-scale, low-cost, in-service training program for teachers and administrators, called Program for Effective Teaching (PET). PET focused on effective teaching and clinical-supervision skills.

The program was voluntary for school districts and had only one staff person to coordinate it. But within four years, more than half the state's teachers, three-fourths of the principals, half the professors at teacher training institutions, nearly all superintendents and all supervisory personnel at the Department of Education had been trained by more than five hundred state-certified PET instructors. PET quickly became an integral component of public education in Arkansas.

Looking back over his first term that summer, Clinton admitted to school superintendents that he was disappointed that the condition of state revenues had hampered what he had set out to do for the public schools. He said, "I had hoped in my first term as governor that I would be able to make a dramatic difference, but the economy finally caught up with us."

Although he did not know it at the time, Clinton was headed for an even greater disappointment.

5

A Snowball of Political Misfortune

CLINTON HAD SPENT TWO YEARS LEARNING TO BE GOVERNOR. HE had set an idealistic agenda, but success in the legislature had escaped him. Learning to deal with the Arkansas legislature and the vagaries of the national economy may have been the toughest course he had ever taken.

Looking back on those two years, most of his friends, enemies, political peers and observers agree that he made one big mistake: the selection of a young, inexperienced, idealistic, eager staff. Starr observed years later:

> Clinton made a major personnel mistake in the begin-
> ning—one from which most of his other problems sprang.
> The nation's youngest governor didn't look for a seasoned
> administrator to run his office. He divided the power of the
> governor's office among three young, bearded, impractical
> visionaries. Rudy Moore, Steve Smith and John Danner were
> intelligent (Smith was brilliant), but they had not a shred of
> common sense among them. Had Clinton been a student of
> history instead of the law, he would not have tried to divide
> the power three ways. Triumvirates didn't work in Rome. This
> one did not work in Arkansas.

Writer David Osborne, who studied Clinton's education program (and served as an adviser in Clinton's 1992 presidential campaign), agreed with Starr's assessment of Clinton's staff. Osborne quoted Tom McRae, then president of the Winthrop Rockefeller Foundation: "He had a staff that was literally out to see where they could pick a fight, and see who they could make mad...There were a whole lot of things they did that were dumb and insensitive."

To Osborne, Smith himself admitted that the staff created political turmoil and opposition to the governor: "We probably did too much head-bashing in the first term. Part of it was that people like me on the staff were sort of smart-ass, and angered a lot of people. We were after every dragon in the land...I used language like 'corporate criminals,' which did not really endear the governor to the timber companies."

Another agreed-upon political mistake Clinton made during this first term was to push through legislation that raised fees on motor vehicle registration and title-transfer fees and gasoline and tire taxes, in order to finance a major highway repair program. For most people, car and truck licenses doubled from about $15 to $30.

Osborne made this observation of the legislation's impact:

> The increase did not appear terribly controversial at the time. But in Arkansas, the 'car tag' tax is an object of hatred. Every year car owners must go down to the courthouse, prove that they have had their car inspected in the previous thirty days, prove that they have paid their personal property tax for the previous year, submit an assessment of their current personal property and—finally—pay their license tax. "It's a nightmare—you stand in line forever," explains Dumas [Ernest Dumas, *Gazette* writer]. "People in the countryside were outraged when they'd finally get to the end of the line and be hit with this increase. That's all anybody talked about for a year, in the countryside. Particularly in poor, rural areas, people drove old cars and pickup trucks, which got the stiffest increases because of their weight. To make matters worse, the title-transfer fee hit the rural poor hardest, because they often bought an old car, drove it until it broke down and then bought another one."

Other changes didn't make Clinton a favorite with special-interest groups. Instead of focusing on recruitment of industries relocating from the North, he changed the old Arkansas Industrial Development Commission (AIDC) to the Department of Economic Development and placed its emphasis on small-business consulting, funding of small farm projects, promotion of agricultural exports and community development. The local chambers of commerce didn't like the new policies and were afraid the governor was ignoring industrial recruitment.

Clinton's administration also set up a network of rural health clinics that proved unpopular with physicians. Doctors clashed with social workers over definitions of responsibilities.

The trucking and poultry industries complained about the higher taxes to finance road repairs. The timber industry became angry over a series of public hearings held on clear-cutting of forests. But Clinton pushed through budget increases of 40 percent over two years for public education, the largest increase in the state's history.

All in all, during his first term, Clinton and his staff set out to effect a large amount of change in a short period of time. Political theorist Osborne described Clinton's "inclination to put good policy over good politics." He cited the highway tax program, which put less of a burden on the poor than a gasoline tax, yet alienated the common people, who did not want the license fees increased and felt the impact more directly.

Old friend and former aide Patty Howe Criner said the highway program would have been "our lifetime highway program. We would never have to raise fuel taxes...He [Clinton] wanted ongoing things. And what he did was try to surround himself with bright people who were specialists...And he went in and he tried to do too much."

* * *

In 1978, a newspaper war broke out that would have an immeasurable effect on Clinton and every other politician in Arkansas.

At the time, Little Rock had two independent newspapers, the morning *Arkansas Gazette* and the afternoon *Arkansas Democrat*. The Patterson family had owned the *Gazette* for years. The *Democrat* had been purchased in 1976 by Walter Hussman, a publisher of several smaller newspapers in Arkansas.

By almost any standard, the *Gazette* was a much larger and much better newspaper. It had been considered Arkansas's newspaper of record for years. The *Democrat*, at the time, was a decrepit old newspaper on its last legs.

Hussman was determined to make the *Democrat* a first-rate newspaper. In 1978, he started head-to-head competition with the *Gazette*. He had also hired John Robert Starr as managing editor. Starr, a seasoned Arkansas journalist, had recently retired as Little Rock bureau chief of the Associated Press. He was a tenacious editor ready to take the *Democrat* to the top. Starr had a young, inexperienced staff that he whipped into a frenzy. They began looking into every nook and cranny of Arkansas politics.

The *Gazette*, with its more experienced staff and its established dominance, was slow to respond. But it could not long ignore the *Democrat*'s growing aggression. The *Gazette* plunged into the fray. The two newspapers put Arkansas government, especially Clinton's administration, under a microscope.

Editor Starr began writing an op-ed column. Much of it was full of vitriol for the competing *Gazette*, but Starr also attacked Clinton and his staff members on a regular basis. He portrayed them as political hucksters, or worse, as determined idiots who were wasting the taxpayer's money and damaging the governmental process.

Articles appeared involving Doug Harp, the head of the State Police, who had been accused of framing a man for murder. The *Democrat*'s articles cleared Harp, but the paper then focused on Martin Borchert, director of State Building Services, who had used his private hardware company to do business with state contractors. The newspaper's investigation forced Borchert to file a conflict-of-interest form. These, and the daily columns, led to what Starr saw as a hostile relationship between himself and the governor and his staff.

Soon, the newly formed state departments became the target of *Democrat* articles about misspending of state money. One article alleged that Economic Development Director James Dyke planned to spend $450 a month for live plants to decorate his office. That order was canceled after news stories appeared in both papers condemning such extravagant spending.

Another story detailed a $2,000 retreat for the employees of the newly formed Energy Department. The topic of the retreat was the conservation of energy. Starr lampooned the Energy Department employees because most of them had driven the seventy miles to the retreat in their individual cars, rather than in a car pool or a van.

The *Democrat* and *Gazette* continued to print stories of wasteful spending by state employees. One example was the purchase of fifty corkscrews—costing $37.50—by the Energy Department to distribute to delegates at a conference in Little Rock so that they could open bottles of wine donated by an Arkansas winery. Starr, in his column, began a series of Sweet William Awards "to recognize wastrels in state and local government."

Starr is often credited with creating the "Slick Willie" label for Clinton's brand of politics. Starr may have used the sobriquet a few times over the years, but he more frequently used the nicknames "Sweet William" and "Billion $ Bill." The Slick Willie name was popularized by Paul Greenberg, an editorial writer for the *Pine Bluff Commercial*. In addition, visitors to the state capital can eat and drink at a restaurant-bar named Slick Willy's only three blocks away. The bar existed long before the nickname became popular for Clinton, and is spelled with a "y" instead of an "ie." The bar's proximity to the capital cannot be discounted as a possible influence on the origin of an appellation that Clinton came to detest.

More problems with the newspapers were on the way. Rudy Moore, Clinton's chief of staff, showed up in police reports in both newspapers after he became involved in an altercation with a woman at a restaurant.

Following that story, another appeared detailing the SAWER (Special Alternative Wood Energy Resources) Project, funded through the now defunct Department of Local Services to train low-income people to cut firewood and distribute it to the needy. The *Democrat* reported that the project had spent $62,000 and produced only six woodchoppers and three cords of wood. The *Gazette* also delved into the project. Clinton fired SAWER's director, Ted Newman, after the story broke, but it was too late to repair the damage the project did to Clinton's political standing.

Despite the growing critical comments and attacks, only one person had filed against Clinton for the Democratic primary for 1980: Monroe Schwarzlose, a retired turkey farmer who had run against Clinton in 1978. Frank White, a Little Rock savings and loan executive and former director of the state Industrial Development Commission, filed as a Republican candidate. White, a former Democrat, had changed parties so he could challenge Clinton in the general election.

The day before the primary election, the worst controversy of Clinton's administration came to a head.

For several weeks, Fidel Castro had been allowing Cubans to leave their home country. Thousands were choosing to climb into leaky boats and head for Florida. The United States government had to find a way of dealing with this influx.

The Federal Emergency Management Agency began placing the refugees in Fort Chaffee, in northwest Arkansas. The fort had once been an active-duty training station, but had been downgraded to a base for National Guard and Army Reserve training. It still contained a number of barracks from the days the place had been an active-duty station. In fact, Fort Chaffee had been used in the early 1970s to house South Vietnamese and Laotian refugees who had fled their countries at the end of the Vietnam War.

The federal government had confined about 19,000 Cuban boat-lift refugees at Fort Chaffee. Most of the Cubans were decent people who were only seeking a better life. But Arkansas residents in the area were fearful of the refugees, because Castro had opened the jails and mental institutions in Cuba and sent those inmates to America as well. It was impossible for American authorities to tell a hardened criminal from a simple, desperate refugee.

The Cubans were angry that they had been sent to Arkansas. They wanted to go to Florida to join the large Cuban community there. The federal government insisted on processing each refugee before allowing him or her to go to Florida. The longer the Cubans remained in Arkansas, the more angry they became.

On May 26, about 350 refugees left the camp and scattered throughout the countryside. They were recaptured within a couple of days by state troopers and local authorities, but Clinton was enraged because the federal authorities at Chaffee had done nothing to keep the Cubans on the base or to recapture them.

The governor ordered two hundred National Guard troops to Chaffee and demanded that the Federal Emergency Management Agency tighten security. He asked President Jimmy Carter to give the Army orders to keep the Cubans on the base.

Patty Criner remembers those days of 1980 as one problem after another. On top of everything else, the state experienced a devastating drought.

"Every time you turned around, there was a disaster," Criner said. "Chickens were dying, cows were starving, a terrible drought, Cuban refugees and then the car tag issue."

* * *

Clinton defeated Schwarzlose in the primary, but the turkey farmer received a surprising 138,670 votes—about 31 percent—to Clinton's 306,736. Schwarzlose campaigned on the car-tag and SAWER issues. He had his picture taken beside his own woodpile to show what could be done for a lot less money. In the Republican primary, Frank White defeated his opponent, Marshall Crisman, 5,867 to 2,310. The Republican Party had been mostly a nonentity in Arkansas since the days of Reconstruction, and those low numbers reflected that fact.

After the primary, more trouble awaited Clinton. On June 1, Fort Chaffee erupted in a riot. Starr wrote, "Most of the fighting took place on the base, but about two hundred Cubans charged down Highway 22 toward Barling [a small nearby community]. They were beaten back with nightsticks less than one hundred yards from the city limits." Clinton again began wrangling with federal officials, demanding that the Army keep the Cubans on base. In August, President Carter told Clinton that ten thousand more Cubans would be sent to Chaffee.

The Cuban crisis was all the ammunition White needed to launch a devastating television campaign.

"When Frank White aired a campaign commercial showing rioting Cubans and criticizing Clinton for not standing up to the president, whose popularity in Arkansas was at an all-time low, there was nothing the governor could say, so he said nothing," Starr later observed.

Further fuel for White's fire was added by another grant program approved by the Department of Local Services. White said the state planned to give $968,189 to the Ozarks Institute of Eureka Springs to teach country people how to grow gardens. Though White did not describe the program accurately, his ridicule whipped up the Clinton opposition. Also drawing criticism was the fact that Steve Smith, the governor's aide, had served on the institute's board before becoming a Clinton employee.

White's campaign fund grew by mid-October to within $15,000 of what Clinton had raised. The Republican stood before audiences and promised he would lower the car license fees. He told them the increases had caused "great pain" for Arkansans, especially the 370,000 people who were on Social Security. He drew loud applause when he told a group that Clinton "should have sued" federal officials when they announced they would use Fort Chaffee as a Cuban refugee relocation center.

A final blow came when two big utilities, Arkansas Power & Light Company and Southwestern Bell Telephone, threw their support to White. Clinton, with his antiutility background, had never been their favorite.

When the votes were tabulated, Frank White had scored Arkansas's first gubernatorial upset in twenty-six years "and brought Camelot down around Clinton's ears," Starr wrote. Clinton drew 403,241 votes; White got 435,684.

* * *

Starr has said Clinton was defeated by the actions of his own staff and his insistence on backing them. "He tended to blame the press, rather than miscreants in his administration, for the bad publicity and consequent negative reaction from the public that dogged him throughout his first administration," Starr wrote.

Much of Frank White's victory must be credited to the 1980 Republican landslide. Jimmy Carter had lost his popularity over the way he handled the Iran hostage crisis, soaring inflation and the Cuban affair. The American voter was ready for a change. An extremely popular Ronald Reagan defeated Carter and marched into office with a lot of Republicans, including Frank White, clinging to his coattails.

In addition, Starr had taken an extreme dislike to Clinton. He was relentless in the final days of the election. He wrote column after column blistering Clinton and ridiculing his administration. Some observers say Starr was single-handedly responsible for

Clinton's defeat, but Starr has said that no newspaper columnist has such clout.

Theorist Osborne pointed out other factors that led to White's victory:

> The campaign subtext was equally important. White painted Clinton as too young, too liberal and too big for his britches. He criticized him for bringing eastern liberals in to run his administration and charged that he was only using Arkansas as a stepping-stone to national office. He exploited the symbolism of Clinton's administration: his youthful, bearded aides, and the fact that his wife had kept her maiden name. "It was ridiculous," says Mahony [Jodie Mahony, a state representative], "but those were the burning issues of 1980: Cubans, car tags and Hillary not taking his name."
>
> Clinton was clearly overconfident. The polls had him far ahead as late as mid-October, and no one—not even White—believed [Clinton] would lose. But as the voters swung to Reagan in the final days, so they swung to White. Arkansas experienced the greatest shift from Carter in 1976 to Reagan in 1980 of any state. In 1978 and 1980, voters all across the nation threw the liberal rascals out, and Clinton became yet another casualty.

Clinton was shocked. So was his staff. His appointees and supporters were shocked. Even Frank White was shocked.

The following day the atmosphere in many state offices was funereal. The idealists Clinton had put in charge of innovative programs felt they had been stopped cold, that all their ambitious efforts had been defeated.

"The loss stung Clinton badly," Osborne wrote. "But it taught him a fundamental lesson: that a reformer must find a way to do what his constituents want, not what he thinks they need...Clinton also learned—many would say too well—that he had to be more cautious, to pick his fights."

One Arkansas editorial writer observed in the *Springdale News*:

> Clinton is an intelligent, competent politician who got caught in a vise between his own complacency and the voters' "throw the rascals out" attitude...Clinton's campaign

misread the state's political barometer and failed to see storm clouds on the horizon. Those clouds boiled out of public anger about the economy and the way a Democratic president and Congress had been attempting to run the nation...Clinton had the image of an overeducated kid with bigger political aspirations than governor.

Clinton himself, in his first interview after his loss, stated four reasons for his defeat: the mood of the times; the increase in automobile license fees; the second influx of Cuban refugees to Fort Chaffee; and the public perception of him as too young, too ambitious, arrogant and insensitive.

I simply didn't communicate to the people that I genuinely cared about them," he said. "I think maybe I gave the appearance of trying to do too many things and not involving the people as I should." Clinton appeared perceptive, naming the reasons many analysts later cited.

But his perception had come too late to save him in 1980.

* * *

Rumors circulated about Clinton's future. Some held that Clinton might be named chairman of the Democratic National Committee or president of a local private college.

In a farewell speech to the legislature, Clinton asked Arkansans to understand what he had set out to do as governor and to recognize that, aside from his own political misfortune, the state had not addressed its basic needs by voting him out of office. An *Arkansas Gazette* editorial writer described the moment:

> It was a poignant scene as Clinton appeared before the joint session of the legislature in a crowded House chamber, his wife, Hillary, holding their ten-month-old daughter, at his side. Just two years earlier he had taken the oath in the same chamber as the nation's youngest governor, one whose intellect and personality were soon to capture national admiration and credit for the state. Now he was beaten, leaving the state government after a narrow upset loss in November, asking the people to "remember me as one who reached for all he could for Arkansas."

The *Gazette* came forth with its assessment of Clinton's first term, naming education as his "finest achievement and his greatest unfulfillment."

The newspaper said Clinton "provided the single largest increase in teachers' salaries ever, extended health insurance to school employees, provided the first incentives for school programs for gifted children, established the first accountability program through standardized testing of students and new teachers, expanded special education and kindergartens and achieved some equity in the distribution of school funds."

Hillary Rodham had been working at the Rose Law Firm since 1977, when Clinton had been elected attorney general and the couple had moved to Little Rock. Now it was Bill Clinton's turn to go into private law practice. He took a position with one of Little Rock's biggest firms, Wright, Lindsey and Jennings. Close friends say he went into a period of depression and partial seclusion. Once filled with hope and optimism, he turned bitter about what he believed was unfair treatment from the people he had tried to serve. For perhaps the first time in his life, Bill Clinton was aimless.

Clinton, seeing his political future vanish overnight, became careless about his actions. He had achieved so much so fast. Now it was gone. Rumors began filtering into the newsrooms and throughout state offices that Clinton was having an affair with another woman. Such rumors about politicians are commonplace, but this one had a persistence about it. Because Clinton was no longer in the public light, the reporters and editors decided to ignore the talk.

But Clinton is known to have asked several confidants, "What am I supposed to do about these women who throw themselves at me?" His friends warned him to resist the temptation and to consider the effect that an affair would have on his family, not to mention his political future. In interviews during the 1992 campaign, Clinton would admit that the "trouble" he brought to his marriage began during these dark days, although he would never be more specific than that.

6

The First Comeback

IF CLINTON HAD SUFFERED AT THE HANDS OF THE MEDIA, THE NEW governor, Frank White, would feel the sting even more.

Although White was an intelligent man—a graduate of the U.S. Naval Academy and highly successful in business—he was depicted in the press and on television as a slow-witted hayseed. He was a big, loud, genial extrovert who loved to tell stories and laugh it up with the guys at the country club.

On the night he was elected, a jubilant White said it was a "victory for the Lord." The 1980 election, both nationally and in the state of Arkansas, was marked by religious overtones. Right-wing evangelist Pat Robertson had initially sought the Republican nomination, but dropped out of the race and endorsed Ronald Reagan. Robertson's fundamentalist Christian supporters gave an immeasurable boost to Reagan.

White belonged to a nondenominational fundamentalist church and had touted that fact during the campaign. Clinton attended the Baptist Church, also conservative and mostly fundamentalist, but he was quiet about his religious beliefs. Virginia Kelley said she once asked her son why he never mentioned his Baptist affiliation while campaigning in a state that was dominated by Baptists. Clinton responded, "I'll never do it. I'll never use this for any political gain."

White's "victory for the Lord" statement made the headlines the next day. The new governor's implication was that Clinton's long-haired liberal administration had been a tool of evil, and that none other than Frank White had conquered the forces of the devil.

That was the implication, but White insisted that the comment was interpreted incorrectly. Yet what did it mean? Reporters hounded White about the "victory for the Lord" statement. A few days later, he said it had only meant that his prayers had been answered.

For the rest of his administration, Frank White's mouth would get him into more trouble than any of his actions.

White realized that he had become governor by accident, and that he had not the slightest idea of how to lead the state. During the campaign he'd promised he would "run the state government like a business." He soon found that politics is chaos, and that the efficiency of the business office doesn't always work in the halls of the statehouse.

The press corps of both newspapers didn't care much for White. Some reporters called him "Governor Goofy" behind his back. Although Clinton's administration had been nearly as inept, Clinton himself had a polished appearance that had captivated the press. Many reporters shared Clinton's liberal views as well. If anything, Frank White was a typical Arkansan in his conservative views, his religious beliefs and his rough-hewn personality. He enjoyed a great amount of support throughout Arkansas.

Bill Clinton, meanwhile, was still in a downward mood swing. Every two years the local journalists produced a gridiron-type show called "The Farkleberry Follies," in which politics and politicians were lampooned. One of the gimmicks of the show was a "mystery guest," usually a well-known person who was disguised during the show and who popped out at the end to deliver a funny monologue.

The show in April 1981, only a few months after Clinton's defeat, was produced by Leroy Donald, the business editor of the *Arkansas Gazette*, who asked Clinton to be a mystery guest. Clinton declined, wanting no reminder of "Cubans and Car Tags," the title of that year's show. Donald got word to Hillary Clinton that her husband was reluctant to join the fun.

"Hillary talked him into it," Donald said later. "He was in a skit where a bunch of inept Cuban hijackers attempted to take over a tiny commuter airplane. Clinton wore one of those old-fashioned leather pilot helmets that covered his whole face. He played a silent role as copilot. Suddenly, he whipped off that helmet and took center stage, delivering one of the funniest speeches of the show, in which he poked fun at himself and at Frank White, who was sitting right in front of the stage. You could see the change occurring in Clinton. You could see his face light up. The crowd was bowled over by him and gave him a loud, long reception. Even Frank White was laughing and enjoying himself." Bill Clinton was coming back.

During the 1981 legislative session, White became infamous for the "Creation Science Act." The legislature approved a bill requiring all public schools in Arkansas that taught the theory of evolution to give equal time to teaching "creation science," a theory put forth by fundamentalist Christians that the universe, the Earth and man were created by God as described in the book of Genesis in the Bible. Supporters insisted that there was as much evidence for the creation science theory as there was for evolution. The legislature quickly passed the bill and sent it to White, who signed it and made it law.

The law created an uproar. School administrators were in a quandary as to how to implement the new program. It stirred a religious debate throughout the state.

Later, while talking to reporters, White overloaded his mouth again. He casually mentioned that he had signed the bill without reading it. Newspaper columnists, including Starr, immediately jumped on him. His failure to read a bill before signing it was cited as proof that White was an incompetent governor.

The creation science controversy also caught the attention of the national press and television. Suddenly, there was Frank White on the evening news, uncomfortable, speaking in circles about science and religion. Arkansans were struck by the contrast between the refined Bill Clinton and the raw Frank White.

The American Civil Liberties Union quickly filed a suit challenging the law. On January 6, 1982, federal Judge William R. Overton ruled the act unconstitutional, saying it "was simply and purely an effort to introduce the biblical version of creation into the public school curricula. Since creation science is not science, the conclusion is inescapable that the only real effect of the act is the advancement of religion." He added, "No group, no matter how large or small, may use the organs of government, of which the public schools are the most conspicuous and influential, to foist its religious beliefs on others."

Attorney General Steve Clark, who had defended the law, announced that he would not appeal the ruling, saying he did not believe the federal appeals court would reverse Judge Overton's ruling.

White abolished most of the state agencies Clinton had created, eliminating programs or combining them with those of other agencies. In addition, school teachers were unhappy with White over what they felt to be inadequate funding for education. Bumper stickers saying "Don't Blame Me. I Voted for Clinton" became popular among teachers.

After White took a free ride in an airplane owned by a utility company, the press began accusing him of being a pawn of special interests.

* * *

Clinton, emerging from his seclusion, began a round of speeches to civic clubs and other groups around the state. He was often quoted in the newspapers as taking issue with White's political decisions.

In addition, Clinton's regular attendance at church provided an unexpected media bonus. He was a member of Little Rock's Immanuel Baptist Church, one of the few white mainline churches that remained in a predominantly black area near downtown Little Rock. Clinton also was a member of the choir. The church's morning services were broadcast on local television ever Sunday morning. The camera angle on the minister included several members of the choir, and Bill Clinton was among the most visible. Every Sunday morning, viewers could see Clinton's face right behind and slightly above the preacher. When his Sunday appearances on television became a minor issue in a later election, church officials and Clinton denied that it had been a calculated maneuver.

In February 1982, Clinton went before the people of Arkansas in a thirty-second television advertisement to announce that he would run for governor again and that he had learned from his mistakes. The ad brought much attention.

"His ploy was a popular topic of conversation," wrote John Brummett of the *Gazette*. "The most common opinion seemed to be that broadcasting a campaign advertisement before actually announcing as a candidate was curious, of course, but that it might turn out to be a smart maneuver. If nothing else, the press was intrigued." The ad was written and paid for by Clinton, but it received considerable free airtime in television newscasts.

Clinton's most formidable Democratic opponent was former U.S. Representative Jim Guy Tucker, who had served as a mentor when Clinton first sought office. Tucker was not impressed by the advertisement and said it was only appropriate that Clinton apologize for the mistakes of his first term. Besides Tucker, Clinton faced Democratic opposition from state Senator Kim Hendren of Gravette and former Lieutenant Governor Joe Purcell.

Clinton, at age thirty-five, again stated during his campaign that his only political aspiration was "to serve as governor a long time." He criticized White for trying to undo some of Clinton's accomplishments in holding down utility costs. One of White's first actions as governor had been to fire three of the former state Energy Department officials who had helped Clinton fight higher utility rates in the Grand Gulf nuclear power plant controversy, which had developed in 1980 when Clinton was in office. Arkansans were forced to pay higher electrical rates because Arkansas Power & Light Company and Mississippi Power & Light Company had, at one time, entered into an agreement to share the energy from the Grand Gulf nuclear plant in Mississippi. The two companies are owned by the same corporation.

White's campaign was not without popular support, however, and it received a boost from Vice President George Bush, who attended a fund-raiser for White before the primary election. The event brought in more than $100,000.

Clinton seemed to concentrate on his own shortcomings as much as White's as the campaign progressed. One campaign theme emerged: "You can't lead without listening," a phrase Clinton had coined. During his campaign stops, he encouraged his audiences to tell him what was on their minds. Once again, he was trying to connect.

Clinton told the people that his issues were "jobs, education and utility rates." He repeatedly blamed White for rising utility rates. "You don't want an antiutility governor, but neither do you want one who takes his cue from the big utilities," he told one group. And, consistent with his first two campaigns for governor, he said education was his major priority, since without it there could be little economic progress.

Surprisingly, teachers' salaries became an issue between Tucker and Clinton. Clinton criticized Tucker for saying he would give the teachers raises without a tax increase. Tucker claimed he could eliminate enough special tax exemptions to cover the cost. The AEA endorsed Tucker. However, many teachers and educators publicly supported Clinton, and one group ran a political advertisement for him in a statewide newspaper.

Tucker's attempt to beat Clinton at the educational-improvement game was not successful. Tucker was eliminated from the race during the primary, which gave Clinton 41.7 percent of the vote and forced him into a runoff with Purcell. It was Clinton's first gubernatorial runoff battle.

Purcell had run a clean, low-key campaign, but was not equipped to deal with the Clinton machine. In the runoff on June 9, Clinton took 54 percent of the vote, with 248,359 votes to Purcell's 212,062. Clinton had gained a rematch with Frank White.

* * *

The second campaign between Clinton and White focused on education issues and utility raises. Clinton was silent on the Creation Science Act issue until September 16, 1982, when he was asked during a radio interview whether he would have approved the act.

"I would not have signed the creation science bill in the form that it was passed," Clinton said. He added that the law "put enormous burdens" on public school teachers because it required teaching a specific version of creation that might not be compatible with all religions. He said the bill was "rushed through the legislature" without parents or teachers being consulted.

The *Gazette* endorsed Clinton over White. The choice was based on the records of both men in the office of governor and Clinton's ability to "bring the ideas and leadership that the state desperately needs." About White, the editorial writer said: "Mr. White's short-coming was that he had nothing much in mind to do as governor. His vision was limited to a few cliches, one being that a government was supposed to be run like a business."

Hillary Rodham became Hillary Clinton and actively campaigned for her husband. A *Gazette* writer observed:

> Mrs. Clinton is almost certainly the best speaker among politicians' wives, probably the only one who can fully engage an audience on her own merits, rather than just as somebody's wife....She is an Illinois native, perhaps a little brisker, a little more outspoken than the traditional Southern governor's lady....The name change indicates that she's working at softening her image a bit...And succeeding, apparently. She has become a good hand-shaking campaigner in the traditional Arkansas style.

White raised $1.2 million for his campaign. Clinton raised $1.5 million, an amount called "impressive when one considers that he managed it without the help of several of the state's traditional political bankrollers," wrote Brummett of the *Gazette*. When the election was over, the candidates had spent about $1.6 million each.

As Election Day neared, Clinton promised that his new staff in the governor's office would be different in personality and function and that he wouldn't attempt to accomplish such a large agenda. Gone were such troublemaking idealists as Rudy Moore and Steve Smith.

Clinton also used one of White's tactics from the 1980 campaign and criticized the Republican's record on such issues as :

- "Selling out" to the utilities, abolishing a key division of the state Energy Department and replacing two of Clinton's appointees to the Public Service Commission.
- Doubling the price of prescription medicine for Medicaid recipients while granting $12 million in tax exemptions to business.
- Taking a job-training program from county governments and giving it to the Opportunities Industrialization Center in

Little Rock, which spent some of the money to build a back porch and a doghouse for OIC officials.

• Not showing sufficient leadership to pass legislation increasing truck's weight limit to 80,000 pounds, which would allow more interstate shipping through Arkansas and provide more revenue for the state.

Clinton picked up support from an unexpected area: *Democrat* managing editor and columnist John Robert Starr, who had been Clinton's most outspoken foe in the previous election. Starr was not pleased with the way White had run the governor's office. In his columns, Starr now soft-pedaled Clinton while bashing White. Readers wondered about the dramatic turnaround. Starr explained that Clinton had apologized for his arrogance and had recognized the error of his ways. In addition, Starr said, White was just not a very good governor.

Starr's change of heart puzzled staffers at the rival *Gazette* as well. There were rumors in the *Gazette* newsroom that Bill and Hillary Clinton had spent much of the last two years courting Starr in an effort to mend fences. It was said that they often visited him in his office and telephoned him frequently, seeking his advice and counsel and ultimately befriending him. Starr and the Clintons have denied that any lobbying occurred.

"After 1980, actually, we saw Mr. Clinton quite frequently," Starr said in a later interview. "He was connected with a law firm [near the *Democrat* offices] and, well, I guess four or five times we saw him during the time he was out of office—going to lunch."

When the votes came in, Clinton's comeback was complete. He captured 431,855 votes, or 54.7 percent, to White's 357,496. He had successfully defended himself from what Starr called White's "arsenal of mudballs."

* * *

Clinton was the first governor in the state's history to be defeated and then come back to regain the office. Clinton made dramatic turnarounds in several counties in which he had done poorly in 1980. The race went on record as being the most expensive in the state's history, with White and Clinton spending over $3 million.

The bulk of the money went to aggressive television and radio advertising.

Gazette writer Ernest Dumas commented on Clinton's comeback:

> Clinton's strength with the voters is still his intelligence, his promise, his obvious effort to be personally esteemed by voters. His final televised talk with the voters Saturday night before the election, a rarity nowadays, may have been pivotal in his victory. As a communicator, he rivals President Reagan.
>
> Clinton had other things going for him this time. The campaign was masterly organized—and this was a tribute both to his having a skilled manager in Betsey Wright and to the revival of the moribund Democratic Party organization.

A guest writer for the *Gazette*, Robert Johnston, a political science professor at the University of Arkansas at Little Rock, wrote, "Bill Clinton won in 1982 for some of the same reasons Bill Clinton lost in 1980 (and Frank White won in 1980 and lost in 1982): State and national tides...The swing nationally back to the Democrats was certainly expected."

After his victory, Clinton thanked the Arkansas Education Association for coming out in support of him against White in the general election. "I think for the rest of my life I will look back on this election with a mixture of disbelief that it happened and with a profound sense of humility and gratitude for people like you who worked their hearts out and went the extra mile to do something that no rational person thought could be done," he said at the group's annual convention that November.

Brummett said Clinton had learned his lessons well, and listed them: "That he had acted too big for his britches, that he became insulated from the people, that he spent too much time garnering national publicity, that he certainly shouldn't have raised the motor vehicle license fees, that he had taken the people's adoration for granted, that he had erred by smugly deciding that he could win reelection solely on the sheer force of his own personality without courting the grass-roots support he needed from traditional Democrats and the labor, teacher and black organizations that formed the core of his earlier political success."

Brummett had kind words for the way Clinton had opened his 1982 campaign with a television message to the people. He praised Clinton's campaign staff for its "unyielding devotion, hard work and efficiency" and attributed much of its success to coordinator Betsey Wright, who told Brummett that the staff "had one central feeling, and that was to leave no stone unturned, no task undone. They took nothing for granted."

Halfway into Governor Clinton's second term, the Associated Press determined that he had accomplished sixty-nine of the 117 promises he'd made during his 1982 campaign, had abandoned five, had unsuccessfully tried to carry out eight but was thwarted by the legislature and was still developing thirty-five. Teachers got a raise averaging $750 each during the first year of his term, a total of $24 million. The AEA was not satisfied and continued to seek a larger increase—an average of $3,000 for each teacher.

Midway through, Clinton himself considered his second term "an exceedingly decisive" one. In education, it proved a turning point for the state.

7

The Education Revolution

IN HIS INAUGURAL ADDRESS TO BEGIN HIS SECOND TERM AS governor, delivered in January 1983, Bill Clinton centered on the hardship of a national recession and high unemployment. He stated that his first priority was "to put the people back to work," but went on to say, "Over the long run, education is the key to our economic revival and our perennial request for prosperity." He continued:

> We must dedicate more of our limited resources to paying our teachers better; expanding educational opportunities in poor and small school districts; improving and diversifying vocational and high technology programs; and, perhaps most important, strengthening basic education. Without competence in basic skills, our people cannot move on to more advanced achievement.

The regular legislative session began that January with the introduction of several bills to reorganize school districts. At the same time, a suit stood before the Arkansas Supreme Court that would call for all children to have equal access to educational opportunities, regardless of the economic condition of their community.

Clinton decided to wait until the court made its decision before developing any education proposal of his own. That summer, the court decided that the state's school funding formula was unconstitutional, and the governor began working with Education Department director Dr. Don Roberts to decided what steps to take to correct the problem. The legislature passed, on its own initiative, a bill to allow teachers to retire with full benefits after thirty years of service. Clinton signed the bill.

The seeds of Clinton's major reform package began to sprout. The governor came out in support of one of the school consolidation bills, but the bill tied consolidation to a requirement that the state Board of Education establish a fifteen-member commission to develop a new set of minimum standards for schools. The standards would not take effect until 1984, and all districts would be required to meet them by 1987 or be forced to consolidate with districts that could meet the standards.

"I think you might see the entire educational community from the state in support of this," Clinton said. The legislature approved the bill and Clinton signed it.

The other education laws to come out of the regular session of 1983 were:

- Act 375: required all districts to offer kindergarten.
- Act 14: allowed students to take up to 50 percent of their courses in another district if the home district does not offer them.
- Teacher Fair Dismissal Act: granted new provisions to teachers on probation (without three years' tenure) for hearings before dismissal and allowed those teachers to transfer to another district and not lose tenure.

Fifteen members were named to the standards committee by the State Board of Education. Most of the members were teachers or school administrators. Some were school board members. Practically all were from smaller communities in the state.

Possibly the most significant member of the committee was the chair: Hillary Rodham Clinton, then thirty-five. The appointment would be Hillary Clinton's political debut in Arkansas. Hillary Clinton had always played a behind-the-scenes role in her husband's career, and a public role in helping him campaign. Now she was clearly at center stage, the leader of Clinton's most ambitious political undertaking.

"This guarantees that I will have a person who is closer to me than anyone else overseeing a project that is more important to me than anything else," Bill Clinton said. "I don't know if it's a politically wise move, but it's the right thing to do."

Hillary Clinton defended her qualifications for the job: "I've gone to school a large part of my life. I've been involved in classroom activities and visiting with teachers as a volunteer." She admitted that the expertise would come from the members of the committee.

* * *

A national report, "Nation at Risk," was released at the same time the committee began its work. The report by the National Commission on Excellence in Education warned of a "rising tide of mediocrity" in the nation's schools. Hillary Clinton said her committee would assess Arkansas's schools in light of the report.

She was critical of President Reagan for not putting "the same kind of leadership in the area of education as he has in defense," and called the report a "blueprint for how we get ourselves out of the serious state of deterioration we're currently in."

At the time of the report, Arkansas students were far below the national average in reading and math scores on the Science Research Associates standardized tests. Although 162 high schools, which educated 76 percent of the state's students, offered the courses that the National Commission recommended, none of the state's 371 districts required students to take all the subjects that the commission said should be required of students.

The report also recommended a longer school day and a longer school year. Few schools in Arkansas were offering more than the state-required 175 days; the commission recommended 220 days per year.

Bill Clinton continually emphasized the importance of the committee's work. It became officially known as the Education Standards Committee. He told its members at their first meeting that their job was "as important as any to be done in public life in the next few years." He said he would not call a special session of the legislature to ask for money for education until the committee members had completed their work. Their target was to finish a draft of the new standards by the 1983–84 school year so that comments could be solicited from the public and incorporated into the final draft.

Committee members started out with the intention of making changes in Arkansas education. "I would be happy if what we came out with caused absolute panic—even in my own house," Hillary Clinton said.

While the committee worked, the governor addressed issues raised by the Arkansas Supreme Court ruling on the state's distribution of funds for public education. The court held that all students in Arkansas have a right to equal opportunity in education, and found inequity in the way tax money was used to fund schools—most problematically, that big communities with a large industrial tax base could offer a better education than small towns with little or no local industry to tax.

Clinton made plans for a special session of the legislature to consider a sales tax increase and a new funding formula for the schools to replace the one invalidated by the court. The disparities in funding had developed over the years because of the varying size of Arkansas school districts. For instance, a high school student in one small community could select from among twenty-three course units; a student at a large high school could choose from as many as 182.

The *Arkansas Gazette* commented: "Mr. Clinton appears to be preparing now to give the state the kind of leadership that will reestablish the public confidence he held when he came to office the first time, in 1979. It is reassuring to think of Mr. Clinton completing the full circle, rekindling those earlier hopes and aspirations."

Clinton himself agreed with the court's ruling, saying that spending unequal amounts of money on students in different districts should be illegal. "We have today an historic obligation to equalize funding and to improve education," he told students and educators at the opening of the fourth Governor's School for the Gifted and Talented.

He asked the state Board of Education to take a public stand supporting the court's ruling and higher standards for public schools. The governor felt the two issues should be tied together. The board did endorse dealing with the two issues together, but asked the governor and legislature to "move as slowly as necessary" because no one knew where the state would get the money for two major operations.

* * *

The Education Standards Committee was proceeding with its work and holding public meetings in all seventy-five counties. Comments were heard from students, teachers, parents, administrators and others on how the schools could be improved. Hillary Clinton told the committee that the state needed to become as "fanatic" about mathematics as it was about high school athletics and extracurricular activities. "High school activities don't last forever, and life goes on after age seventeen," she said.

Governor Clinton traveled the state making public appearances to ask the people for support of educational reform. He was attempting to prepare them for a tax increase. In Hot Springs that summer, he asked state labor union leaders, traditionally opposed to higher sales taxes, to "search your hearts and go home and look at your children" before taking a stand on a possible tax increase to support education. The governor told the AFL-CIO members, who had been among his strongest supporters, that he was convinced that better public schools and better adult education were crucial to the state's economic development.

In July, the governor came on even stronger, speaking to about 450 public school administrators. He told them that he was prepared to lead the state in a dramatic and once-in-a-lifetime effort for major progress.

"We are in the midst of what I believe to be the most dramatic improvement in our system of education in our lifetimes," he said. "At times like these, when you have opportunities like this, you have to seize them, because they come along only rarely."

Bill Clinton had taken up the torch for the single most dramatic cause of his political career in Arkansas.

School administrators in the audience did not appear as enthusiastic as the governor. Many were worried about how the changes that were developing in funding and standards would affect their districts. Clinton asked the administrators for "unity" on the issue.

Clinton also made plans for a special session of the Arkansas

General Assembly to address the school funding formula problem and the need for money to finance the new standards. The governor had to work closely with the Department of Education and two legislative committees—the Joint Interim Committee on Education and the Joint Interim Committee on Revenue and Taxation.

Because the Arkansas legislature meets only every two years in regular session, several joint interim committees must carry on its business when it is not in session. Such major legislation as Clinton was proposing would need the imprimatur of the interim committees before Clinton could take it to the legislature.

When the proposal to revise the funding formula came before the Joint Interim Education Committee in July, it was only two votes short of gaining on-the-spot adoption. Under the new formula, about 150 districts would lose money unless $100 million could be added to the total aid package. Plans were to seek a sales tax increase of 1 percent to fund the needed $100 million. The revision of the formula placed minimum levels for tax rates that local school districts assess on real, personal and utility property. The new formula also called for a phaseout of special funding given in the past to districts with fewer than 360 students.

The Standards Committee set a September 1 deadline for the completion of its preliminary proposals for the new standards. This deadline would allow for public review of the proposals and give the state Board of Education time to follow new procedures for adopting new policies. The public hearings were still going on. Some lasted as long as nine hours. Recommendations ranged from requiring a longer school year to requiring a foreign-language offering in each district.

Among the few people asking the committee not to impose standards that were too strict were superintendents of small districts. Most of the public participants asked for such standards as stronger requirements in math, science and social studies, tighter restrictions on the hiring of noncertified teachers, more instruction time and lower student-to-teacher ratios.

* * *

One of the big issues the Standards Committee addressed was the requirement of a minimum competence test for eighth-graders to pass to be promoted to the ninth grade. Students also would be tested at the third grade for competence in reading and mathematics. They would be tested in the sixth grade in reading, language arts, math, social studies and science. At any of the three levels, those who could not pass the tests could be kept from being promoted to the next grade. Teachers, counselors and principals would be required to develop individualized remediation plans for those students.

The eighth-grade competence test also was formulated as a key to measure the performance of schools. Those schools that could not achieve an 85 percent pass rate on the test would be required to change teaching practices to improve students' performance. If, after two years, the school could not achieve the 85 percent pass rate, it could lose accreditation, putting it in danger of being consolidated with another district.

The Standards Committee completed its preliminary report and released it to the public on September 6, 1983.

"Our schools are not doing as good a job as they must," Hillary Clinton said at a press conference. "While there may be many causes for our dilemma, there is only one solution. We Arkansans have to quit making excuses and accept instead the challenge of excellence once and for all."

A school that "passes illiterate or semiliterate students commits educational fraud," she said. "There is a feeling of urgency and a need for changes in education. If we do not seize the opportunity we have now, we will go backward."

Public opinion of the new standards was overwhelmingly favorable. *Arkansas Gazette* columnist Ernest Dumas praised the committee for "not limiting its vision and not being oppressed by the practicalities of Arkansas's low station." He did warn, however, that "legislative interference" could prevent the standards from being implemented. Dumas wrote:

> Not that the standards are radical. The requirements on curriculum, graduation, faculty staffing and length of school terms are in line with what are generally required across the country....But most Arkansas school districts don't meet those requirements now, and the standards may be beyond the reach of fifty or more tiny districts....

What is innovative and refreshing about the recommendations of Mrs. Clinton's committee is that the state for the first time will not only measure paper staffing and classrooms but how well every school actually performs in educating children....The criticism will be that schools often will resort to devoting exorbitant attention to teaching the tests. But the result will be that everyone in the educational system, from the teachers to the state Education Department, will have a stake in every child's development. It will not be bad if the schools must redouble their attention to the needs of each child.

The state Board of Education enthusiastically endorsed in principle the recommendations made by the Education Standards Committee. Board member L. D. Harris of Blytheville said Hillary Clinton was "the best thing to come along for education in Arkansas in the last fifty years." The board was supportive in spite of estimates by the Department of Education that the cost of implementing the standards would be about $100 million more than what was then being spent on education, plus an undetermined additional amount for capital improvements.

The legislative Joint Interim Committee on Education unanimously endorsed "in principle" the new standards. Hillary Clinton went before the committee to say that the legislature and education agencies should begin work on several standards that needed immediate attention. This would allow enough time for the standards to be implemented by the 1987 school year.

* * *

It was time for the recommendations to be considered by the full legislature. It would be an uphill battle for Bill Clinton.

The special session was called in October 1983. In a televised address to the legislature, Clinton opened the session by trying to sway public opinion in favor of his education and tax program. He called the session "a magic moment" that could "change the face" of the state's history. Yet, as he looked over his audience, only about a dozen legislators were wearing the blue satin ribbons that were symbols of support for the governor's education and tax program. Legislators told the press that the task of writing a new funding formula to satisfy enough school districts would be the governor's toughest challenge, even tougher than trying to raise the sales tax from 3 percent to 4 percent.

The measure that Clinton supported contained some compromises, but remained essentially the same as the earlier version of the funding formula.

The governor's legislative package for the session would have required $179.4 million to fund. He proposed these ways to get funds that would amount to $180.2 million:

- Raise the state sales tax from 3 to 4 percent (producing $91 million the first fiscal year and $161.7 million per year thereafter).
- Raise the "severance" tax on natural gas. (Natural gas companies use the word "severance" for gas that has been pumped from the ground. A severance tax is one that taxes gas according to a fixed formula as it is pumped from the deep gas reservoirs that are plentiful in Arkansas.) Under Clinton's plan this severance tax increase would produce about $6 million the first year and $9.3 million thereafter.
- Raise the corporate income tax for corporations with $100,000 or more annual income from 6 to 7 percent (producing about $3.7 million the first year and $10.8 million thereafter).
- Tax membership in country clubs and other private clubs (producing $200,000 the first year and $300,000 thereafter).
- Eliminate all but $200 a month of the 2 percent of total sales tax collections that retailers keep for administrative costs (producing about $1.6 million the first year and $2.7 million thereafter).
- Tax services now excluded from the sales tax.
- Place the sales tax on cable television bills (producing $600,000 the first year and about $1 million thereafter).

A coalition of consumer, labor and community organizations announced its opposition to the sales tax increase because it wanted exemptions for food and utility bills. Clinton's reluctance to support such exemptions was then and has continued to be a political thorn for him, recurring in nearly every legislative session and, years later, in his presidential campaign.

Clinton told the press at the end of the first week of the special session that his proposed $180 million tax increase for education was "the most important thing I've ever tried to do. It's more important to me personally than whatever political consequences will come of it....It's something that's worth putting myself and whatever career I might have on the line for."

Most of the governor's tax proposal did not make it through the legislature. The increase in the severance tax on natural gas was blocked by gas lobbyists and defeated in both houses.

All that was left was the one-cent sales tax increase.

In a quirk of Arkansas law, it only takes a one-third majority of both houses to approve a sales tax increase, but it takes a two-thirds or a three-fourths vote to approve other kinds of tax increases. It is almost impossible to get a two-thirds vote of the Arkansas legislature on any tax increase.

So, the lowly sales tax became the whipping boy—the easiest way to raise revenue. Food and groceries were not exempt from the sales tax in Arkansas. Critics called it a "regressive tax," because it had its greatest effect on lower-income people, the people who could least afford it.

But if Bill Clinton's reforms were going to be realized, they would have to be paid for with a sales tax. The corporate interests of Arkansas had declined to pay for school reform.

For all his talk of risking his career for the program, Bill Clinton was not ready to risk it in a major fight with the business community. This was a watershed. Bill Clinton's "idealism" had vanished, to be replaced with an expedient pragmatism.

* * *

The part of the Clinton education package that turned out to be the most difficult to pass and that brought him the most controversy was the requirement that all teachers take a competence test.

This proposal first called for all teachers to take the National Teacher Examination. Clinton said he felt "it is a small price to pay for the biggest tax increase in the history of the state and to restore the teaching profession to the position of public esteem that I think it deserves."

Immediate opposition came from the AEA. "We teachers are being laid on the altar of sacrifice for political expedience," said AEA President Peggy Nabors after the governor outlined his program in his address to the General Assembly. The Arkansas Black Caucus also came out in opposition to the test, saying such standardized tests were skewed by cultural bias.

Clinton's original proposal was for teachers to go through a one-time evaluation by taking two tests. The first would evaluate basic skills—reading, writing, mathematics. The second would be a subject test in the area of certification. It had not been decided at that point whether the subject test would be the National Teacher Examination or a test developed in Arkansas by Arkansas teachers.

The test proposal was not totally lacking in support from teachers. A group of teachers at Little Rock's Central High School presented a letter to the governor saying that they would not object to having to take the NTE. The letter was signed by sixty-six of eighty-five faculty members. A group of teachers in the Monticello School District also endorsed the testing requirement. All but two of the Monticello district's 137 certified staff members signed petitions supporting the test.

Hillary Clinton appeared before a legislative subcommittee to defend teacher competence testing, although, oddly enough, her original Standards Committee had never suggested teacher testing, but had only addressed the issue in vague terms, such as recommending that all teachers be certified and that teachers acquire additional educational experience in their subjects.

But Hillary Clinton was firmly behind her husband's decision on teacher testing.

"The problem of teacher accountability begins in higher education, and we think teacher education is inadequate in many respects," she told the subcommittee. "The governor is quite properly looking at teacher accountability in the context of his overall recommendations."

On October 27, after weeks of debate, the legislature broke a deadlock over teacher testing and passed the proposal, and the Senate approved the one-cent sales tax increase. Bill Clinton called it "a great day." He said he expected the House also to approve the bill.

The Arkansas Education Association was outraged and worked to block passage of the Senate bill through the House. Clinton was even more outraged and publicly announced that if the AEA defeated the teacher testing bill, he would kill his own proposed one-cent sales tax increase and thereby leave teachers without raises and schools without funds to implement the new standards.

"There will be no tax increase without a testing bill," Clinton told the press.

Arkansas Education Association Executive Director Dr. Kai Erickson called the governor "irresponsible" and said he was "hot and overreacting." The AEA had stopped a vote on the House version of the teacher testing bill by supporting a filibuster in the Senate. The AEA also had distributed letters to the Senate quoting the Educational Testing Service (ETS) as advising Clinton that his proposed use of teacher tests was improper and perhaps illegal.

The governor pushed ahead: "The AEA leadership apparently cares nothing about teacher raises, more money for standards or more money for higher education." He accused Erickson of being hired "solely to protect a few teachers who might be incompetent." He expressed resentment that the AEA had failed to support any of his tax bills and had only supported one of the proposed new standards. The Arkansas Education Association held firmly to its position that the teacher testing proposal was a "witch hunt."

On the last day of October, the governor won his battle with the AEA and got his teacher testing bill through both houses of the legislature. (Although it is commonly called the "teacher testing law," the regulation required all public school educators, including principals and superintendents, to take the test.)

The tax bill, however, was delayed. Clinton had wanted the tax to take effect November 1, but he ran into trouble. The tax bill also had passed both houses, but the emergency clause to make it take effect immediately was not approved. Without the clause, the sales tax would not take effect for ninety days, allowing time for opponents to circulate petitions to refer the tax to a vote of the people.

Yet Clinton was smiling as he met with reporters after the legislature recessed for the evening. One reporter suggested that

Clinton had been "more politically assertive" during the last few days than ever before. But some of the legislators did not feel that the governor should be so overjoyed. Senator Nick Wilson, a major power broker in Arkansas politics, said he hated to see the teacher testing bill ruin the political career of "a fine young man in the governor's office."

After much wrangling, final passage of the sales tax bill came on Friday, November 4, and an emergency clause was enacted. Although both houses had approved their own versions of the tax increase, final passage had been stalled because the two chambers could not agree on a "grocery amendment"—an effort to give a rebate to low-and moderate-income families for the sales tax on food. The amendment was dropped. The state would begin collecting the tax on Monday.

And so, in the end, the sales tax paid for the new education reforms, with no exemptions for food. Still, the sales tax increase would leave Arkansas in fiftieth place as the state with the lightest state and local tax burden.

Clinton's education package was law. The money was there.

The funding formula bill that became law also ordered school districts to spend 70 percent of their total revenue on salaries. After a district hired new teachers and administrators to meet the requirements, 80 percent of the salary money was required to be divided equally among teachers and administrators, unless the school board and a majority of the teachers agreed on a different distribution. This was a built-in guarantee that teacher salaries would not stagnate.

The special session of the Arkansas General Assembly adjourned November 10, 1983. "You've done a lot to assure a better future for the young people of this state—and for the rest of us, too," Clinton told legislators on the thirty-eighth and final day of the session. The governor expressed regret that his only major tax proposal to pass was the sales tax, but expressed gratitude that the legislature had given him much of what he had asked.

Still, he pointed out: "This is a beginning, not an end, to the work we must do." Clinton pledged not to give up his fight for a more equitable tax system, citing the state's low severance tax as "an example of what is wrong with the system."

Although the teacher test was now law and the legislature had gone home, Bill Clinton's fight with the teachers had only begun.

John Brummett of the *Arkansas Gazette* observed at the time that the relationship between Clinton and the 17,000-member AEA had developed into one of "harsh public bitterness and nasty private name-calling, totally the result of Mr. Clinton's insistence on requiring teachers to take a basic skills test in exchange for the nice raises most of them will likely get from his tax program."

Clinton told Brummett: "I was exceedingly disappointed when they testified against some of the standards, disregarding the fact that I'd appointed three people to the Standards Committee [whom] they wanted. And I was equally disappointed when they made no concerted effort in support of any of the revenue bills."

AEA President Peggy Nabors said Clinton was looking to give the appearance of toughness in seeking accountability and competence in exchange for higher taxes and that he "picked on" teachers and used them as a "scapegoat." She said that many good teachers would quit rather than take the test.

At an AEA convention in Little Rock in November 1983, Ermalee Boice, assistant executive secretary of the AEA, told that teachers they and Bill Clinton were "at war." Clinton, speaking before another group the same day, predicted that the tests "will show that the overwhelming majority of our teachers are well-prepared to do the job they have been hired on to do, and that will bolster public support."

Partially in response to the Clinton-AEA controversy, the Arkansas Association of Professional Educators, a rival organization with about four hundred members, asked its members to "actively promote" their willingness to take competence and subject-area tests. The letter to members said, "The too-much-publicized campaign of the AEA against teacher testing is doing irreparable harm to our profession."

Clinton, famous for his diplomacy and warmth, was ready to give the rebellious teachers an unforgettable taste of the cold shoulder.

On November 19, Clinton got his chance. He was to speak to a group of about eight hundred AEA delegates at its convention in Little Rock. Virginia Kelley had received warning that her son would receive the silent treatment—that there'd be no welcome and no applause and that the teachers would instead studiously ignore the governor. Kelley warned him what to expect. She then seated herself among the teachers.

As Kelley recalls it:

> He came in the back door, walked directly to the stage, made his speech, did not go up and down the aisle to visit with people, did not open it [the speech] to questions and answers and totally ignored Peggy Nabors. And he just made his speech and left by the same way....I'll never forget it as long as I live....I was with a group of people, and we were walking out of this meeting. And I usually keep my mouth out of Bill's affairs....But there was a professor walking right behind me, or a teacher...so help me, his words were, "I ain't gonna take no damn test!" I couldn't help it. I turned around, and I said, "Sir, that's a double negative, and that means that you will take the damn test."

Clinton had, indeed, received the silent treatment. He'd walked onto the stage, delivered his remarks and left. But in that short span, he'd listed areas of accord between himself and the AEA, defended teacher testing and pleaded with members not to put the issue ahead of working with him for a better future for Arkansas's children, teachers and schools.

The National Education Association soon followed suit in condemning the testing law. The NEA said it would work for repeal or amendment of the law and would consider a legal challenge to it. The law, being the only one of its kind in the nation, was criticized as "an educationally unsound testing statute that will not contribute to educational excellence in the Arkansas public schools" and as a measure that "demeans the education profession, deceives the public and is detrimental to the teaching and learning process."

The Educational Testing Service announced in November 1983 that it would no longer permit the use of its National Teacher Examination (NTE) to evaluate teachers who were already on the job. The exam was designed only to test new teachers, fresh out of college, not experienced teachers, the group maintained. ETS President Gregory Anrig said, "It is morally and educationally wrong to tell someone who has been judged a satisfactory teacher for many years that passing a certain test on a certain day is necessary to keep his or her job."

New York Times writer Edward Fiske said the announcement was directed at the state of Arkansas and the Houston (Texas) Independent School District, both of which had used sections of the NTE as part of new efforts to improve the quality of their teaching staffs.

The ETS's position did not seem to bother Clinton. "We don't need their tests," he responded. "We can get them from some other state or school district."

* * *

Hillary Clinton's Education Standards Committee officially completed its nearly nine months of work and approved a final version of its proposed new standards for accreditation of Arkansas public schools on December 10, 1983. There were no major changes from the preliminary report it had released in September. The report was ready to present to the state Board of Education and the legislative Joint Interim Committee on Education for action by March 1.

"I think we have a really good set of standards—a blueprint that Arkansas can follow over the next few years," Hillary Clinton said. "This is a move toward competency-based education and the requirement of more accountability and responsibility from students, teachers, the school systems and parents."

Some of the major components of the standards were:

- A maximum class size of twenty students in kindergarten; an average of twenty-three and maximum of twenty-five in grades one through three; and an average of twenty-five and maximum of twenty-eight in grades seven through twelve, with an exception for classes such as band or choir.
- A specified 13½ units that must be taken for graduation: four of English, five of mathematics and sciences, two of social studies, one of practical arts or a third unit of social studies, a half-unit each of physical education, health education and fine arts.
- Lengthening of the school year from 175 days to 180 by 1989–90.

- Provision of one counselor for every 450 high school students and every 600 elementary students.

Looking back, Bill Clinton said it had been "a very good year" for the state of Arkansas. He said his biggest disappointment had been the failure of the legislature to pass his entire tax program during the special session. Still, the legislation and the sales tax increase would, he said, constitute "a great first step in a continuing effort to reform and improve our educational system."

The income tax question would come back to haunt Clinton throughout his career. Clinton put the blame on the legislature; his critics said he was not willing to push the lawmakers to force them to drop their own self-interests long enough to vote a tax on business and industry.

In assessing his success in getting his 1983 reform package through the legislature, Clinton credited a $130,000 public relations campaign with gaining the support necessary for his victory. The campaign had been financed by private donations from hundreds of individuals who had been solicited by Clinton's staff and supporters. He told a conference on education at the Kentucky General Assembly in January 1984 that the campaign of television, radio and newspaper advertisements and printed brochures helped explain his proposals for educational reform and higher taxes. A total of 26,000 brochures were mailed, and others were handed out at county fairs and distributed at meetings.

"I cannot overemphasize how important I believe this component of the program was," Clinton told the legislators. He said the money for the campaign was raised in four days by telephone calls to financial institutions and others in the business community. "The business community was phenomenally interested in being supportive of the program....People really appreciated being told what was happening to them and why, before it happened."

Betsey Wright, who was Clinton's chief of staff at the time, remembers the public relations campaign and its contribution to the success of the 1983 legislative session:

Before the session really convened at the legislature...we did a public campaign for the governor's standards and program and for the tax with a blue-ribbon campaign. We bought radio ads, newspaper ads, TV ads; we did a lot of direct mail across the state. We had people doing postcards and letters to their legislators. We had them wearing the blue ribbons...and rallied meetings across the state—all meant to snowball into the beginning of the legislative session so that by the time those legislators convened, each of them had a constituency in their district begging them to raise their taxes for education. Never has a legislature convened with it being so easy to raise taxes. Their district wanted them to do it for education. Even at that it was a struggle. We had to vote several times on the sales tax to get the majority and make it happen. But it happened because the people brought it to the legislature....We did phone banks at night in the districts of recalcitrant legislators and had them just snowed the next day. To get it done was a very well-planned campaign.

* * *

The year 1984 dawned. It was an election year and Clinton was running again. Clinton's opponents were sure to capitalize on his unpopularity with teachers and school administrators.

They got an early start. On January 18, school superintendents and the AEA appeared before the legislative Joint Interim Committee on Education to chip away at the standards. Hillary Clinton rose to defend her work.

State Representative Jodie Mahony contended that the interim committee should not be the body to accept or reject anyone's objections to the standards and that the job should be left to the state Board of Education. The committee decided to send the state board a synopsis of five major objections raised by school superintendents and to let the board consider them.

The interim committee had sent letters to school superintendents asking for written comments, and received fifty-two responses. The five most recurring complaints were:

1. Extending teacher contracts from the current 180 days to 190 would be too costly.
2. The proposed class-size restrictions would be too costly because new facilities and more teachers would be needed.
3. The proposed high school graduation requirements needed to be changed, because no clear provision had been made

for students without aptitude for complex mathematics courses and for those specializing in vocational training.
4. The proposed requirement for counselors in elementary schools would be too costly, and the requirement was impractical.
5. The proposed new state regulations for remedial instruction jeopardized federal funds for remedial instruction that specified the type of instruction.

Hillary Clinton quickly defended the proposed standards, especially those limiting kindergarten class size to a maximum of twenty students and the high school graduation requirements. She said those two would be her top priorities if she could save only certain standards based on available money.

Opposition also was voiced at the committee meeting by the AEA, which took the stand that some of the standards were too rigid and beyond the state's financial means.

Public meetings were held throughout the state by the Board of Education to hear comments on the new accreditation standards. Many people, parents among them, praised them and said they looked forward to their implementation. Others expressed fear of monetary problems for the schools in meeting some of the standards.

On February 22, 1984, the Board of Education approved the proposals, giving Arkansas schools their first comprehensive new standards since 1969. They were to take effect on June 1, 1987.

"It's a great, great day for Arkansas," Clinton told the assembled when the meeting drew to an end. "I'm very pleased. The board was under enormous pressure to water the standards down. In my heart of hearts, I could have gone a little further, but the committee and the board did a good job."

More trouble came as the National Education Association began its investigation in Arkansas of the teacher testing law. Clinton met with members of the NEA executive committee in Little Rock, sparred politely with them and left after a round of "friendly but firm disagreement," in the words of *Gazette* reporter Brummett. The education officials had accused Clinton of having purely political motives.

Clinton countered by saying that when people disagree with a public official's action they allege "political motivation," but when they agree they laud "statesmanship." He held strongly to his position, saying: "This law is nothing but right. I believe in it very strongly." He went on to say that the controversy "has caused me a great deal of pain."

The NEA asked Clinton why he had insisted on the law when his own Department of Education director, Dr. Don Roberts, had been opposed to it. The governor said he had weighed Roberts's arguments but "decided I simply disagreed with them."

The NEA team decided that the law should be repealed or amended and that Clinton should either call a special legislative session for that purpose or delay the testing until after the 1985 regular session (possibly counting on Clinton being defeated in 1984 and a more sympathetic governor occupying the chair in 1985). Clinton responded that he would back teacher tests in spite of the NEA's position.

A poll conducted in June 1984 showed that the public favored the tests two to one. A total of 369 registered voters around the state were polled by telephone. Of those, 65.5 percent said they favored the concept. When asked if they would favor national standards for teacher testing, 61.5 percent said yes. Those who opposed teacher testing frequently cited as reasons the belief that a suitable test could not be designed and the conviction that teachers who had taught several years should not be tested.

The issue drew national attention. A three-hour ABC television documentary in September 1984, "To Save Our Schools, To Save Our Children," featured a segment on teacher testing. The show attempted to explore both sides of the question. Phil Donahue devoted an entire episode of his show on NBC to the controversy. ABC's "This Week With David Brinkley" invited Clinton to answer questions about the testing law. The presidents of the NEA and the American Federation of Teachers also were allowed to speak on the show.

Meanwhile, the state's educational television network was airing programs to help teachers prepare for the test. The year was 1984 and teachers would be given several opportunities to pass the test by June 1, 1987.

The idea of taking a test was unacceptable to many teachers, especially those with careers of thirty or forty years. Many vowed they would never take the exam. Others quit their jobs rather than take it. Teachers were highly vocal about it in their communities, but found little sympathy among taxpayers, who saw the test as a tangible evaluation of how well their tax money was being spent.

It was the single most emotional issue in public education in Arkansas since the civil rights era.

8

Preserving the Standards

IN 1984, AT AGE THIRTY-SEVEN, BILL CLINTON FOUND HIMSELF IN HIS fourth race for governor, making his bid for a third term.

After his defeat in 1980, Clinton had come back with a vengeance in 1982. His main objective had been to install a program that would revolutionize education, and he had. Now he had to preserve that program.

Clinton had plenty of trouble on his hands, primarily from two powerful teacher unions—the AEA and the NEA.

He also had some serious trouble of a personal kind: His younger brother, Roger Clinton Jr., had become deeply involved in illegal drugs.

The State Police and other investigators had been watching Roger Clinton for several months. When it became clear that he was participating in serious cocaine trafficking, the State Police decided to inform Bill Clinton.

The governor was distraught. He told the State Police to continue their investigation in order to acquire evidence on all the suspects, as well as his brother. The probe lasted for another month. "I couldn't tell my mother, or her husband, or my brother. It was a nightmare," Clinton told writer Joe Klein. "But it was the right thing to do. He had a four-gram-a-day habit. They said if he hadn't been in incredible physical shape, he would have died."

Roger Clinton Jr., then twenty-eight, was arrested in August 1984 on five counts of distributing cocaine and one count of conspiracy to distribute it. He pleaded guilty and served a little over a year in a federal prison.

Friends have said this was another time of personal trouble for Bill and Hillary Clinton. Bill Clinton has stated many times that "I was forty when I was sixteen." He had tried to be a mature adult when he was still a child in an effort to bring order to the chaos generated by his alcoholic, fearsome stepfather. His brother's arrest triggered all of the old doubts that he had worked so hard to keep behind the facade of supreme self-confidence. Intimates say the vacuum of a lost childhood finally drained him of his self-respect. He began to see himself as a failure. He hit a low in his mood swing and became self-destructive. Rumors of an extramarital affair again swept through state offices and newsrooms. Reporters kept a close watch on Clinton, but came up with no credible evidence to support the rumors. Clinton's family and his vigilant circle of friends closed ranks to protect him from himself.

A period of intense family therapy began when Roger Clinton Jr. was released from prison a year later. Bill Clinton has said in several interviews that this therapy forced him to wrestle with the dark forces inside him. Friends say he still reads books and medical studies on children of alcoholics, searching for clues to his own behavior.

The arrest of his brother brought more negative headlines for Bill Clinton at a time when he was seeking reelection. But the general population reacted with sympathy for the Clinton family. In the midst of the cocaine epidemic of the mid-1980s, many families who had been touched by the destruction of drugs could understand Clinton's agony. The case was never a factor in the campaign.

Roger Clinton later said he had been angry with his brother for not using his influence to protect him. But he also declared that he came to realize that the governor had done what was right and necessary. In 1992, Roger Clinton's arrest and his association at the time with other cocaine users would become an issue in the presidential campaign.

Bill Clinton marshaled his energies to prepare for the reelection campaign. The competition he faced in the Democratic primary was not particularly threatening: Monroe Schwarzlose, whom Clinton had defeated before; Kermit Moss, a retired accounting teacher; and Lonnie Turner, who campaigned on a platform of opposition to Clinton's education reform. Two Republicans, Jonesboro contractor Woody Freeman and Erwin Davis, a Fayetteville lawyer, also filed for the 1984 race.

Even in the face of this light competition, Clinton said he would run with gusto. "I'm going to run as if I were starting out as an unknown and as if I were behind. I enjoy this and I'm ready," he told supporters.

The 1980 election had taught Clinton a valuable lesson: Never take anything for granted. In 1980, Schwarzlose was considered a joke candidate, but he captured much of Clinton's Democratic vote. Clinton was determined not to let that happen again.

And he didn't. He collected 64 percent of the vote in the 1984 primary. His closest competitor was Turner, with 24 percent. Freeman got the Republican nomination.

Education standards became an issue in the 1984 campaign between Clinton and Freeman. Clinton predicted the 1984 election would be a referendum on his educational reform package, saying the standards would be watered down if Freeman were elected. Freeman denied Clinton's charges and said he would not lower the standards if elected. He said that he did oppose consolidation of small school districts, which would take place if those districts did not raise the local tax money needed to meet the standards by the 1987 deadline.

Clinton won the 1984 election with 554,561 votes (64 percent) to Freeman's 331,987. The Arkansas Education Association had failed in an attempt to find a candidate to successfully oppose the teacher-test governor.

John Robert Starr, writing in his book on Arkansas politics, *Yellow Dogs and Dark Horses*, said some were surprised that Frank White "sat this one out." But Starr was not. "Like the experienced Democratic politicians, he [White] realized that the education issue had made Clinton too strong to handle."

In January 1985, at age thirty-eight, Clinton again found himself on the steps of the Capitol on a bitterly cold January day, taking the oath of office for a third term as governor of Arkansas. He made it clear that he would "brook no tampering with the education programs," in the words of a *Gazette* editorial writer, who added that Clinton seemed "surer of himself."

Clinton told the people of Arkansas: "Our administration will pursue an ambitious agenda for Arkansas's future, an agenda based on our commitment to economic growth, our commitment to excellence in education and our commitment to increased security and stability for our people."

Of the ambitious education program he had begun, the governor said: "Our education program has a simple goal: to retain the progress of the special session on education and build on it....We must not weaken the standards or repeal the testing laws."

*   *   *

All across the state, teachers were furious with Bill and Hillary Clinton over the test. The Clintons would not give in.

Hillary Clinton said: "I don't want to pick up another project and devote a lot of time to it until I feel like I have carried through on my responsibility to the people of Arkansas—as well as to my own daughter—to do what I can to make sure these education standards are in place and that they do what we hoped they would do when we passed them."

She also said that part of the reason for the education standards was to "provide a better-educated work force in Arkansas so we can be more competitive for jobs," adding that Arkansas still had "a long way to go to convince ourselves, as well as people outside of Arkansas, that our citizens are educated to the point that will enable them to compete with workers from not just around the country, but around the world."

As the time for the initial testing drew nearer, Hillary Clinton stated that public support for the test had become stronger as opposition by the Arkansas Education Association had grown more vociferous. Speaking to a meeting of education reporters in Atlanta, Hillary Clinton said she and her husband "sort of feel like combat veterans." She was critical of the AEA for not supporting many of the standards involving school curriculum. Yet she praised proposed legislation that would prevent test scores of teachers and administrators from being released to local school districts.

On occasion, the governor also found himself defending the test outside of Arkansas. He spoke to a group of educators in Chicago in April 1985 and told them, "Objections are academic, and not very important when you look at what's important for a child."

On March 23, 1985, a total of 25,077 educators took the test, a threatened boycott having failed to materialize. Administering the test was not without its difficulties. At the last minute, there were allegations that copies of the test had been leaked in advance. The state Department of Education released a statement saying that the integrity of the test had not been compromised.

In another eleventh-hour development, a lawsuit challenging the constitutionality of the test was dismissed by a state court judge the day before the test was given. The lawsuit had claimed that the testing law "created a separate class of citizenry" and violated constitutional equal-protection guarantees by not including private-school teachers, future teachers or teachers who were unemployed or on a leave of absence during the 1984–85 school year. The a court dismissed the case because the legislature had passed a law a month earlier specifying that those categories of certified personnel were also required to meet the provisions of the law.

When the test was finally given, a higher rate of failure for black teachers brought more criticism. Clinton said during an appearance on the CBS television program "Face the Nation" that the failure rate did not mean the test was discriminatory.

"I agree that would be discriminatory if the test was given once and then if you didn't pass it you couldn't be recertified....I believe the evidence is that black teachers can learn these skills and can do just as well as white teachers....Black children and poor white children in our state...have no other shot but the public schools to have a decent education and a decent opportunity in life. We're doing this for them."

Over a period of a year, teachers who failed the test were allowed to take it as many times as was necessary to pass. Roughly 10 percent of teachers failed each time the test was given. When the testing was finished, 1,315 teachers (3.5 percent of the state's total) had been forced to leave teaching because they could not pass the test. Failure rates were higher in areas of Arkansas that had large black populations.

Democrat columnist Starr said that in the original plan for educational reform, the state was to take responsibility to retrain teachers who failed the test:

> If they graduated from an Arkansan educational institution and were certified to teach by the...state Board of Education, then the state was going to take responsibility and say, "We gave you a diploma that said you had qualified as a teacher. We gave you a teacher's certificate, and if you thought you were a teacher and you aren't, it's our fault. So we will pay the full cost of remediation....You've got to put in the time, but we'll pay...the full tuition in the summertime at [a local college] or wherever else you want to go. We'll set up a special program to retrain the unqualified teachers. Well, that got lost in the AEA's battle against teacher testing. I mean, all common sense flew out the window.

Three reporters for the *Arkansas Gazette* took the test without officials knowing who they were. All three, including a "reporter intern"—a college student working at the newspaper for the summer—reported that the test was surprisingly easy, and all three received top scores.

The test was divided into sections on reading, writing and mathematics. The math questions focused on such skills as telling time, calculating the cost of a school field trip, reading a thermometer, figuring percentages and calculating test scores. The reporters said that in the first math question, three basketball players scored a total of 84 points and teachers were asked how many each made if all three scored the same amount.

The reading section focused on differentiating between facts and opinions, culling the main idea from a reading passage and using reference materials. It also included questions on educational vocabulary. Teachers were asked to define such terms as "correlation," "inservice," "median," "criterion-referenced testing" and "cognitive objectives."

The essay portion asked the teachers to write a memo: "Last month you attended an educational conference. You think that many of your colleagues would benefit from some of the information provided at the conference. You would like to schedule a staff meeting to present some of this content. Write a memorandum to your supervisor to explain what you would like to present and how your presentation would benefit your colleagues." The response was to be about two hundred words long and would be graded on organization, mechanics, word usage and legibility.

The *Gazette* reporters said the teachers "were given between nine A.M. and two P.M. to take the test, with all parts of the test given to them at the beginning. All were allowed to continue through each section at their own pace, and most finished early—the first test-taker left the room at ten-forty-five A.M."

*   *   *

Looking back today, AEA officials still express bitterness over the test, but have put the issue behind them and joined forces with the governor in his fight for educational reform. Sid Johnson, president of the AEA in 1991, said teachers resented the test because "they really felt like this was a slap. Here you had the lowest-paid teachers in the country having to prove that they could do the job in the classroom when you had [teachers in] states making twice as much as we were making and they weren't having to be subjected to this sort of thing."

AEA Executive Director Cora McHenry agreed with Johnson, saying the test was "a critical mistake" that caused many teachers to leave the profession rather than submit to it. McHenry believed that the test was "a trade-off. The business community always wants something for something, and he [Clinton] thought that would not have the kind of repercussion that it really had and he had done an even trade."

Today, however, the AEA has high praise for Clinton's achievements in education. Johnson said of the governor's grasp of the education issue:

> He was extremely knowledgeable, and even though at the time he was relatively young, I felt like he talked and had enough facts in his head that it was someone who should be around sixty years old, and he just amazed me. Not only could he talk about K-12 [kindergarten through twelfth grade], but he was talking about higher education, and he was talking about early childhood. He was talking about all phases of education and seemed to be knowledgeable in all areas of it. So I felt that he had a vision for the state, and I felt

that he could do something for us; and I wholeheartedly supported him in almost all of his campaign [for education reform].

* * *

Bill Clinton's contemporaries offer varying assessments of his success in educational reform, ranging from unlimited praise to highly negative criticism.

For instance, two of the people who were Clinton "insiders" and who worked closely with the governor on the reform efforts gave divergent opinions. Dr. Paul Root, who was on the governor's staff during the 1983 reform initiative, gave a positive assessment. Dr. Tommy Venters, who was director of the Arkansas Department of Education after Dr. Don Roberts left that position and during the period the standards were being implemented, gave mixed reviews.

Root said Clinton's experience at Georgetown, Oxford and Yale allowed him "to understand the education problem because of competition with other countries." He said Clinton's Rhodes Scholarship was fundamental "in the shaping of the information and understanding that helped him get...where he is." Root refers to this ability as "the all encompassing look."

As an example, Root recalled the time when Clinton was putting together his reform package: "Don Roberts would be in the meetings; Venters was sometimes there;...and the AEA was there. And there were times when he thought of things that all of us were [overlooking]."

To critics who say Clinton hasn't done much for higher educa-tion, Root's response was: "I think he feels very strongly about the need for improvement in higher education, but I think he believes the public school is the beginning place until that job is done....I think he believes [that] in...improving the public schools, you will be improving higher education."

In the beginning, Root felt that Clinton might have tried to do too much too fast. Having taught history to him at Hot Springs High School, Root said that during the 1983–84 gubernatorial term:

I kept reminding him, as his history teacher, that the king who tried to make too much change in the first year was beheaded in the second year. And he kept saying to me, "We only have two years. That's the nature of this job and...politics, you know? We have two years to try to do what we're going to do. That's all we're guaranteed. We'll try to get more, but we...only have what we have. So we need to try to do all that we can do within this period of time." And my concern, of course, was that he would do so much that he would draw such reaction from public school people that once he was not there, it would...mostly be reversed. But, of course, he has been there long enough and enough people have bought the idea [of what] he was trying to accomplish that I think it could not be reversed now.

Root is also a firm believer in the purity of Clinton's motives:

[Education is] still on the front burner....The public has stayed with us, and that probably is a result of television, radio coverage, newspaper coverage and...it's the governor's leadership and his wife's...who probably are, to some degree, responsible for that. When I went to work for him in '83, I thought this is just something that he has looked at and seen. He's read the [national report on the schools], and he wants to try and fix this. But, eight or nine years later he's still working on it. So I see it as a real dedication—a long-range dedication with a great deal of understanding behind it. A lot of people have talked about the governor as waffling; and from day to day, if you studied him in the legislature, he would seem to do that. But if you study him over a ten-year period, he's still pushing the same basic ideas he was then. So I see him as being consistent and his purposes still being intact.

Venters, on the other hand, downplayed Clinton's role in educational reform. He said a lot of the leadership came from Hillary Clinton. "She actually carried the ball, along with Dr. Roberts and me, when we were both directors of the Department of Education. I can remember periods of time where the governor's wife would be out on the road every night making meetings along with me and others. So I think that the credit for being the person that...works with the legislature and the leader goes to Governor Clinton, but the actual groundwork goes to other people."

Venters saw Clinton's national ties as having a negative impact:

> The governor is easily influenced by outside people on educational issues. Anytime he goes to a meeting or goes to a Southern Governors Conference or anywhere else that he sees something that somebody thinks is good, he wants to immediately implement [it] in Arkansas, regardless of the research or regardless of the money involved. And this, I think, is a shortcoming that I see in the governor.

Venters also criticized the forming of the new standards:

> We put too much weight in what a few people said. Let's take global studies, for example. We had a group that went around from meeting to meeting to talk global studies and, in turn, we got a global studies mandate; and we had no one to speak for driver education or some of the other courses, and, therefore, it was left completely out—not even in the elective criteria. And, so, I think that we put too much emphasis on the input that we got and didn't weigh that input against good common sense. The thing that I think we lacked most was listening to the educational leaders. You know, they would listen to the public...And [Clinton] would get this small group of advisers around him, and they would not be educational leaders. And they would have input, and he would go from there.

Still, Venters said Clinton's major accomplishment had been an "improvement in education." He believed the governor's early-childhood initiatives would be positive.

Overall, Venters said "the governor strived real hard to...put a quality program in every school. I think the shortcoming is that he really wanted consolidation. He really wanted to cut down the number of schools, but he didn't have guts enough to do it. Or he didn't want to fight the political machine....The other thing I think is a mistake is that we didn't ask for enough money to do both the equalizing [of school funding] and the standards. I think the standards were too costly. We should have gone out and once we got the one-cent sales tax, we should have gone ahead and got the severance tax and some of the other taxes. I know that the governor can't do that by himself. But his leadership would have helped in that area."

Among other Arkansans, opinions vary. Starr said Clinton's biggest mistake is "in failing to sit down and tell himself that he's the governor of Arkansas and that he should act like the governor of Arkansas every day and that he shouldn't put up with a bunch of little piddlin' stuff from legislators. He should grab them by the front of their shirt and slap their faces left and right and tell them this is what we need to do, let's do it. Symbolically, that's what...good governors have always done. Now, he hasn't done that."

9

Fine-Tuning an Election Machine

CLINTON'S NEXT CAMPAIGN, FOR A FOURTH TERM, CAME IN 1986, the year he turned forty. Until that year, he had been serving two-year terms, but the legislature had recently changed the law, allowing the governor and top state officials to serve unlimited four-year terms.

One of Clinton's Democratic opponents was former Governor Orval Faubus, the 1950s symbol of segregation. Faubus had served six terms as governor before retiring in 1966. In succeeding years he had run for governor periodically, only to be defeated each time. *Gazette* writer Brummett called Faubus the man "who set the state back anywhere from a decade to fifty years."

Clinton's other opponent, W. Dean Goldsby, was the former head of a disgraced antipoverty agency that had misspent government funds.

Still bearing the scars of his defeat in 1980, Clinton threw himself into the campaign with all of his considerable energy. "The governor seldom fails to seize an opportunity to publicly level a broadside attack on Faubus and his record," Brummett wrote. "The last thing Clinton wants is to revisit 1980."

At political rallies around the state, Clinton and Faubus argued about the education issue. Faubus called the school standards "a back-door effort to force consolidation" of small school districts.

114

Clinton was successful again. He soundly defeated Faubus and Goldsby in the primary, with 315,397 votes; Faubus received 174,402 and Goldsby 30,829.

Clinton then stepped into the ring with White.

While the two were participating in a debate, the issue of drug testing surfaced. President Reagan was championing his "Just Say No" campaign against drugs and had taken a drug test to prove that he was clean.

Clinton announced that he and Chief of Staff Betsey Wright had also taken the test and would make the results public. Clinton insisted that drug abuse was an important issue to him because it had touched his family. Roger Clinton Jr. had only recently been released from a federal prison after serving his one-year sentence.

White charged that Clinton had been governor too long. If reelected to a fourth term, White worried aloud, Clinton would serve four years. Clinton hit back at White, saying that if elected White would "delay this school program to death, and a generation of schoolchildren will suffer....That's why I'm running."

Starr recalled an observation by a prominent Arkansan, oil magnate Charles Murphy of El Dorado. Murphy said he had changed his support from White to Clinton because White represented the past and Clinton the future.

In September 1986, Clinton told the public that when he'd decided to run for reelection, he'd removed himself from contention as a candidate for president. "The person who's going to be nominated by the Democratic Party in 1988, barring a total abandonment of the last twenty-five or twenty-six years of history, is somebody that's been out there [running] already for a year," he said.

Again the governor stated that he wanted to see his education program through. White charged that Clinton was seeking the vice presidential nomination and would abandon the office of governor to run. Clinton said he was not running for vice president and that running mates are chosen by the presidential nominee, not elected. He also said that if offered the nomination for vice president, he would consider taking it. The governor flatly denied he would run against U.S. Senators David Pryor or Dale Bumpers in 1990.

But Clinton also said he had no specific plans to run for governor again in 1990, adding, "I don't have any particular plans at all. I'm not worried about it. I'm having a good time, and one of the things I've learned is that you can't foresee the future. I'm really happy about it."

In the general election, Clinton won 64 percent of the votes, 439,882 to White's 248,427.

In his victory speech on election night, Clinton declared, "This election was a clear, unambiguous and almost stunning mandate, but not for me. It is a mandate for better schools, more jobs and a better future for our state."

On Wednesday, January 14, 1987, the day of his fourth inauguration as governor of the state of Arkansas, Clinton told legislators that this might be his "last trip to the lectern under these circumstances," indicating that he might not run for governor again.

He had chosen for his inaugural theme, "Making Arkansas Work: Good Beginnings, Good Schools and Good Jobs." In an address that day to the General Assembly, Clinton said the need to raise money to finance the education program was evident. This was not really news to the lawmakers, since he had already proposed legislation to raise the sales tax.

* * *

By 1987, the time was drawing near for Clinton to make a decision on taking the next big step. The logical move was a senatorial or presidential campaign.

Because the two Arkansas senators, Bumpers and Pryor, had been steadfast friends and supporters of Clinton , it was not likely that he would challenge them, although back-stabbing is a long-honored practice in politics.

To broaden his recognition, Clinton remained active in regional and national political organizations and took visible positions on national issues, appearing in the major newspapers and on the television networks to comment on whatever topic was capturing headlines at the moment.

In turn, his activities outside of Arkansas had brought criticism from Arkansas political enemies and newspaper columnists, who

In 1964, Bill Clinton and close friend Carolyn Yeldell Staley, seniors at Hot Springs High School, won the Elks Youth Leadership Award. (Photo courtesy Carolyn Y. Staley)

Clinton's mother, Virginia Kelley, with her fourth husband, Dick Kelley. She has been widowed three times. Clinton's father was her first husband, Bill Blythe.

Bill Clinton (center) playing saxophone with the boys in the band, Randy Goodrum (left) and Joe Newman (right). The jazz trio call themselves the "Three Blind Mice." (Photo courtesy Carolyn Y. Staley)

Clinton was also "band major" of the high school band, the highest office a band member could hold. (Photo courtesy Carolyn Y. Staley)

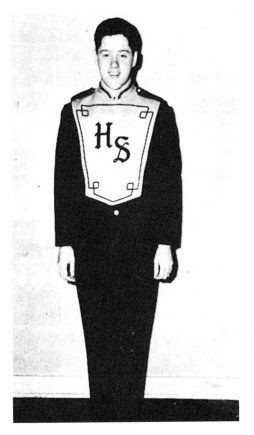

Clowning around at the high school's annual Band Variety Show, Clinton is seen here holding friend Paul David Leopoulos. (Photo courtesy Carolyn Y. Staley)

Central Avenue in downtown Hot Springs, where Clinton and his friends once cruised to the music of Elvis Presley. (Photo by Jonathan Portis)

The old Hot Springs High School, where Clinton graduated. A new high school has since been built. (Photo by Jonathan Portis)

Clinton's childhood home at 213 Scully Street in Hot Springs. (Photo by Jonathan Portis)

A pivotal moment in Clinton's young life: On a trip to Washington, D.C., with Boys Nation in the summer of 1963, Clinton had the good fortune to meet his idol, President John F. Kennedy. He told his mother on his return to Arkansas that because of this encounter with the President he was determined to enter politics. (Photo *Arkansas Democrat-Gazette*)

Clinton during his first campaign for governor in 1978. (Photo courtesy Billy Simpson)

Bill Clinton, at age thirty-two, the youngest governor in the nation is seen with wife, Hillary, thirty-one, at his first inauguration as governor of Arkansas in 1979. (Photo *Arkansas Democrat-Gazette*)

On the campaign trail in 1982, Bill and Hillary attempt to regain the governor's office. The Comeback Kid was the first governor to be defeated and than regain the office in the state's history. (Photo *Arkansas Democrat-Gazette*)

The Clintons pose with Donald Duck at Disney World in Orlando, Florida, in 1984. Hillary (left), Bill (right), and daughter, Chelsea, at age four, holding Donald's hand. (Photo *Arkansas Democrat-Gazette*)

In his inaugural address in January 1983, Clinton pledged to reform the state's educational system. The Board of Education would establish a fifteen-member commission to set up standards for a new set of minimum standards for schools. At age thirty-five, Hillary Clinton would make her political debut as the committee's chair, though not an educator herself. The proposal Clinton accepted was received favorably for the most part, but the competence test for teachers met angry opposition. Hillary firmly defended her husband's position. The teacher-testing law was the most emotional issue in Arkansas history since the civil rights movement. Hillary Clinton (above) speaks to an educational committee meeting in 1990. (Photo *Arkansas Democrat-Gazette*)

saw Clinton's efforts as an exercise in self-aggrandizement at the expense of taking care of business back home.

That same year, a *Time* magazine article listed Clinton as one of fifty top leaders. The article referred to *Gazette* cartoonist George Fisher's often-used depiction of Clinton "as a brat furiously pedaling a tricycle." The article listed among Clinton's achievements his passage of $47 million in new taxes and his regaining power for the governor's office "that had been usurped by the legislature." The magazine speculated that Clinton would run for Congress.

Arkansas media paid close attention to Clinton's out-of-state trips to meetings of various organizations, sifting for clues as to whether he was going to run for president.

Clinton, who was chairman of the National Governors Association, made plans to attend the association's public hearing on economic development in Iowa and to speak at a meeting of the Education Commission of the States in Scottsdale, Arizona, during the same month, February 1987. The *Gazette* pointed out that Iowa would hold the first presidential caucus in 1988, giving the governor a good reason for going there. The newspaper said those two trips would raise the number of Clinton's out-of-state ventures to six since early December 1986.

Later that year, Clinton traveled to Traverse City, Michigan, to another meeting of the National Governors Association. Democratic Governor Rudy Perpich of Minnesota called Clinton "the best governor in the United States." Republican John Sununu of New Hampshire, who took over as the new chairman, praised Clinton for his "style and capacity to deal with his colleagues to get results." During his chairmanship, Clinton had formed task forces that developed recommendations to improve social programs and economic development initiatives.

Another highlight of the Michigan meeting for Clinton was getting to play the saxophone with the musical group Junior Walker and the All-Stars.

The Little Rock news media were trampling each other to gather information on rumors of a presidential campaign. Every time Clinton left the state, reporters and columnists strained to be the first to find evidence of significance in the trip.

One example is a trip Clinton made out of state that year to a mock Democratic National Convention put on by students at Washington and Lee University in Lexington, Virginia. Clinton delivered an inspiring address and later socialized with students, dancing and playing the saxophone. Brummett noted in his *Gazette* column that Clinton "can't go anywhere and have a good time without some yahoo back home writing about it."

As the speculation about Clinton's presidential ambitions reached a fever pitch in 1987, the phantom candidate himself remained silent.

Brummett wrote about Clinton's out-of-state appearances in key presidential primary states, but also noted that if Clinton were serious about running for president, he would have made more frequent visits to those states. Brummett asked, "Are we in Arkansas going to be the last to know? About Governor Bill Clinton's running for the Democratic presidential nomination in 1988, I mean."

Senator Dale Bumpers's name also kept popping up as a likely presidential candidate in 1988. "Men like Bumpers and Clinton continue to help the state's reputation and offset the ravages of the Faubuses...," wrote senior editor James Powell in the *Gazette*.

Powell guessed that Clinton would be more likely than Bumpers to make a bid for president in 1988, partly because he felt secure in his present position and partly because of his position as chairman of the National Governors Association.

However, at the National Governors Association Conference in Hilton Head, South Carolina, in August, Clinton made no indications that he was a candidate. He delivered a well-received speech upon taking over the chairmanship at the closing of the convention, but made no attempts to attract national attention.

"Why all the hoopla anyway?" That was the question of John Brummett in noting that other prominent Arkansans down through the years had been mentioned as presidential or vice presidential possibilities—J. William Fulbright, Wilbur D. Mills, Dale Bumpers, Winthrop Rockefeller, Joe T. Robinson.

"Something about Governor Bill Clinton seems to rub people the wrong way," Brummett wrote in his political column. "Otherwise, why would there be all this hoopla about his being potentially prominent in national politics, perhaps a presidential or vice presidential candidate someday?"

Brummett offered four prevailing theories about Arkansans' attitudes toward the subject and decided the answer probably lay in a combination of some or all of them:

- That many Arkansas people are jealous of Clinton; that they feel they have given him too much too soon.
- That the Arkansas people consider Clinton too transparently ambitious, too transparently expedient in his political actions and pronouncements; that they consider him a pure political animal, albeit glib and impressive, and not a statesman like Bumpers or a man of actual in-government hard work and accomplishment like Mills or Fulbright; in brief, that they think Clinton is using them, and selling them short in the process.
- That Arkansas people don't believe Clinton has paid his dues; that they know of him only as a political candidate and officeholder, unlike Bumpers, who had a life before politics, spending time in the military, practicing law and raising a family for several years before running for governor.
- That Arkansas people assign higher standards to him because they had such high hopes.

Brummett also said, "The reason Clinton gets national attention is that he is impressive at first blush. It is reminiscent of the fascination many of us had with him when he burst on the scene at age twenty-eight and darn near beat John Paul Hammerschmidt for Congress."

The time for running drew shorter. During a trip to Washington in February 1987 to a National Governors Association meeting, Clinton encountered a throng of reporters in the lobby of his hotel. They were shouting questions about possible presidential nominees. Clinton evaded their questions about his own intentions by saying he would not "even think" about running until after the Arkansas General Assembly had adjourned.

Clinton did make observations about the other candidates, saying former Senator Gary Hart of Colorado and Governor Michael Dukakis of Massachusetts both had plenty of support. New York Governor Mario Cuomo had just decided not to run, a move that Clinton said "surprised" him.

Brummett commented back home that Clinton's experience in the hotel lobby "would be a dream come true for many people, especially those who are ambitious young politicians. Or ambitious old politicians. Or just plain everyday politicians. When you are forty years old and have only been the governor of a small, poor Southern state, it is a heck of a deal for the big-time press to consider you worthy of shouted questions, and for those questions to have to do with the presidency."

* * *

The speculation that Bumpers would seek the presidency came to an end on March 20, 1987, when the senator announced that he would not seek the nomination, citing family reasons.

In April, Clinton told reporters in Little Rock that he was exploring the possibility of putting a campaign together. He was invited to speak that month at the New Hampshire State Democratic Committee's quarterly meeting in Manchester. Gary Hart, who was officially running for the Democratic nomination, had been the speaker at the last quarterly meeting. Also in April, Senator David Pryor came out in support of Clinton's running, saying Clinton's ability on the podium would impress people and make him a standout in a crowd of would-be candidates.

Clinton said that his mail was running three-to-one in favor of his making the bid for the presidency, adding that he would not resign as governor if he chose to run. The Democratic Party's State Committee adopted a resolution urging Clinton to seek the nomination.

Possibly the most telling indication of Clinton's shifting alliances was offered when Jerry Maulden, president of the Arkansas Power and Light Company, said he would support his bid for the presidency. Only seven years before, Clinton had been on the utility's enemies list, and AP&L had supported his opponent, Frank White. In the intervening years, Clinton had reached a settlement in the Grand Gulf nuclear plant controversy that had been favorable to the parent company of AP&L, and that had increased rates for electricity in Arkansas. Clinton had learned how to play ball with the big boys.

Toward the end of April 1987, Clinton stopped evading reporters' questions about the presidency.

"Oh, yes, I'd very much like to do it," he said, adding that if he did run, he would have a plan "to permit me to discharge my responsibilities to the people of this state." The governor said his staff told him the letters encouraging him to run were about eight-to-one in favor.

Hillary Clinton told the press that she would support whatever decision her husband made, noting that he was "very deliberative when faced with a difficult decision." She pointed out the problems her husband would have serving as governor and running for president at the same time. But she added, "I have no doubts that he would be an excellent president."

The *Arkansas Gazette* took the position that "Bill Clinton is not ready to be president of the United States....He has strong potential, to be sure, and it could suddenly blossom into prospects for strong national leadership. While we are waiting for that to happen, the memory of the early Clinton comes to mind." The editorial writer went on to say that "Governor Clinton is needed in Arkansas."

Brummett brought out a reservation he had about Clinton's assuming the responsibilities of the office of president—his indecisiveness. He used as an example a favorite story he had heard about Clinton some time ago.

The story, as Brummett told it, went like this: "In 1985...he [Clinton] vetoed a bill, then sent a state trooper to fish the bill out from under the door of the clerk of the House of Representatives, using a coat hanger, so the governor could un-veto it by marking through the prefix in the 'disapproved' stamp. Then a couple of months later, Mr. Clinton had to call a special session to undo the veto."

(Clinton, in a televised interview, criticized Brummett for bringing the story up a hundred times, but Brummett insisted he had only written about it *six* times.)

Brummett posed the question of "whether this man is equipped to deal with, as an example, the Soviets on questions having to do with the very security of the world." Clinton said that everyone makes mistakes and that Brummett had done a great job of repeatedly resurrecting the incident, and told the columnist he ought to get a doctoral degree in Bill Clinton criticism. Later he called Brummett to apologize, which Brummett used as another example of Clinton's not sticking with his decisions. The governor told media representatives the next day that he had been embarrassed by the incident of the "un-veto" and had changed his mind only because he had promised to support the bill.

On the other hand, some have defended this characteristic as not indecisiveness but, perhaps, deliberativeness. Billy Simpson of Stuttgart, Arkansas, a bank board member, State Police commissioner and lobbyist, commented:

> Bill Clinton has been criticized repeatedly for his long delays in taking a position on an issue, for being slow to reach decisions and for his inability to see a matter all the way through. He has also been known to change his mind on certain issues. So, basically the decision-making process of the Clinton administration is slow. Clinton seems to require so much data to be compiled, studies to be made and reports from task forces. So, I must say Governor Clinton does make informed decisions.

* * *

When Democratic contender Gary Hart of Colorado dropped out of the race in May because of a sexual scandal, some of his supporters urged Clinton to run.

The issue of public scrutiny of the private lives of candidates was raised. Clinton said he would expect the cocaine conviction of his brother to be "rehashed" if he ran, and he remained undecided. *Newsweek* magazine reported a week later that Clinton had decided to run. Clinton said he had not.

As far as the perception of him by the public, Clinton fared better in other states during those days than he did in Arkansas. Even in Boston, where presidential candidate Michael Dukakis's popularity was expectedly strong, Clinton was praised and compared to John F. Kennedy.

Clinton also traveled to Wisconsin, Montana, Indiana and Nashville for speaking engagements. The Wisconsin press carried glowing accounts of Clinton's reception there. Speaker Thomas Loftus of the Wisconsin legislature was quoted as saying, "He about stole the convention. Clinton can obviously do something."

In July, the *New York Times* reported that Clinton was running. Clinton again said he hadn't decided. In a newspaper interview, Bumpers brought up the issue of Clinton's family considerations, calling Hillary "a beautiful wife who is one of the most intelligent women in the country" and referring to Clinton's "lovely daughter" and his devotion to her.

The announcement came on July 15, 1987: Bill Clinton would not seek the Democratic presidential nomination.

"My heart says no," Clinton told the people of Arkansas in a press conference.

He continued: "Our daughter is seven. She is the most important person in the world to us and our most important responsibility. In order to wage a winning campaign, both Hillary and I would have to leave her for long periods of time. That would not be good for her or for us."

He also mentioned the toll that fifteen election contests had taken on him in the past thirteen years. "I hope I will have another opportunity to seek the presidency when I can do it and be faithful to my family, my state and my sense of what is right," he said.

The press, the governor's staff and his friends were surprised. They had expected him to run. The only person in Arkansas who had not expected him to run was probably his brother, Roger, who had told a longtime friend of the governor that he did not think his brother would run "because of Chelsea," the governor's daughter.

Clinton answered many questions from the press about his decision. He said he had undergone a "mental tug-of-war" but had decided not to go against his instincts, which told him not to run.

The Republican Party of Arkansas used the governor's announcement to criticize him: "This bears out his indecisiveness by deluding his most ardent supporters into believing one thing and at the last moment doing another."

Though many debated whether Clinton had given the true reason for his decision, Brummett wrote that he felt the governor was sincere. "The man choked up when he said he had made a promise to himself that if he were ever lucky enough to have a child, that child would not grow up with an absentee father," Brummett wrote. But Brummett also wrote that Clinton "still wants to be president and expects another opportunity."

Political consultant Raymond D. Strother of Washington, whom Clinton had retained to serve as media consultant for his presidential bid, said that the governor's decision not to run had been made for personal considerations and made on his own.

He said that he and a group of political figures and friends were having lunch at the Governor's Mansion the day before Clinton's announcement and that the governor had suddenly pushed away his egg salad and said, "I'm not running." Strother advised the governor that people would think that he had been threatened with some form of bad publicity or damaging information, causing him to back out at the eleventh hour.

"This indicates to me that this was not the case," Brummett wrote. "Again, a sudden lunchtime announcement of noncandidacy, one catching associates by surprise, indicates the decision was made as a result of personal doubts, reached introspectively, not in reaction to a specific development of that day or the night before."

10

"I Fell on My Sword"

CLINTON MAY HAVE DECIDED NOT TO SEEK THE PRESIDENCY, BUT AT the age of forty-one he was still a young man on the run.

He spent much of 1988 traveling around the nation, speaking, receiving awards, generally keeping a high profile across America while irritating the folks back home, who felt he should be in Arkansas working as governor.

At one ceremony, he and Hillary Clinton jointly received the National Humanitarian Award from the National Conference of Christians and Jews. Mayor Andrew Young of Atlanta, a speaker at the national meeting of the conference in Little Rock, said the Clintons symbolized the best of the South. He characterized them as full participants contributing to society yet still devoted to each other, and said this symbolized what families would have to be like in the future if they were to survive.

Clinton aligned himself with Governor Michael Dukakis of Massachusetts and traveled extensively with the Democratic candidate as both an adviser and promoter. The Little Rock reporters shadowed Clinton as though he were a candidate.

When the delegates gathered in the Omni in Atlanta from July 18 to 21, 1988, for the Democratic National Convention, it was clear that Dukakis had the nomination sewed up. Dukakis asked Clinton to make the nominating speech.

It was an exciting time for Clinton. This oration would give him the opportunity to do what he does best: make a national appearance demonstrating the mysterious Clinton aura that television so enhances.

Clinton was now on his own turf. He had acquired a certain "magic" for performing on television. He knew the environment, and was not distracted by the pressurized electronic atmosphere surrounding a television production. He was skilled at speaking directly to the camera, and thus, directly to the viewer, projecting the appearance of a handsome, likeable, accessible and sincere statesman. He also knew, as did his advisers and longtime observers, that he could give a political speech that would make even the most bored television watcher sit up and take notice.

On July 20, 1988, Clinton stepped up to the podium in Atlanta. The governor, who usually speaks from notes or outlines, or extemporaneously, carried with him a ten-page, thirty-minute speech that Dukakis had approved.

Clinton had worked on the speech all day in his hotel room, putting in revisions that Dukakis and his staff requested. His assignment was to introduce Michael Dukakis to the nation and tell it exactly who this man was. Dukakis told Clinton that he liked the speech and that he wanted Clinton to deliver all of it.

Within seconds after he arrived on the podium, the Clinton television magic was gone. Everything went wrong.

The rowdy, out-of-control delegates were in no mood to listen. They frequently interrupted Clinton with chants of "We want Mike!"

Clinton had to stop twice to ask the delegates to be quiet so that he could let the rest of the country know "why they should want Mike." It only got worse, with many delegates signaling the "cut" sign to Clinton and others simply not listening at all.

It was clear to television viewers that Clinton was confused and frightened. Viewers could see that he was wondering whether he should continue the speech or stop. Bill Clinton, the master manipulator of the media, had lost control. He decided not to stop—and instead he seemed to go on and on.

Clinton later insisted that the original speech was shorter, but that screaming delegates, by taking up airtime, had caused it to run longer. The only applause came when Clinton said: "In conclusion..."

NBC analyst John Chancellor said on the air, "I am afraid Bill Clinton, one of the most attractive governors, just put a blot on his record."

When it was all over, Clinton told the Associated Press, "I just fell on my sword. It was a comedy of errors, one of those fluky things."

National media follow-up was vicious. "The Numb and the Restless" was the *Washington Post* headline. Pulitzer Prize columnist Tom Shales said that while Jesse Jackson's speech had electrified the audience, Clinton's had "calcified" it.

Hillary Clinton had been on the convention floor when the time had come for her husband to speak. She was alarmed when the houselights were not dimmed as they had been for Ann Richards and Jesse Jackson, who had spoken before the Arkansas governor. As she accompanied her husband to the podium, Hillary Clinton asked the woman who was escorting them to the stage if the houselights were going to go down, which would put the emphasis on the stage. The woman said she would check. Hillary Clinton recalled:

> The lights did not go out. The Dukakis campaign whips—
> the people who keep delegations in line—were not telling
> their delegates to listen. In fact, in several instances, they were
> telling their delegates to yell every time Bill mentioned
> Dukakis's name—which was a lot since it was a speech about
> Dukakis. The platform, the Democratic National Committee
> people, who actually run the platform, had not been told that
> Bill was going to talk for seventeen minutes. Something was
> wrong in the signals that were given....And I sat there
> knowing that there was something really, really wrong,
> because if the lights had gone down, if the crowd had been
> quiet, if the speech had been given the way we had been told
> that it was supposed to be given, it would have done exactly
> what Bill had prepared for it to do....Bill had told Dukakis
> he'd give the speech; so he gave the speech.

Johnny Carson made a joke of the incident on "The Tonight Show," saying the surgeon general had just approved Governor Bill

Clinton as an over-the-counter sleep aid. "What a windbag," Carson cracked. After two nights of jokes about Clinton's speech, Carson invited the governor to appear on "The Tonight Show," and Clinton accepted. When Carson told his audience he had invited him, he said if the governor accepted, "we won't have to book any other guests."

The appearance a few nights later went well. Carson began the show that night with an introduction of Clinton that was a parody of his speech and included a rambling biography and several facts about Arkansas.

Clinton entered the set laughing. The television magic was back. He was relaxed. He seemed perfectly at home with the witty "Tonight Show" host. Clinton joked that Dukakis had asked him to deliver the nominating speech for Republican rival George Bush. He also said that his speech made Dukakis look good when Dukakis delivered the acceptance speech the next night.

Clinton spoke of the support the people in Arkansas had given him following his ill-received speech. Carson told the governor, "Your saving grace is that you have a good sense of humor." Then Clinton played "Summertime" on the saxophone after promising "a short song."

After the performance, which included a session with Doc Severinsen and the orchestra as well as a solo, the audience applauded warmly and at length. Carson said Clinton had been such a good guest he would have to find new targets for his monologues.

After the show, Harry Thomason and Linda Bloodworth-Thomason, the creators and producers of the CBS television shows "Designing Women" and "Evening Shade," threw a party for Clinton. On a wall in the garden was a sign with a picture of the White House saying, "On the Road Again...Clinton '96."

"We got lemons, and we made lemonade," Clinton told the people at the party.

When the governor walked into the state Capitol the next morning, the operator of the souvenir stand near the entrance broke into applause. "This whole experience has brought me closer to the people of the state than ever before," Clinton said. The media-drubbing he had received after the Atlanta speech was followed by an outpouring of letters and support from Arkansans.

"If you don't ever fall on your face, you forget how hard life is for a lot of other people all the time," Clinton said on a radio talk show.

The "Tonight Show" staff received hundreds of letters from Arkansans in support of Clinton. Carson even read one, from Sharon Rector of Little Rock, on the air. Clinton was happy that Carson's parody had gotten in "a lot of good information about Arkansas."

Clinton also admitted, "I've wanted to play with Doc Severinsen longer than I've wanted to be on 'The Tonight Show.'" Playing the sax earned the governor an extra $475, in addition to the $200 he was paid for the appearance. He donated the earnings to the Children's Defense Fund.

Brummett was not as optimistic about the redeeming value of the Carson show, writing that the Atlanta speech exposed "the real Bill Clinton" and that it turned "the big-money people in the Democratic Party" against him. "His Arkansas-reinforced arrogance deluded him," Brummett wrote.

Things went much better in the public-speaking arena the next year. Clinton's views on education earned him a standing ovation at a 1989 meeting of the Democratic Leadership Council, a group of moderate Democrats primarily from the South and West who came together to discuss ways to get the party back on the winning track to the White House. Several of them asked him for copies of the speech after he presented it in Philadelphia. He had none, because he spoke, as usual, from notes and not a prepared text.

Clinton's address had stressed the need for continued public pressure on government leaders to improve the nation's schools and to increase the international competitiveness of the U.S. in the 1990s. "We must do more, better and differently than we have in the past," he said. "We have to have a nationful of Einsteins to stay even with the rest of the world."

Clinton admitted that the people of Arkansas had become tired of hearing about the need for better schools, but added that nonetheless he would keep preaching it.

11

The Fire of an Election

IT IS DIFFICULT TO BELIEVE, BUT IT WAS JANUARY 1989 BEFORE Clinton, as experienced as he was in dealing with the General Assembly, was to have any real measure of success with the legislative body. During the regular session of 1989, "virtually all" of his educational reform, health care and criminal justice proposals passed, the governor told the press after the session concluded.

However, Clinton still had not achieved what he was looking for in order to fund education and was disappointed that the legislature failed to provide "anything approaching adequate funding" for pay raises for teachers, college faculty and state employees. The legislation that had pleased Clinton were programs to increase scholarships, to give students a chance to choose schools they wished to attend and to let the state take over districts in which students performed poorly on standardized tests.

The governor saw no alternative but to call a special session that autumn to address the need to raise taxes, but was again unsuccessful in passing needed funding measures. He called the House and Senate together for a lecture after his proposal had been defeated, and scolded them like disobedient children. "Let me tell you something," he said. "I care about this state....I try to get things done the best way I know, person to person. All I want is results. I don't care who gets the credit for it. I just want results."

As 1989 drew to a close, Clinton's longtime adviser and chief of staff, Betsey Wright, resigned. Wright said she was exhausted, but there was speculation that she had had some differences with Clinton. The Clinton staff hermetically sealed off information about the rift, but reports leaked out that Clinton and Wright had clashed over Wright's brusque treatment of legislators. Wright was a strong woman, did not fail to speak her mind, and in doing so irritated many lawmakers, who were mostly middle-aged white males unaccustomed to such straight talk from a woman. After she departed Clinton's office, she took the job of chair of the state Democratic Party. She later left that job to become a fellow at Harvard University, teaching a course in political science.

As the fourth year of his fourth term began, a popular topic of conversation was whether Clinton would seek an unprecedented fifth term. Brummett predicted in January 1990 that the governor would run again. "Like most observers, I think he is running, because he acts too much like a candidate and talks privately about the ominous specter of a governor named Tommy Robinson." Robinson was an Arkansas congressman known for his publicity stunts and unpredictable actions. He had only recently switched from the Democratic Party to the Republican Party and was hinting that he would run for governor.

Attorney General Steve Clark, who had earlier announced his candidacy for governor, had had to withdraw after a scandal over misuse of a state credit card.

When Clinton announced his plans in March 1990, at age forty-three, he faced Democratic opposition from former U.S. Representative Jim Guy Tucker, whom he had defeated in a Democratic primary years earlier, and Tom McRae, former director of the Winthrop Rockefeller Foundation, an Arkansas-based think tank. McRae was a respected intellectual, but an extremely low-key personality.

The Republicans were running two firebrands: Congressman Tommy Robinson and Sheffield Nelson, a former utility executive who had been wanting to run for some time. Both were onetime Democrats who had recently joined the Republican Party in what was undoubtedly a ploy to attract some of the popularity of President George Bush. They knew, also, that Clinton's powerful Democratic machine could eliminate them in the primary. By running as Republicans, they figured at least one of them would get the chance to face Clinton in the general election.

Clinton announced that he would seek a fifth term, even though "the fire of an election no longer burns in me." He told the people of the state that he "decided that I just didn't want to stop doing the job." No one had known what Clinton's decision would be before the announcement—except Hillary. Even his mother and staff had been kept in the dark.

Reporters and columnists made much of the "fire of an election" comment. Did it mean Clinton, the indefatigable campaigner, was growing weary?

Some observers saw it as another example of his famous "waffling." He seemed to be saying he wanted to run, but he didn't *really* want to run. What did he mean?

Clinton explained to reporters that his remarks were meant to point out that his decision was based on his desire to see the state move securely into the 1990s, and not motivated purely by his own political ambitions. He had chosen, he added, to ask the voters of Arkansas to let him remain governor in spite of the fact that political advisers had told him that another four-year term might ill-serve his political future.

Brummett attacked Clinton for the "fire" remark.

"I think the remark was candid, sane and human," Brummett wrote. "But I do not think it was a smooth political move to verbalize such a thought. It exposed Clinton to two valid crit-icisms: one, that he had been in office too long, since he admits to burnout on one of the main components of holding political office, that being the age-old process of running for it; and, two, that it is arrogant to have the attitude, much less express it, that you do not really want to actually campaign for governor, but will do the people the kind favor of staying on the job."

Brummett also speculated on the possibility of a Clinton-Robinson general election battle. "Robinson demonstrates nearly every time he opens his mouth that he will say just about anything, regardless of truth, proof or responsibility," Brummett warned. If Clinton no longer had the "fire," Brummett opined, taking on Robinson was a losing proposition.

Ironically, Clinton had launched the congressman's political career in the 1970s by appointing Robinson, a former state trooper, as director of public safety, a position that put him in charge of the State Police, the State Crime Laboratory and other agencies.

Robinson went on to become sheriff of Pulaski County, where Little Rock is located. During his tenure in that office, he was known for pulling stunts to capture media attention, such as the time he personally hauled a group of Pulaski County jail inmates to a state prison unit and shackled them to the guard tower, in an effort to draw attention to the overcrowding problem in county jails.

Nelson, Robinson's Republican opponent, wasted no time in criticizing Clinton for education goals that were "too lofty and too expensive." Tucker, on the other hand, seized on the idea that ten years in the governor's office was too long and that all of the appointees to state boards and commissions would soon be Clinton's.

During the 1990 campaign, rumors about Clinton's sex life began to increase. Ever since the Gary Hart affair, newspapers had debated among themselves whether a candidate's private life was of importance to the public. At about the same time, a former state employee, Larry Nichols, who had been fired two years before, filed a suit against Clinton, ostensibly to get his job back. But the lawsuit accused Clinton of having affairs with five women. One of those women was named Gennifer Flowers.

Local media reported the lawsuit, but played it down, not naming the women and not even mentioning the allegations. Nichols, who had been pressured to quit after allegedly using state telephones to raise money for the contra rebels in Nicaragua, was considered by the media to be a disgruntled ex-employee with a grudge and without a shred of evidence.

The rumors were so pervasive that both the *Gazette* and the *Democrat* put teams of reporters on the story. The *Gazette* reporters came back with no evidence and firm denials from all the women mentioned in the lawsuit. Columnist Starr has said the *Democrat* reporters also found no credibility in the allegations and rumors. Nothing about the rumors was written in either paper, other than vague references by columnists to Clinton's "personal life."

All of the women, including Gennifer Flowers, denied having affairs with the governor. Flowers even threatened to sue a radio station that had used her name in reporting the lawsuit.

Brummett, in his *Gazette* column, warned of another issue that could surface during the campaign—Clinton's evasive answer when asked by the press if he had ever used illegal drugs. Clinton's answer was that he had not used them "as an adult in Arkansas." Brummett felt that since Robinson once had a drinking habit that had been made public, Robinson would bring up the drug question and use it against Clinton. Brummett put the issue to rest as follows:

> What matters is that he does not use drugs now, and has not for at least a very long time. For twelve years in the public eye he has shown himself to be in constantly sober control of his mental and physical faculties.
>
> Clinton is too much in love with himself, too timid in his personal habits and too concerned about his political health to take such a chance—physically, socially or politically. A couple of beers put him to sleep. A glass of wine with dinner activates his allergies and makes his face puffy.
>
> It may be that his direct and honest answer to the question is an absolute *no*, in which case it would be in his best interest to clear up that curious answer about adulthood in Arkansas.
>
> But it may be that his direct and honest answer would be that more than two decades ago—as a lad or college student—drug use was prevalent among people of his age and station in life, and on one or a few occasions he inhaled from what was commonly called a joint.

Brummett proved to have remarkable insight. Two years later, during the 1992 presidential campaign, Clinton finally admitted that, while at Oxford University, he had "experimented with marijuana a time or two and I didn't like it."

But Clinton did give a straight answer to another question.

During a televised interview on October 15, 1990, newsman Craig Cannon asked Clinton: "Will you guarantee all of us that if reelected, there is absolutely, positively no way that you'll run for any other political office and that you'll serve out your full term?"

Clinton responded: "You bet. I told you when I announced for governor that I intended to run, and that's what I'm gonna do. I'm gonna serve four years. I made that decision when I decided to run. I'm being considered as a candidate for governor. That's the job I want. That's the job I'll do for the next four years."

This became known as "the promise." Like his bumbling old enemy, Frank White, Clinton had overloaded his mouth, and it would hurt him in the years to come.

* * *

A report by *Financial World* magazine ranked Arkansas among the most poorly managed states, placing it forty-first out of fifty. Robinson made the article public, sending copies to the press. Clinton was furious.

A magazine spokesperson said the rating was based on fiscal policy and social factors, such as Medicaid and Medicare dependency, the poverty rate and student dropout figures. The article was not entirely critical, naming job creation, the booming poultry industry and the ability to lure industry as "bright spots" for Arkansas. But it criticized the state's use of tax-exempt bonds and tax abatement as incentives to industry.

No longer content to let criticism sit unanswered, Clinton immediately issued a four-and-a-half-page news release to counter the article. He blamed the ranking on "a lack of understanding of the state's budget process," pointing out the legal mandate—of which the magazine must have been unaware—that Arkansas had to operate on a balanced budget. He said that much of the rating was based on the state's not having a "rainy day" fund and explained that the state based spending on revenues actually taken in and acted on this mandated method of spending, making a reserve fund unsound fiscal policy.

Meanwhile, Tucker dropped out of the governor's race, leaving

McRae as Clinton's principal Democratic opponent. Four other candidates also joined the primary race. If Clinton were to go on to win the general election and serve a fifth term, he would outstrip the twelve-year tenure of Orval Faubus and set the record at fourteen years.

It would be one of the nastiest campaigns Arkansas had ever seen.

12

The Mud Hits the Fan

THE NATION'S EYE WAS ON THE 1990 RACE IN ARKANSAS BECAUSE Clinton was considered—in the words of *Washington Post* writer David Broder—"a perennially rising star on the national scene." Broder noted that Clinton, in this race, was "without the support of labor or teachers."

Hillary Clinton returned to the spotlight briefly when she broke up a news conference held by Bill Clinton's opponent, Tom McRae. When McRae started listing charges against Clinton, Hillary, standing in the crowd, interrupted by reading back to McRae his past words of praise for Clinton. McRae attempted a back-and-forth exchange, but soon realized that Hillary was upstaging him. He ended the press conference.

Hillary Clinton had kicked up a storm. The newspapers and radio talk shows were dominated by comments as to whether her actions were appropriate. Bill Clinton appeared to be amused by it all.

Clinton won a clear majority at 54.8 percent of the primary vote, but it was the smallest percentage of the vote he had ever garnered in a primary, with the exception of 1982, when, with 41 percent, he was forced into a runoff with Joe Purcell.

Broder noted, however, that the Democratic campaign was "sissy stuff" compared to "the personal warfare between the two newly minted Republicans who were vying to face the Democratic winner in November. Businessman Sheffield Nelson and Representative Tommy F. Robinson are challenging each other's ethics, honesty and mental balance—as well as the motives of their big-money backers—in a fashion that may leave permanent scars on a Republican Party that is still trying to get a foothold in the state."

The Nelson-Robinson battle was classic Arkansas politics. It was so complex that it was difficult to keep the players straight.

Nelson grew up in poverty in East Arkansas. Fresh out of college, he went to work at Arkla, Inc., a huge natural gas distribution company owned by the powerful Stephens family of Arkansas. He quickly worked his way up to president of Arkla. In the early 1980s, he signed a deal with Arkoma, a gas drilling and production firm owned by oilman Jerry Jones. Arkoma acquired gas leases from Arkla, agreed to share development costs and was guaranteed a high price from Arkla.

Natural gas prices plunged. Arkla, still paying the high prices to Jones, was losing so much money on the deal that it was forced to buy its way out of the agreement. Jones made millions of dollars.

Jones and Robinson had grown up together in a poor section of the city of North Little Rock and had been best friends all of their lives. Jones became a political patron of Robinson and loaned him money to purchase a farm. Robinson hired Jones's twenty-three-year-old daughter for a $60,000-a-year staff job in his congressional office.

When both Robinson and Nelson switched to the Republican Party and announced as candidates for governor, everything turned upside down.

Although Nelson had long since stepped down as president of Arkla and had gone into private law practice, the Stephens family was still steamed over the Arkoma deal, which had cost them millions while enriching Robinson's old friend, Jones. They put their money on Robinson, who began attacking Nelson over the Arkla-Arkoma deal. This ended his lifelong friendship with Jones.

Nelson and Robinson began attacking each other personally. The struggling Arkansas Republican Party, which was trying to establish itself with credible candidates, was embarrassed by the almost childish display of name-calling and stunts.

Nelson defeated Robinson for the Republican nomination. Both Republicans and Democrats gave Clinton a hard race, reminding voters, as Broder put it, that "after ten years of Clinton's leadership, Arkansas teachers are still the lowest-paid in the nation and schools rank low on many ratings." There were also charges that Clinton had "lost his clout with the legislature and neglects the state because of his national ambitions."

Broder summed up Clinton's challenge:

> Many longtime Clinton allies concede that time has taken a toll on him....At the national level, Clinton is known as a leading voice for school reform, Bush's Democratic partner at the national "education summit," a former chairman of the National Governors Association, the new head of the Democratic Leadership Council, almost a candidate for the 1988 presidential nomination and on everyone's list of future White House possibilities.
>
> But at home, Clinton has had a rocky time. The legislature repeatedly has refused to pass his school-finance program because it involved higher taxes. Teachers unions, angry at his requiring competency testing of their members, withheld their endorsement in the primary. In a state desperate for jobs, the Clinton administration approved a big loan to a company in the middle of a labor dispute—angering unions enough that the governor lost their endorsement.

Spectrum Weekly, a small Little Rock newspaper, brought out the issue that Clinton had an ironclad political machine in place:

> With [the] expected win over Sheffield Nelson, Clinton is assured of at least fourteen years in office. By the middle of his fourth consecutive term, each and every one of the roughly two thousand gubernatorial appointees in Arkansas will owe their positions to Clinton. From the powerful Highway Commission to the lowly Podiatry Examining Board, Clinton has packed the state's regulatory bodies with his own hand-picked appointees....The appointed bodies have a hand in virtually every aspect of life....While most appointees do not receive salaries, they often choose well-paid directors to head their commissions.

In the last days of the campaign, Nelson began televising the famous "raise and spend" advertisement. The Nelson publicity machine had found a videotape of Clinton speaking to the legislature. During that speech, he had randomly used both the words "raise" and "spend," but not in the same context. Nelson's media people patched together a videotape "loop" that portrayed Clinton as saying "raise and spend, raise and spend, raise and spend" over and over again.

The Clinton camp went ballistic, and immediately began seeking some emergency campaign money to counter the Nelson ads, which were extremely damaging. The last-minute effort was credited with saving Clinton's job, and perhaps his political career. Clinton took 59 percent of the vote to defeat Nelson.

*   *   *

Clinton's unprecedented tenure was sealed. He immediately established his priority as raising money for education. He called on the legislature to make its biggest financial commitment to that cause since 1983, saying he wanted to give teachers an average 10 percent pay raise both of the next two years.

"We cannot...ever hope to have the education system we want if we try to add new standards, new programs and new opportunities on the backs of the schoolteachers," he said. "They have done all they can do, and they have produced for you more results with less money than any state in the United States of America."

Thus Bill Clinton, at age forty-four, took the oath of office before the legislature on Tuesday, January 15, 1991, his left hand on a Bible held by his daughter Chelsea, age 10. The ceremony had been moved inside the Capitol because of rain. Hillary Clinton was there to support her husband's embarkation on a second four-year term and a fifth term in office.

Since 1983, when Clinton's education reforms were put into effect, school administrators had complained that most of the tax money was being used to pay for the new school programs and that little was going to teachers. In 1987, about twenty of the state's top business leaders formed the Arkansas Business Council. One of the council's goals was to devise methods for the business community to assist in improving education in the state. John

Brummett nicknamed the group "The Good Suit Club," an epithet that became more familiar than its real name.

During the legislative session of January 1991, Clinton set out to address the problem of teacher pay. He proposed a $145 million "Educational Excellence Trust Fund" that would be paid for by a half-cent increase in the state sales tax, a new sales tax on used cars and an increase in the corporate income tax from 6 percent to 6.5 percent for companies with annual pretax earnings exceeding $100,000. The Arkansas Business Council had approved the latter tax increase as its contribution to education.

A howl went up immediately. Critics said Clinton was again taking the easy way out with the income tax and pointed out that there was still no exemption for food. Meanwhile, new industries that had moved to Arkansas were granted certain tax exemptions, and wealthy Arkansans were paying a lower income tax on their gains.

The half-cent sales tax was trouble enough, but Arkansans were especially displeased with the tax on the purchase of used cars. Once again, those people who could least afford to pay a tax were asked to pay it. Clinton was upbraided by antitax groups, who accused him of unfairness and of "waffling" on tax issues.

Columnist James Powell, a longtime Clinton supporter, wrote in the *Gazette* that he was disappointed that "this time Clinton didn't even try" to find a more equitable way of paying for the education program. Quoting an old friend, Powell said, "...what we do in our society is tax the poor, because they expect it, but not the rich, because it makes them mad."

But the governor was adamant. He was going to have his Educational Excellence Trust Fund, and the sales taxes were going to pay for it. The Arkansas Education Association linked up with Clinton, and teachers and administrators began lobbying. On the other side, several groups opposed to the sales tax increase pleaded with Clinton to develop new ways of finding the money.

Clinton tossed them a bone. His legislation would remove about two hundred fifty thousand low-income Arkansans from the state income tax rolls. The proposal also lowered the state income tax on Arkansans who were just above the federal poverty line.

The legislature acted before the controversy got out of hand.

Within two weeks of its proposal, the Educational Excellence Trust Fund was approved and the tax measures were law. Critics were furious, but schoolteachers were jubilant. Teacher salaries in Arkansas ranked fiftieth among the states and the District of Columbia in 1990. The new legislation meant that they would get raises totalling about $4,000 over the next two years, depending on how tax collections panned out.

Clinton, who had been vilified by teachers in 1983 over the teacher testing program, had now become a hero in education circles. But many Arkansans remembered Nelson's "raise and spend" advertisement, and wondered if they had been duped by Clinton.

13

The Question and the Promise

CLINTON'S VISIBILITY ON EDUCATION ISSUES HAD WON HIM SEVERAL leadership roles in the late 1980s. President George Bush had asked him to cochair a national summit of the governors set for September 1989 to address ways to reverse "the decline of our educational system." The summit marked only the third time that a president had sat down with state governors to address a single issue.

Just before the summit, Clinton traveled to Wilmington, Delaware, to play a key role in the Southern Governors Conference fifty-fifth meeting. He chaired a session of the Corporate Coalition on Infant Mortality and hosted a meeting of teenagers to discuss teen pregnancy and drug abuse.

Clinton again addressed the need to improve education on a national level in 1990 during a meeting of the National Governors Association. The governors drafted a set of national education goals, many of which were crafted by the Arkansas governor. Clinton had been serving as the main go-between for the governors and the White House. The governors called for the federal government to take money from a reduced military outlay and spend it on education.

By 1990, Clinton again found himself mentioned as a national hope. *Time* magazine wrote that Clinton represented a new breed

143

of "mainstream" Democrats trying to win back the conservative vote.

That same year, Clinton was named chairman of the Democratic Leadership Council, the group of "moderates." The *Time* article went on to say that "Clinton is the perfect front man for an organization that celebrates the work ethic of the common man while relying almost entirely on the Fortune 500 for operating funds."

Clinton was the first governor to chair the Council since its inception in 1985. He said the reason for his selection was to mobilize a broader base of elected officials, including governors, legislators and mayors, and to build a better partnership between those local officials and Democrats in Congress.

After taking over the chairmanship of the DLC, Clinton traveled to New Orleans for a Council meeting. He declared victory in the organization's quest to steer the Democrats to a new national philosophy. Clinton said that the Council must "move beyond the old liberal-conservative debate."

The DLC called for government to spend more on education to attract math and science teachers and to expand tax credits to bring the working poor above poverty level.

Clinton's DLC chairmanship brought him unwanted controversy. The Rev. Jesse Jackson, a contender for the 1988 Democratic presidential nomination, was not invited to speak at the annual DLC convention, set for Cleveland in May. It was reported that Jackson was being shunned as an "old-style" ultraliberal Democrat.

Clinton wrote a letter of apology to Jackson and assured him that he was welcome to attend the convention. But Clinton did not ask him to speak. Jackson accused the DLC of trying to divide the Democratic Party into liberal and conservative factions.

When Clinton filed for reelection to a fifth term in March 1990, he responded to reporters' questions about his plans for national office by saying that he would not run for the Senate in 1992 and by pointing out that "George Bush is at eighty percent in the polls."

The governor was visibly angry with the reporters. "Do you think there's going to be a presidential race in '92? Besides that, I'm doing what I'm interested in doing. I think all this election speculation is, again, your efforts to divert people's attention from the real issues so you'll have another story to write, and I think that's sad."

Later that day Clinton said, "I'm going to be governor four years. We're going to have a good four years, and we're going to have a great legislative session in '91, I think."

But the presidential rumors abounded. During a trip promoting the DLC, Bill Clinton "sounded every bit like a candidate on the stump," wrote a reporter for the Salem, Oregon, *Statesman Journal*. Oregon's Secretary of State, Phil Keisling, called Clinton "one of the brightest, most thoughtful, most energetic people in our party." But Clinton himself said, "I'm not running for anything."

Later, the *Gazette* reported:

> The Clinton presidential watch has been an overtime job lately, what with the governor's flurry of trips, his flap with Jesse Jackson and appearances and reappearances in political columns and talk shows.
>
> The latest sighting of the looks-like-a-candidate, sounds-like etc., noncandidate from Arkansas was in Friday's *Los Angeles Times*.
>
> The newspaper's Washington bureau chief, Jack Nelson, writes that Clinton had told friends that he thinks Bush can be beaten and will "take a hard look" at whether to run for the 1992 Democratic presidential nomination after the May 5–7 Democratic Leadership Council's national meeting in Cleveland."

*　*　*

On August 2, 1990, Iraq attacked and annexed the tiny kingdom of Kuwait. The leaders of the Western world, and many Middle East leaders, feared Iraq's leader, Saddam Hussein, would next target Saudi Arabia and jeopardize the world's oil production.

The United Nations, pushed by President Bush, set a deadline for Iraq to withdraw from Kuwait by January 15, 1991, the day Clinton was to sworn in for a fifth term. The United States and a coalition of nations began a military buildup in the Persian Gulf. Trade and other sanctions were placed on Iraq.

Congress voted to authorize Bush to go to war against Iraq. But the two Arkansas senators, Dale Bumpers and David Pryor, voted with the minority, which believed the United States and the United

Nations should allow more time for the sanctions to work. They also advocated a total blockade of ship and air movements before resorting to war.

Gazette columnist Max Brantley asked Governor Clinton how he would have voted had he been in Congress.

"I guess I would have voted with the majority if it was a close vote," Clinton said. "But I agree with the arguments the minority made."

He added: "It seems it would have been in error for the U.S. government to say, well, the UN set a deadline, but we're going to put it off."

The U.S.-backed coalition attacked Iraq on January 17, 1991. The majority of Americans supported the war. President Bush's ratings in the polls began to soar.

On May 21, 1991, Clinton told a group of five hundred elementary school students in Little Rock, "I wouldn't mind running [for president], but I haven't made a decision. I'd like to be able to do it someday."

On that same day, Hillary Clinton said it seemed unlikely that her husband would run in 1992. "I haven't thought about it very seriously because I don't think it's a very likely possibility," she said. "Bill is personally very capable, obviously, along with a number of qualified Democrats who would be certainly in a position to do an excellent job. But what's more important to me is that we have something to say and that we have policies that are responsive to the needs of people."

The talk of a Clinton presidential candidacy began to grow louder. But although many of his political peers—Governor Ray Mabus of Mississippi, for example—saw Clinton's future in national politics as promising, many Arkansans did not share that view.

Starr said, "I don't see anything for him. He can't run for president, and if he had any sense he would know that. He can be governor, I guess, as long as he wants to be, and I think he'll probably go on wanting to be."

Sheffield Nelson, Clinton's 1990 Republican opponent, shared Starr's opinion:

I don't think Bill Clinton can make it on a national level. I really don't. First of all, he's from a little state with very little

clout from a state standpoint....I think he's got some weaknesses or substantial weaknesses that will be the death knell
for any attempt to be president. I don't think that a guy can
say I will not answer "have you ever" questions and run for
president. That's been proven in past years. The press is going
to demand that he open up his personal life, and I don't think
that Bill Clinton will do that. And if he does not, he cannot
successfully run for president.

I think he can try this DLC approach and try to tout
himself as a more moderate person than he is, but the truth of
the matter is that he is a liberal, tax-and-spend candidate
regardless of what he is running for. And that will not fly once
the national press puts the spotlight on him. I don't think that
Clinton can fool the national press. They'll look at his
background, look at his tax-and-spend propensities, look at
where he has taxed the people and how he has taxed them—
and I'm talking about the regressive-type taxation that we've
got in this state—and I think it will be impossible for him to
ever sell himself as a moderate candidate.

*   *   *

In July 1991, Clinton addressed the National Women's Political
Caucus in Washington and made it clear that he had strong pro-
choice views on abortion.

"I think the majority of the American people are with this group
on the issue of choice," Clinton said, adding, "I am opposed to
overturning Roe v. Wade. I think it's the right decision. I think we
should leave it intact."

In 1989, Clinton had said he was personally opposed to abortion, but would allow it in cases of rape and incest and to save the
mother's life. In 1990 he had said: "Under the present Arkansas law,
abortion is illegal when the unborn child can live outside its
mother's womb. I support that. While I have also supported
restrictions on public funding and a parental notification requirement for minors, I think the government should impose no further
restrictions....I believe the decision on abortion should be the
woman's, not the government's."

Clinton, in his Washington remarks in 1991, made no mention of
his previous support for some restrictions on abortion, including
parental notice and the use of public money for abortions.

The governor was accompanied to the caucus by national media consultant Frank Greer, but Clinton dodged questions about a presidential race.

"I think the whole thing will be set before long," he said. "I think everybody who will be in, will be in before long."

Later that month, Clinton acknowledged publicly for the first time that he was considering running for president. But he said he had not begun the preparations for a national campaign. He said he would make a decision by Labor Day.

The next day, reporters asked Clinton if he would answer questions about extramarital sex and illegal drug use if ran for president.

The *Gazette* and the Associated Press responded that Clinton said: "It's none of your business." He accused the press of being "the moral police of the country."

"I think the people who ran in '88 kind of resented it and chose not to answer those kinds of questions. And I would expect most people who run in '92 won't," Clinton added.

He said he believed people in public life should "try to draw some reasonable lines between their public and private lives."

A week later, Clinton backtracked on his responses. He denied having said "It's none of your business" or having called the press "the moral police." He took a softer tone by saying reporters "have to ask whatever questions you consider relevant—that's what the First Amendment is for. But I have to give the answers that I think are appropriate." He then reiterated that he would not answer such questions.

The questions persisted. On July 22, *USA Today* published an interview in which Clinton said he'd never "broken any drug law." During the 1990 campaign, he had said he "never violated the drug laws of the state as an adult in Arkansas."

The next day, *Gazette* reporter Scott Morris asked Clinton if the *USA Today* interview represented a broadening of his drug-use statement.

"It is accurate to say that I haven't broken any drug laws," Clinton said. "I will say that because it is a legal question. I literally thought what I said was consistent with what I said in 1990."

Morris asked Clinton if he had used marijuana or any other illegal drug as a college student.

"The answer to that question is no," Clinton said. "That's the question you asked, and I'll give you the answer."

* * *

As early as August 1991, Clinton heard New Hampshire calling.

He was planning a trip to Concord to open a chapter of the Democratic Leadership Council in New Hampshire. He was going to do so in defiance of that state party's executive committee, which had voted not to recognize any group that claimed to represent Democrats or the party's ideals unless it first got the approval of the state committee.

Chris Spirou, chairman of the New Hampshire Democratic Party, believed the chapter was unhealthy for the party and was dividing it. The group was not allowed to use the word "Democratic" in its name, so it adopted the initials and called itself the "New Hampshire DLC."

Spirou was not happy that Clinton was coming to the state in apparent defiance of the state party. Clinton's press spokesman, Mike Gauldin, said Clinton had been invited by DLC members in New Hampshire.

"People in New Hampshire formed the DLC chapter. It was not formed by Bill Clinton or the DLC staff in Washington," Gauldin said, adding that Clinton was going to Concord not to stir up trouble, but to speak during an issues forum given by the new group.

Clinton headed for Concord and spoke to the maverick group. The dispute had created so much attention that the meeting drew a huge national and state media contingent, who were curious about this Clinton fellow.

After delivering his talk to the DLC, Clinton strolled down the street to the state party headquarters for a brief, closed-door meeting with Spirou. The two emerged to say that they had come to more agreements than disagreements, and that they were united in the goal of defeating President Bush. Clinton again said he would reveal his presidential plans, if any, by Labor Day.

Since May, Clinton had traveled to the politically important states of California, New York, New Hampshire, Illinois and Texas carrying the message of the DLC.

On August 15, he quietly announced that he was resigning as chairman of the DLC so that he could form a presidential exploratory committee. Clinton explained that tax laws prohibited the tax-exempt DLC from being identified with any specific candidate.

Clinton emphasized that he hadn't made a decision on a presidential campaign and that his DLC resignation was no big deal. "The news today is this was a practical necessity. We'll be exploring whether people would contribute if I should run," he said. A few days later, Robert Farmer, the chief fund-raiser in the Democratic Party, became chairman of the exploratory committee.

Despite Clinton's downplaying of the action, most observers said it was the first step to a presidential candidacy.

Labor Day came and went, with no announcement. After a trip to Seattle to the National Governors Association, Clinton returned to Arkansas and began traveling around the state, asking Arkansans what they thought about his potential candidacy. There was the problem of "the promise," and he was asking them if they would release him from the pledge he'd made in 1990 that he would serve a full four-year term if reelected governor.

Clinton kept his Arkansas travel itinerary secret from the press. He did not want reporters tagging along. "The governor is trying to talk to people about their honest opinions," a staff member explained.

Reporters who caught up with Clinton in Fayetteville after he'd been traveling for several days asked him about the mood of the people he had talked to.

"I think most people, in the end, say that if you believe what you're doing is best for us and you, we're with you," Clinton said. He was also realistic about his chances: "I might get my brains beat out—probably will. It's difficult for a sitting governor to be elected president."

As the time for a decision drew near, Clinton found himself spending more and more time dealing with "the question"—the issue of his relationship and rumored extramarital affairs—and "the promise"—his pledge to serve four years as governor.

In mid-September, Bill and Hillary Clinton attended a breakfast in Washington with several of the nation's top political writers. Bill

Clinton was interrogated about his knowledge of foreign affairs, taxes and other policy issues. "The question" arose.

"What you need to know about me is we have been together for almost twenty years and have been married almost sixteen, and we are committed to our marriage and its obligation, to our child and to each other. We love each other very much," Clinton said.

"Like nearly anybody that's been together twenty years, our relationship has not been perfect or free of difficulties. But we feel good about where we are. We believe in our obligations. And we intend to be together thirty or forty years from now, regardless of whether I run for president or not.

"And I think that ought to be enough."

After returning to Little Rock, Clinton had to face the local press about his answer to "the question." He had told them in July that he was never going to make another response to questions about his personal life, yet he had talked to the Washington writers about it.

Clinton had another problem: *Newsweek* magazine reported that his advisers had urged Bill and Hillary Clinton to appear together in Washington in an effort to sidestep the rumors about his personal life.

"I didn't volunteer anything. I was asked. I didn't know for sure what they were going to ask. My staff had nothing to do with that decision," Clinton told the local press. "I made a decision and Hillary made a decision that we would go to that meeting."

He said his response in Washington would be his final one:

> I have nothing else to say about this. That's not what this election would be about and I have nothing else to say about it. It's not a very important thing. It's not important to most Americans. They haven't said anything to me about it. Most people in Arkansas haven't. But I've got to say it's very important to me personally and I didn't want people to think that it wasn't important, so I said what I believed and I have nothing else to say.

Clinton had one more fence to mend in the Democratic Party before he could run for president. Jesse Jackson was still miffed over Clinton's efforts to move the Democratic Party to the middle of the political spectrum. Jackson had been calling the Democratic Leadership Council the "Democrats for the Leisure Class" and the "Southern White Boys Club." In early October, Jackson came to Little Rock to talk with Clinton.

After a seventy-seven-minute meeting behind closed doors in the Governor's Mansion, Jackson and Clinton walked outside to tell reporters that they had come to a mutual understanding.

"It is resolved because it's behind us," Jackson said. "I certainly cannot go forward looking backward. The stakes right now are much higher than the feelings of leaders."

Jackson said their misunderstanding had grown out of Clinton's public opposition to racial hiring quotas. Clinton's statements had led some people to believe that he wanted the Democrats to abandon affirmative action.

"I reassured him that was not the case, and I do believe that we have more common ground than divided," Clinton said, although neither he nor Jackson explained what "common ground" they had reached.

Jackson made it clear that he wasn't endorsing Clinton or anyone else, but that it was important that the Democratic Party have a show of unity.

"This is an intersquad game," Jackson said. "Ultimately, the big game is with the other team, and we cannot lose so many players in practice until we forfeit the big game."

Two days later, Bill Clinton would be in the big game.

14

The New Covenant

ON MAY 6, 1861, THE ARKANSAS LEGISLATURE GATHERED IN THE building in little Rock that is now the Old State House to vote to secede from the United States and join the Confederacy. The vote was 69 to 1, with only Isaac Murphy of Huntsville holding out. Within two years, the conquering Union Army had occupied Little Rock. General Frederick Steele converted the Old State House into his headquarters. Union soldiers bivouacked on the grounds around the building.

At high noon on October 3, 1991, the area around the Old State House was once more choked with an army, this time an army of people carrying banners, placards, flags and television cameras. A crowd estimated at 4,500 had come to see Bill Clinton announce for the presidency.

A high school band played and a college choir sang. Several people mounted the platform on the steps of the Old State House and gave speeches introducing Clinton. Among them were his childhood friend, Carolyn Staley, and Hollywood producer Harry Thomason, one of his most ardent supporters.

Directly in front of the main platform was an even larger stage brimming with television cameras and newspaper photographers. When the last introductory speaker finished, Bill Clinton, forty-five, headed for the lectern amid the roar of cheers. The moment was broadcast live on national television by CNN.

Backed by twelve American flags and flanked by the huge white columns of the Old State House, Clinton stepped up to the microphone and into the campaign for the presidency.

In a thirty-five-minute speech, Clinton outlined where he had come from and where he was going:

> All of you, in different ways, have brought me here today, to step beyond a life and a job I love, to make a commitment to a large cause: preserving the American Dream, restoring the hopes of the forgotten middle class, reclaiming the future for our children.
>
> I refuse to be part of a generation that celebrates the death of communism abroad with the loss of the American Dream at home.
>
> I refuse to be part of a generation that fails to compete in the global economy and so condemns hardworking Americans to a life of struggle without reward or security.
>
> That is why I stand here today, because I refuse to stand by and let our children become part of the first generation to do worse than their parents. I don't want my child or your child to be part of a country that's coming apart instead of coming together.

Clinton began a theme that he was to carry throughout his campaign, that the middle class had carried the economic load for too long and that he would change all of that:

> Middle-class people are spending more hours on the job, spending less time with their children, bringing home a smaller paycheck to pay more for health care and housing and education. Our streets are meaner, our families are more broken, our health care is the costliest in the world and we get less for it.
>
> The country is headed in the wrong direction fast, slipping behind, losing our way, and all we have out of Washington is status quo paralysis. No vision, no action, just neglect, selfishness and division.

In an ironic nod to his backdrop, the Old State House, where his forerunners had voted to make Arkansas part of the Confederacy,

Clinton called for a unity of the races that had eluded Americans for 130 years since the Emancipation Proclamation:

> For twelve years, Republicans have tried to divide us—race against race—so we get mad at each other and not at them. They want us to look at each other across a racial divide so we don't turn and look to the White House and ask, why are all of our incomes going down? Why are all of us losing our jobs? Why are we losing our future?

Clinton insisted that a new approach was needed to solve old problems. The nation needed a fundamental change in the way it looked at itself and at the world:

> The change we must make isn't liberal or conservative. It's both and it's different. The small towns and main streets of our America aren't like the corridors and back rooms of Washington. People out here don't care about idle rhetoric of "left" or "right" and "liberal" and "conservative" and all the other words that have made our politics a substitute for action....We need a new covenant to rebuild America. It's just common sense. Government's responsibility is to create more opportunity. The people's responsibility is to make the most of it.

Clinton offered such solutions as tearing down trade barriers; providing preschool to every child who needs it; an "apprenticeship" program for people who don't want to go to college but who want good jobs; and a "domestic GI Bill" under which anyone could borrow money to go to college and pay it back as a small percentage of his or her income or through national service.

He promised to make taxes "fair," saying, "For twelve years Republicans have raised taxes on the middle class. It's time to give the middle class tax relief."

The way to solve rising health costs was to "take on the big insurance companies and health care bureaucracies and get some real cost control into the system," Clinton said. He pledged that in the "first year of a Clinton administration, we will present a plan to Congress and the American people to provide affordable, quality health care for all Americans."

The crowd was with him all the way, cheering and waving

placards. When he finished, the Fleetwood Mac rock song "Don't Stop Thinking About Tomorrow" boomed from the sound system, nearly drowning out the crowd. Clinton had selected it as the theme song for his campaign. The governor then turned and hugged his wife and eleven-year-old daughter.

* * *

Clinton's ambitions received the endorsement of the *Gazette*. But the *Democrat*, in an extra addition published on the day of the announcement, said, "We don't for a moment believe that the governor will see the inside of the White House this time around. George Bush bestrides next year's presidential horizon like a colossus."

Columnists for both newspapers noted that Clinton had not addressed his 1990 promise that he would serve his full term as governor. *Gazette* columnist Max Brantley, who was generally sympathetic to Clinton, wrote, "He can run for president. But he can't hide from the people back home. They deserve straighter talk."

The political columnists for the rival *Democrat* had already taken a strident anti-Clinton position over the issue of "the promise" as it had become clear in the preceding weeks that he was going to run for president.

On the day of Clinton's announcement, *Democrat* columnist Meredith Oakley put it bluntly: "His word is dirt."

She called Clinton a "common, run-of-the-mill, dime-a-dozen politician." And of his supporters, she wrote: "The bleaters who care more for celebrity than veracity are basking in a false and empty light. They trumpet the basest form of political expediency, for they revel amid the debris of a broken promise."

Starr denounced Clinton for breaking "the solemn oath that he made to the people of Arkansas, and a private pledge he made to me, in order to go in blind pursuit of personal political ambition."

Both newspapers' coverage of the announcement portrayed it in anticlimactic tones. Clinton had actually been on the campaign trail for months and the reporters had been dogging every step. His presidential announcement was described in the *Gazette* as a "slowed-down summary of the speeches he has been giving around the country since March."

It was noted that Clinton had used the words "middle class"

thirteen times, "responsibility" twelve times, and "opportunity" ten times.

"The thirty-five-minute speech was often rousing, but too long," wrote *Gazette* columnist Brantley. "It was three minutes longer than the disastrous nominating speech Clinton gave for Michael Dukakis in Atlanta in 1988."

Clinton supporters were enthusiastic about the moment. "It was a hell of a crowd," said Frank Greer, Clinton's media consultant. Greer said it was the largest crowd that any of the six announced Democratic candidates had drawn.

The speech was called "inspiring" and "outstanding" by others in the crowd. Lieutenant Governor Jim Guy Tucker defended the length of the speech by saying, "He was as specific as presidential candidates ever get. That will satisfy journalists who chide politicians for not being specific."

* * *

Clinton became the sixth declared Democratic candidate. The others were former Senator Paul Tsongas of Massachusetts; Senator Tom Harkin of Iowa; Virginia state Senator L. Douglas Wilder; Senator Bob Kerrey of Nebraska, and the mayor of Irvine, California, Larry Agran.

A few weeks later, on October 21, former Governor Edmund G. "Jerry" Brown Jr. of California would join the race and take an unusual stand: He would accept no contributions larger than $100.

Except for Agran and Wilder, Clinton was probably the least known, nationally, of the candidates.

The day after his announcement, Clinton addressed the problem of "the promise." For most of the day, he used a satellite TV hookup to provide interviews with television reporters and anchors around the nation. It was a novel approach that put him on the air in the presidential nominating states as well as the big markets.

During a lunch break, local reporters asked Clinton why he had not addressed "the promise" in his presidential announcement.

"I knew I would have an opportunity to talk about it today, and because [the presidential announcement] was the first opportunity I had to speak to the whole country.

"The conversation about the pledge [to serve his full term] is a conversation that's completely between me and the state. I do think that a majority of the people now will understand and accept and support the decision I made in the end, after talking to literally hundreds of people."

He also said he was confident that his staff and Lieutenant Governor Tucker would make a "good team" that could manage the state while he was campaigning.

The next day, a Saturday, Bill Clinton began the grueling nation-wide campaign with a trip to Des Moines for a speech. After that, he headed to New Hampshire for his first trip there as an announced candidate.

Clinton was way behind. He had taken too long to get out of the starting gate. He had little name recognition and came from an obscure state.

But he had one thing in his favor: The national media were curious about him, and soon were captivated by him. That old Clinton magic was working again.

Back home, he had nothing but media trouble. On October 18, the Little Rock newspaper war came to an abrupt end. That might have been a relief to most public figures, as it would mean less media scrutiny. But it was not the case with Bill Clinton.

The *Arkansas Gazette*, whose editorial page had been a constant Clinton supporter through the years, was sold by its owner, the Gannett Company, to Walter Hussman, owner of the competing *Arkansas Democrat*. The *Gazette* was shut down and the majority of its seven hundred employees lost their jobs.

Hussman changed the name of the *Democrat* to the *Arkansas Democrat-Gazette*. The newspaper's editorial page was ambivalent about—and seemingly bored by—Clinton's presidential aspirations.

But its three main political columnists were virulently opposed to Bill Clinton. Former *Gazette* columnist John Brummett believed Clinton was not presidential timber. He denounced him as "timid, indecisive, wishy-washy, vacillating and a chameleon who tried too hard to get everyone to love him."

Columnists Oakley and Starr had numerous complaints against Clinton, the chief one being that Clinton had broken "the promise." Both had stopped using the word "governor" in front of his name because they believed he had abdicated his responsibility for that role.

So, while Clinton was scrambling to seek national media endorsement, the editorial page of the *Democratic-Gazette*—the biggest media outlet in Arkansas, the last remaining statewide newspaper—was yawning at his run for the presidency. That is, it was yawning when its three top op-ed columnists weren't actively opposing Arkansas's favorite son.

* * *

Late in October, Clinton returned to his old school, Georgetown University, to deliver the first of three policy statements that he called "The New Covenant."

The statement hammered at Clinton's familiar themes: the greed of the Reagan-Bush years; the burden of the "forgotten middle class"; the abandonment of the troubled urban neighborhoods; making more education available to anyone who wanted it, regardless of cost; the endless "cycle of welfare"; and promoting free trade.

It was clear that Clinton had become a student of the "new paradigm" political theory, a complex concept first put forth in 1988 by David Osborne in his book *Laboratories of Democracy*.

Simply explained, a new paradigm emerges to replace a system that is becoming ineffective, or worse, detrimental to society. Osborne cites the New Deal's replacement of the sinking industrial age, with all its economic problems such as the Depression, as a new paradigm.

If a new paradigm is emerging now to replace New Deal liberalism, the traditional concepts of liberal and conservative may no longer apply. New paradigm politicians seek to step outside the established boundaries such as liberal and conservative to seek answers to problems caused by the dynamics of change. Osborne believes Clinton is a prime example of a new paradigm politician.

A new paradigm usually evolves out of a crisis and replaces the old paradigm. Osborne sees the "glimmerings" of a new paradigm now, especially in "new partnerships between the public and private sectors."

In his first New Covenant statement at Georgetown, Clinton said:

More than two hundred years ago, our founders outlined our first social compact between government and the people, not just between lords and kings. More than a century ago, Abraham Lincoln gave his life to maintain the union that compact created. Sixty years ago, Franklin Roosevelt renewed that promise with a New Deal that offered opportunity in return for hard work.

Today we need to forge a New Covenant that will repair the damaged bond between the people and their government and restore our basic values—the notion that our country has a responsibility to help people get ahead. That citizens have not only the right but a responsibility to rise as far and as high as their talents and determination can take them, and that we're all in this together. We must make good on the words of Thomas Jefferson, who said, "A debt of service is due from every man to his country proportional to the bounties which nature and fortune have measured him."

Make no mistake: This New Covenant means change— change in our party, change in our national leadership and change in our country. Far away from Washington, in your hometowns and mine, people have lost faith in the ability of government to change their lives for the better. Out there, you can hear the quiet, troubled voice of the forgotten middle class, lamenting that government no longer looks out for their interests or honors their values....

This New Covenant can't be between the politicians and the established interests. It can't be just another back-room deal between the people in power and the people who keep them there. This New Covenant can only be ratified by the people in the 1992 election. That is why I'm running for president.

Clinton never said anything about paradigms, but his mention of Jefferson, Lincoln and FDR—people who have brought about positive and beneficial results by eclipsing the established patterns—clearly indicated that variations of the theory were on his mind. Osborne, in his book, says Bill Clinton is a classic "new paradigm liberal" who is seeking a "synthesis" of the national and state governments to solve problems.

Under Clinton's New Covenant, the government would use incentives and rewards to empower the people to climb the economic ladder on their own.

Carrying this bag of lofty ideas, Clinton entered the fray in New Hampshire in November, and immediately got into a tangle with Douglas Wilder over, of all things, a newspaper article.

The *Arkansas Democrat-Gazette* had published an Associated Press article that quoted Wilder as criticizing Clinton's "workfare" reform. Clinton supported a welfare program that would require welfare recipients to perform public service work, if they are able, after receiving welfare for two years. An experiment with this "workfare" program has been conducted in Arkansas and other places.

In the article, Wilder was quoted as saying Clinton "said he was going to put people off welfare and put them to work. He didn't start coming on strong like that until he saw what happened down in Louisiana with David Duke. Why make poor welfare recipients the whipping boy of the country's economic downturn?"

Clinton was outraged that Wilder would criticize the program and mention him in the same breath with David Duke, the Louisiana ex-Nazi-turned-Republican.

"I've worked on welfare reform since Arkansas was one of the first demonstration states in 1980," Clinton said. "I've got an eleven-year record on this. Secondly, I was the Democratic leader of the governors' welfare reform effort, which became the Family Support Act of 1988."

Clinton said Wilder had only been a governor for two years and didn't have the experience to be running for president.

The fight spilled over into the debate the next night—the eve of the New Hampshire state Democratic convention. It was the first of the televised debates, and only Clinton, Tsongas and Wilder participated in it. Brown, Harkin and Kerrey had business elsewhere.

At times, the debate became a series of petty disputes, with Clinton and Wilder carping at each other. They haggled over the definition of negative advertising, with Wilder saying he would not participate in it. An agitated Clinton charged that Wilder had already used negative advertising against him, namely the David Duke statement. Wilder said: "I will never engage in negative campaigning, period."

Clinton countered: "Yesterday, you were quoted in my hometown paper as saying I had never expressed any interest in welfare reform until David Duke won in Louisiana."

Wilder said he had not made the statement.

"So you never made any reference critical to my emphasis on welfare reform? Clinton asked.

"Never," Wilder said, adding that he would like to see the newspaper article.

"Well, I didn't bring it with me," Clinton said.

It went downhill from there, dissolving into a childish tit-for-tat argument. Tsongas came off looking like a diplomat. He stayed above the squabble and even managed to address some important issues. Tsongas clearly won this first debate. Clinton and Wilder merely looked foolish.

Clinton quickly realized he had made a major misstep. One of his most successful strategies is to analyze his mistakes, catalogue them in his memory and devise methods to surmount them. Friends say Clinton gets as little as four hours of sleep most nights. He and his crew must have spent much of that postdebate night preparing new tactics.

The next day, a reconstituted Bill Clinton appeared at the state convention. He would be the last speaker, a bad slot because the crowd would be restless and bored after so much political speech-making. Within minutes, Clinton had captivated the audience with a short talk that hit the high spots of his populist beliefs. He then brought in a husband and wife who had just been thrown into the economic wringer after the husband had lost his job. They were the perfect illustration of the effects of the recession. Bill Clinton had come back again.

Clinton was struggling to overcome his lack of name recognition. Two weeks later, a poll of New Hampshire voters put him in sixth place. The other candidates were chipping away at his New Covenant, accusing Clinton of dreaming big, but offering no specifics.

The recession had become the big issue. President Bush had lost nearly all of the popularity he had gained during the Persian Gulf war. The Democrats blamed the Republicans for the economic hard times. Bush took a licking in the media for seeming to be ignorant of the troubles in America and being more interested in foreign policy.

Clinton was quick to take part in the Bush-bashing. But he also took aim at the old-line Democrats in Congress.

"We have to move away from George Bush's and Ronald Reagan's failed experiment in trickle-down economics and political neglect," he said. "It didn't produce growth or upward mobility. It didn't prepare average Americans to better compete in the new world economy. But we must also move beyond the old Democratic theory that says we can just tax and spend our way out of every problem we face."

He offered a five-point plan to end the recession:

- Rebuild consumer confidence with an immediate infusion of much-needed cash by cutting taxes for middle-class Americans and for families with children.
- Create hundreds of thousands of jobs by accelerating current highway spending and opening up the housing market to more first-home buyers.
- Institute measures to protect, for a period, the health care coverage and mortgage or rent payments of those who lose their jobs.
- Expand credit by urging banks to continue serving sound businesses and to offer fair credit card rates to good customers.
- Increase U.S. production by insisting that Japan and Germany do their part to maintain global economic growth, by stimulating their economies to purchase more exports from the United States and elsewhere and by immediately paying more of the costs of their own military security.

As if that wasn't enough, Clinton added five more points for a "long-term" strategy:

- Empower every American to be more productive by changing the way children are educated and workers are trained.
- Revolutionize government so that it becomes an "engine of opportunity," not an obstacle.
- Encourage American companies and American workers to reorganize the workplace and the way they do business, "to make sure corporations behave responsibly and to increase

genuinely productive investment and innovation throughout the economy."

- Stand up for American workers and businesses by expanding trade on just and fair terms.
- Define a new national security policy that preserves the United States as the world's leader, while retaining efforts to take care of the people in America.

Clinton was on a roll. He practically demanded that the president and Congress adopt his program at that very moment. On November 20, he delivered the second part of this three-part New Covenant. The thrust of the second part was economic change and the policy was an expansion of his five-point recession plan.

* * *

On the day before Thanksgiving, while Clinton was campaigning in Texas, a variation of "the question" popped up again, but in an odd way.

Penthouse magazine published an article by Connie Hamzy of Little Rock, a self-described groupie who claims to have had sex with hundreds of rock stars.

Hamzy, known as "Sweet, Sweet Connie" because a rock group, Grand Funk Railroad, had called her that in a popular song, said in the article that she had had an encounter with Bill Clinton on August 31, 1984. Hamzy said she was sunbathing by a hotel pool in North Little Rock when one of Clinton's aides appeared and said the governor wanted to meet her. According to Hamzy:

"You're kidding," I answered and, looking at my skimpy purple bikini, added, "I don't have any clothes on."
"I'm sure that's fine with him," [the aide] said, motioning for me to follow him inside.

Hamzy said she and Clinton engaged in "small talk" until the men around them left the area. Then:

After they were out of earshot, our governor really 'cut loose,' I wrote in my diary that day. He said 'I'd love to get with you. Where can we go?' We walked down the hall and he opened a few doors of meeting rooms. He closed them pretty quickly, so I guess folks were [inside].

Hamzy said she and Clinton were unable to find a room, but she fondled him, then they talked a bit and she kissed him. At that point, she said, he got in his car with his aides and drove away.

The account was so bizarre and suspicious that the *Democrat-Gazette* editors debated whether to publish it all, although local radio and television stations were already reporting it. When Clinton's staff issued a denial, the newspaper decided to run the story.

Clinton's press secretary, Mike Gauldin, issued a statement that said:

> The allegations published in *Penthouse* are baseless and malicious lies. As three witnesses traveling with the governor on the date in question have stated, Ms. Hamzy introduced herself to the governor and accosted him in the lobby of the North Little Rock Hilton as he was leaving a lunchtime speaking engagement. Governor Clinton rebuffed the advance and promptly left the hotel.

A state representative and two aides to Clinton said in sworn statements that they were with Clinton on that day, but only the legislator, Jimmie Don McKissack, said he'd witnessed Clinton's version of the incident. All three said that if anything happened, Hamzy had instigated it.

McKissack said Hamzy accosted the governor, pulled down her bikini top for a moment, then propositioned him. "I was astonished. The governor was dumbfounded," McKissack said. "He turned red. She reached for his groin and backed off. There were other people in the hallway. We left immediately. The governor was completely taken aback by the entire event and he was embarrassed."

The lurid little story sparked quite a bit of talk around Arkansas, but it came and went without much effect. The national press buried it, if they used it at all.

Bill Clinton would not be so lucky the next time.

15

Up and Down
in New Hampshire

THE THREAT OF MARIO CUOMO LOOMED LARGE IN THE MINDS OF the announced Democratic candidates.

The New York governor was an "established name," a nationally recognized heavyweight who would step into a ring full of middleweights, if he could ever make the decision to fight. Even the Bush administration, watching the president's ratings plummet, had an understandable fear of Cuomo.

Cuomo was bogged down in an important budget wrangle with Republicans in the New York legislature. Still, he was finding time to make feints and jabs at the Democratic contenders and at Bush. More to the point, he was doing well in the polls in New Hampshire.

Clinton insisted he wasn't worried about Cuomo and that he welcomed the test. That may have been true, but in early December, Clinton hired James Carville and Paul Begala as "general consultants" to help his media presentation. In a few weeks, as the media began gnawing at him, he would need all the help he could get.

Carville had managed to keep a low profile over the years, but he was known to insiders as "the Democrats' Lee Atwater." (Atwater, a Republican operative, gained fame in Bush's first run for the presidency by launching a series of damaging attacks on Michael

Dukakis, including the Willie Horton advertisement that portrayed Dukakis as soft on crime.) In November, Carville and Begala had engineered the U.S. Senate race of Democrat Harris Wofford against Republican Dick Thornburgh. Wofford didn't seem to have a prayer in this matchup with the powerful Thornburgh, a former U.S. attorney general, a former Pennsylvania governor and one of the best-known politicians in the state.

Wofford was a former college president and had served as an aide to John F. Kennedy, but he had never run for elected office before. The race started with Wofford lagging forty-four points behind Thornburgh.

When it ended, Wofford had demolished Thornburgh with 55 percent of the vote. Not only was it an upset for Thornburgh, but it was perceived as a direct message from voters to President Bush that they didn't like Republican attitudes on the country's economic troubles.

Much of the credit for Wofford's upset went to Carville and Begala. Analysts said Carville had a way of tapping into the resentment of the middle class and using that anger to motivate the voters. Carville had realized that Pennsylvanians, knocked for a loop by the recession, were worrying about health insurance. Wofford offered a plan for health care that appeared affordable and feasible.

The Senate race was Carville's tenth consecutive Democratic victory in Pennsylvania, and he had won gubernatorial races in Kentucky and Georgia as well.

Carville, a native Louisianan, was known for his tough approach to campaigning, especially in the structuring of television ads and in confrontations with the media. He once said that it was hard for someone to hit you when you had your fist in his face. "Opposition research and money," he has said, are the keys to a successful campaign.

Carville also said he would have considered working for Cuomo. "If the governor had called me, I would have talked to him."

But Bill Clinton called, and Carville answered. With Carville installed as resident pit bull, Clinton had created a strong-willed staff of veteran campaigners. At the top was campaign manager David Wilhelm, who had been in politics since the Carter years.

Wilhelm, who came from Chicago, was considered by some to be the best organizer and campaign manager in politics. He could help define political policy as well as take care of such managerial duties as motivating staffers and solving the million logistical problems, both large and small, that a campaign encounters.

Bob Farmer, the campaign treasurer, was famous in Democratic circles for his ability to raise money. He had gathered millions of dollars for Michael Dukakis in 1988.

Frank Greer was already aboard as Clinton's top media consultant. He was most effective in helping Clinton establish a television image, but Greer was no slouch in handling the print media, either. Greer's wife, Stephanie Solien, was Clinton's political director. Clinton had policy advisers all over America, as well as being a policy expert himself. It was Solien's job to coordinate this influx of advice so that it became cohesive.

Clinton had established his national headquarters in Little Rock, and most of his top people worked out of those offices when they weren't on the campaign trail. To balance his staff, Clinton had included some Arkansans who were veteran Clinton campaigners. He chose as campaign chairman his old friend and law partner, Bruce Lindsey, who had been a Clinton supporter and money-raiser for years. His wife, Bev Lindsey, was also as a top staffer. She had worked in all of Clinton's campaigns as well as several other national presidential campaigns. The finance director was Craig Smith, a young Arkansan who had served on Clinton's gubernatorial staff before resigning to join the campaign.

In later months, as the Clinton campaign hit numerous rocky shores, there would be rumors of friction between the "outsiders" and the Arkansans. But at the beginning it was a formidable team.

Already, Clinton had delivered two parts of his three-part New Covenant. He had created an economic plan to deal immediately with the recession, and he would soon offer a health care program.

Clinton became known as a "policy wonk," a politician who could spout data and statistics nonstop, a man with a quick answer for every question. Members of the national press were amazed at his ability to formulate answers to complicated questions seemingly without thinking. He never carried notes during interviews. Where did all of these ideas come from?

Over the years Bill and Hillary Clinton had created "platoons of friends," as one magazine writer described them. These friends, including David Osborne of the "new paradigm" theory, were often experts and authorities in various social, educational and political realms, and the Clintons would have numerous discussions with them.

But it appeared that much of the policy came from the governor himself. Clinton is a voracious reader. Since his Georgetown days, when he received a bachelor's degree in international studies, he has focused on position papers concerning foreign and domestic policy, but has found time to read history, the ancient classics and the great novels. He has said his favorite book is Tolstoy's *War and Peace*.

Longtime friend Patty Criner helped Clinton move his household several times and always noticed the many books he took with him.

"I've helped them move three times, and I'll never do it again, just because of the books," Criner said. "He had them in alphabetical order at one time. Then he had them by subject matter. Every time they've moved, that's been the biggest thing, because he reads nonstop. He reads nonfiction. He reads fiction. He reads historical things. He reads political publications. He's always been that way. Since he was a kid, he always had another book under his arm."

Hillary Clinton agreed with that assessment. "If he could get away with it he'd read when he drove," she said. "He is insatiably curious about everything. He reads constantly."

She said Clinton can perform multiple tasks and still concentrate.

"He'll be watching some obscure basketball game, and he'll be reading and talking on the phone all at the same time and knowing exactly what is going on in each situation," she said. "If you stopped him and said, 'What's the score?' he'd tell you. If you stopped him and said, 'What did the person you were talking to just say?' he'd repeat it verbatim, and if you stopped him and said, 'What did you just read?' he'd say what he read."

His wife also finds incredible her husband's ability to catnap and not miss out on what is going on around him. "Bill often falls asleep if he gets a minute to rest and he's been on the road, if he sits down in a car, if he has a minute off." Hillary Clinton believes this ability "is part of what keeps him fueled up."

She recounted an incident during a legal seminar the couple

had attended: "The fellow was showing us a problem on the screen, and it was a pretty hard problem and Bill was asleep. Well, I wasn't going to wake him up. It was a little embarrassing, but the lights were off, so I didn't think anybody would know he was sleeping. And the fellow was asking about the answer to this problem. None of us were really catching on. Bill woke up, answered the problem, and fell back asleep."

With Clinton's ability to devour information, his power of concentration and a tough, experienced national campaign team, he was able to walk into the New Hampshire primary campaign with a huge amount of confidence.

*   *   *

But in New Hampshire, trouble was just as confidently waiting for Clinton. A group of Arkansans who disliked Clinton had bought ads in the New Hampshire media. An ad in the *Manchester Union-Leader*, New Hampshire's largest newspaper, accused Clinton of foisting a myth of an "Arkansas Miracle." The ad accused Clinton of raising taxes without providing results. Similar ads were broadcast on radio and television.

The group behind the ads was called ARIAS, which stood for Alliance for Rebirth of an Independent American Spirit. It was headed by Cliff Jackson, an Arkansan who had attended Oxford when Clinton was there. The two had been friends at Oxford, but had become bitter enemies in recent years. Jackson, a conservative Republican of the Reagan stripe, despised Clinton's Democratic politics.

Jackson, saying his group feared that the national press would overlook Clinton's record, created a series of thirty-second radio spots and bought time on a New Hampshire television station. The radio and TV ads said Clinton created tax increases of $214 million in one month while allowing $400 million in tax breaks to big industries.

Clinton's staff saw the group as a front for the Republican Party.

"If they didn't believe that Clinton is the most credible challenger to George Bush, they wouldn't be running ads around the country," said Richard Mintz, a Clinton spokesman.

While Mintz said the ads had no effect on the Clinton campaign, the governor was taking no chances. The day after the ARIAS ad appeared in the *Union-Leader*, the Democratic Party of Arkansas ran an ad of similar size.

"Bill Clinton is the only candidate who can bring middle-class voters back into the Democratic Party," the ad said. "And that has Republicans scared. That's why they took out a big negative ad in yesterday's *Union-Leader*."

Greer, Clinton's chief media man, then sent letters to media outlets warning them that if they ran the anti-Clinton ads, they might be obligated to provide equal response time for Clinton under Federal Communications Commission regulations. This was clearly untrue—media outlets are under no obligation to offer equal time for advertising—and ARIAS leader Jackson saw it as an effort to intimidate broadcasters. He fired off a letter to the law firm that had written the warning letter for Greer.

"I believe the message you were *really* sending between the lines and not too subtly, was, 'You've got to choose. You can run these piddling ARIAS ads, and you risk thousands and thousands of dollars of Clinton's campaign advertising,'" Jackson said.

The controversy stirred up trouble in Little Rock, where columnists accused Greer of trying to infringe on the First Amendment rights of the New Hampshire media outlets. Greer denied that was his intent. But ARIAS had accomplished a goal: It had stirred up a controversy and had gotten itself noticed.

While these bomblets were dropping, Clinton was in New York and Washington, attempting to discuss issues, specifically foreign policy.

On December 11, he gave an address to the Conference of Presidents of Major American Jewish Organizations in which he attacked Bush for saying Israel should be grateful for American military support.

"Israel should never be grateful to the U.S. for defending it in the Gulf war, " Clinton said. "The U.S. should be grateful to Israel for its forbearance of the Gulf war."

Columnist Pat Buchanan had announced his Republican candidacy the day before, and Clinton wasted no time in tackling him.

"Did George Bush want to create David Duke? Of course not. It took part of his political base away," Clinton said.

"What gives rise to a David Duke? What gives rise to some of the intemperate remarks of Pat Buchanan? The misery and anxiety and frustration and sense of futility of ordinary working men and women in this country," Clinton told the group.

Clinton's New York speech was a prelude to the third part of his New Covenant, which he delivered at Georgetown on December 12.

Part three of the New Covenant dealt with America's superiority and its military dominance. Again, it defined crumbling "old paradigms" such as the Cold War and communism. Again, it dealt with "new paradigms" such as forging "a new economic policy to serve ordinary Americans by launching a new era of global growth. We must tear down the wall in our thinking between domestic and foreign policy."

Everything is changing everywhere, Clinton was saying, and the ordinary American should be more than prepared for it—he or she should be participating in the change and directing it:

> This spring, when the troops came home from the Persian Gulf, we had over one hundred thousand people at a welcome-home parade in Little Rock. Veterans came from all across the state—not just those who had just returned from the Gulf, but men and women who had served in World War II, Korea and Vietnam. I'll never forget how moved I was as I watched them march down the street to our cheers and saw Vietnam veterans finally being given the honor they deserved all along. The divisions we have lived with for the last two decades seemed to fade away amid the common outburst of triumph and gratitude.
>
> That is the spirit we need as we move into the new era."

Clinton offered some insight into the tumultuous change occurring in Central Europe:

> We need a New Covenant for American security after the Cold War, a set of rights and responsibilities that will challenge the American people, American leaders and America's allies to work together to build a safer, more prosperous, more democratic world.
>
> The strategy of American engagement I propose is based on four key assumptions about the requirements of our security in this new era:
>
> • First, the collapse of communism does not mean the end of

danger. A new set of threats in an even less stable world will force us, even as we restructure our defenses, to keep our guard up.

- Second, America must regain its economic strength to maintain our position of global leadership. While military power will continue to be vital to our national security, its utility is declining relative to economic power. We cannot afford to go on spending too much on firepower and too little on brainpower.
- Third, the irresistible power of ideas rules in the Information Age. Television, cassette tapes and the fax machine helped ideas to pierce the Berlin Wall and bring it down.
- Finally, our definition of security must include common threats to all people. On the environment and other global issues, our very survival depends upon the United States taking the lead.

Clinton wanted to show that he was not naive about developments in Europe, and advanced the view that events there had demonstrated that revolutionary change occurs when least expected. He stressed that all Americans should be watchful for, and even fearful of, global instability. And he had a plan for dealing with this anxiety:

The world we look at today is not the same world we will see tomorrow. We need to be ready to adjust our defense projections to meet threats that could be either heightened or reduced down the road.

Our defense needs were clearer during the Cold War, when it was widely accepted that we needed enough forces to deter a Soviet nuclear attack, to defend against a Soviet-led conventional offensive in Europe and to protect other American interests, especially in Northeast Asia and the Persian Gulf....

However, a new consensus is emerging on the nature of post-Cold War security. It assumes that the gravest threats we are most likely to face in the years ahead include:

- First, the spread of deprivation and disorder in the former Soviet Union, which could lead to armed conflict among the republics or the rise of a fervently nationalistic and aggressive regime in Russia still in possession of long-range nuclear weapons.

- Second, the spread of weapons of mass destruction, nuclear, chemical and biological, as well as the means for delivering them.
- Third, enduring tensions in various regions, especially the Korean peninsula and the Middle East, and the attendant risks of terrorist attacks on Americans traveling or working overseas.
- And finally, the growing intensity of ethnic rivalry and separatist violence within national borders, such as we have seen in Yugoslavia, India and elsewhere, that could spill beyond those borders.

To deal with these new threats, we need to replace our Cold War military structure with a smaller, more flexible mix of capabilities, including:

- **Nuclear deterrence.** We can dramatically reduce our nuclear arsenals through negotiations and other reciprocal actions. But as an irreducible minimum, we must retain a survivable nuclear force to deter any conceivable threat.
- **Rapid deployment.** We need a force capable of projecting power quickly when and where it's needed. This means the Army must develop a more mobile mix of mechanized and armored forces. The Air Force should emphasize tactical air power and airlift, and the Navy and Marine Corps must maintain sufficient carrier and amphibious forces, as well as more sealift. We also need strong special-operations forces to deal with terrorist threats.
- **Technology.** The Gulf war proved that the superior training of our soldiers, tactical air power, advanced communications, space-based surveillance, and smart weaponry produced a shorter war with fewer American casualties. We must maintain our technological edge.
- **Better intelligence.** In an era of unpredictable threats, our intelligence agencies must shift from military bean-counting to a more sophisticated understanding of political, economic and cultural conditions that can spark conflicts.

Clinton also picked up on the subject he had been discussing with the Jewish organization in New York the day before:

In the Middle East, the [Bush] administration deserves credit for bringing Israel and its Arab antagonists to the negotiating table. Yet I believe the president is wrong to use public pressure tactics against Israel. In the process, he has raised Arab expectations that he'll deliver Israeli concessions and fed Israeli fears that its interests will be sacrificed to an American-imposed solution.

We must remember that even if the Arab-Israeli dispute were resolved tomorrow, there would still be ample causes of conflict in the Middle East: ancient tribal, ethnic and religious hatreds; control of oil and water; the bitterness of the have-nots toward those who have; the lack of democratic institutions to hold leaders accountable to their people and restrain their actions abroad; and the territorial ambitions of Iraq and Syria. We have paid a terrible price for the administration's earlier policies of deference to Saddam Hussein. Today, we must deal with Hafez Assad in Syria, but we must not overlook his tyrannical rule and domination of Lebanon.

We need a broader policy toward the Middle East that seeks to limit the flow of arms into the region, as well as the materials needed to develop and deliver weapons of mass destruction; promotes democracy and human rights; and preserves our strategic relationship with the one democracy in the region: Israel.

It was time, Clinton said, to realize that America has the ability to grasp control of global economic change, and that this power lies in the hands of each individual American:

> Now we must understand, as we never have before, that our national security is largely economic. The success of our engagement in the world depends not on the headlines it brings to Washington politicians, but on the benefits it brings to hardworking middle-class Americans. Our "foreign" policies are not really foreign at all....We can no longer afford to have foreign and domestic policies. We must devise and pursue national policies that serve the needs of our people by uniting us at home and restoring America's greatness in the world.

* * *

The next day, Clinton went before his former archenemies, the National Education Association, at a meeting in Washington. The NEA was not endorsing Bush. The support of the nation's biggest teachers union was a valued prize for the Democratic candidates.

Clinton, through successes in raising teacher pay and by participating in numerous educational conferences across the nation, had salved some of the wounds he had opened in 1983. But there was still some residual doubt.

Two top officials of the Arkansas Education Association circulated a "Dear Colleague" letter among AEA members attending the conference. The letter said: "We believe that Governor Clinton is the most qualified candidate and that, if elected president, he would have a national education agenda, not just in words, but an agenda that would bring significant improvements to America's public school system."

It was clear that, in Arkansas at least, the bad old days of teacher testing were over. Clinton had finally sealed a "new covenant" with this group of people who had for so long disliked him, with a fervor often bordering on hatred.

In an interview, Senator Bob Kerrey of Nebraska took a shot at Clinton's "domestic GI Bill," the one that would allow anyone to go to college and to pay for it in small increments later or by performing public service. Kerrey questioned whether it was a "bribe" to force students into participating in public service.

"It's not a bribe," Clinton said, adding, "I may be wrong, but when I go to college campuses, I find legions of young people who are dying to serve their country and would love to be a part of this system. It's totally optional."

He promised the NEA that he would "scrap the inadequate, wasteful and often broke student loan program." The NEA made no endorsement that day. As Randy Lilleston, a reporter for the *Arkansas Democrat-Gazette*, pointed out, Senators Harkin and Kerrey, because of their positions in government, held a great deal of power to assist education. In addition, Harkin supported collective bargaining for teachers, and Clinton did not. Nevertheless, Clinton had made an impression on the educators.

Throughout Clinton's fledgling campaign, there had been foreshadowings of potential problems. In early December, two reporters for the Little Rock newspaper *Spectrum Weekly* were looking into Clinton's draft background. The reporters, Mark Oswald and Joe Nabbefeld, found some discrepancies in Clinton's own descriptions of his draft status. They also said they had found a University of Arkansas law professor who claimed he had a letter from Clinton to Senator J. William Fulbright in which Clinton asked for help in evading the draft. The professor later denied that he had any such letter. The article's questions about Clinton's conflicting accounts of his draft status remained open, and it appeared that the Clinton staff paid little attention to it.

Clinton got some good news on December 15, when he won a Florida straw poll with 53 percent of the votes of the Democratic delegates. Cuomo, still unannounced, had received only 21 votes. Although it was in Clinton's territory, the South, the poll showed his strength in a big state. Harkin came in second with 31 percent. During the short campaign in Florida, Tsongas had criticized Clinton's plan for a tax cut for the middle class, calling it "Twinkie economics."

"It tastes great, but [has] no nutritional value. Why do we do it? Because it sells. If we replace 'voodoo economics' with 'Twinkie economics,' we don't deserve the White House," Tsongas said.

The six Democratic nominees headed to Washington for another televised debate. The television camera has its limitations, and those limitations were challenged by the visual format of the debate. It was difficult to get all six candidates in one television frame without pulling the camera so far back that the picture lost definition. The candidates contributed to this problem by wearing similar dark business suits and rep ties. Viewers had a hard time recognizing which candidate was speaking, or how each one was reacting to what was being said, except when the director called for close-ups.

Jerry Brown overcame this handicap by twice holding up a card with his toll-free telephone number and repeating the number over the air, violating ground rules established by NBC. Brown said he had never agreed to the rules.

Clinton, apparently mindful of the contentious impression he had made during the previous debate with Wilder, maintained a low-key performance, making it difficult for him to stand out from the crowd. The debate broke down several times into squabbles, with all of the candidates talking at once. Kerrey again attacked Clinton's student loan program, saying students who participated would be "told to serve" in public service positions, rather than volunteering. Clinton tried, again, to point out that they had the option of repaying the loan.

Harkin, who, like Tsongas, opposed the tax cut for the middle class, held up a dollar bill as a symbol of the cut, estimated at $300 to $500 a year. "A dollar a day for a family is a joke," Harkin said.

On the tube, as the debate collapsed into squabbling, Clinton seemed to fade from sight. There was no clear winner, although Brown attracted the most attention with his phone numbers and his shouts of "This is a campaign of insurgency!"

At a press conference later, Clinton defended his performance, saying, "I got to make my points, differ with people and not get into a lot of personal back-and-forth that I think undermines the dignity of the office of president." He said the other candidates acted like a bunch "of school kids in a school yard."

A scheduling conflict prevented Clinton from attending a health care conference in New Hampshire, where all the other candidates explained their plans at a forum attended by hundreds of people in the health care field. But Clinton made up for it by heading to New Hampshire the next day and spelling out his plan. Under "a Clinton administration," he said:

- Every American would have access to health care. It would be paid for by demanding insurance reform to end "the administrative waste of the current system, control the unnecessary spread of excessive technology, stop drug prices from going up at three times the rate of inflation, reduce billing fraud that may account for up to $75 billion a year and force the people who send bills and the people who pay them to agree on how much health care should cost."
- Primary and preventive care would be provided in inner-city and rural areas. Children's access to health care would be increased by putting clinics in schools.
- "We should provide health care to the elderly when they need it—before they spend themselves into poverty. Our senior citizens should make their own choices about how to spend their health care benefits. In Arkansas, we created a program that gives seniors the right to take money which used to be used...for nursing home care and spend it on home health care, personal care, transportation to senior centers, hiring a nurse or attending an adult day care center. I want a federal

health system that gives seniors all over the country the same choices."

Kerrey had proposed a universal health insurance program that would be funded by the government, and had criticized Clinton's proposals as empty and nonspecific.

At last, on December 20, Cuomo announced that he would not enter the campaign. He blamed the state budget woes for his decision. "It's my responsibility as governor to deal with this extraordinarily severe problem," Cuomo said.

Clinton said he felt sorry for Cuomo, but he must have been rejoicing at the same time. A little more than two months earlier he had entered a race with little money and less name recognition. Now his relentless style of hand-to-hand campaigning was paying off. He had raised nearly $3 million. A New Hampshire poll released on December 23 showed him second, with 25 percent of the vote, behind Tsongas, with 29 percent. Another poll, taken a few days after Christmas, showed them neck-and-neck, with Tsongas at 23 percent and Clinton at 21.

The pace picked up after the New Year. Wilder dropped out on January 8, lacking the money to continue. This was a windfall for Clinton, who had always enjoyed the support of black voters. With Wilder out of the race, Clinton could look for an even better showing in the Southern primaries—Super Tuesday—on March 10.

Then, on January 13, the supermarket tabloid *Star* appeared on the stands with a report that Clinton had had extramarital affairs with five women. The allegations came from the lawsuit filed in 1990 by Larry Nichols.

The story was buried by the New Hampshire newspapers. The Arkansas newspapers put it on the front page, but didn't give it much credibility. The *Arkansas Democrat-Gazette* said it had investigated the allegations for months and had found nothing. Clinton called the tabloid stories "rehashed lies." Many mainstream newspapers found themselves in a dilemma. Should they report something that had originated in a tabloid?

The Clinton camp held tight, hoping that this storm, like the others, would blow over.

For weeks, it had been granted that Tsongas would capture New Hampshire. He came from a neighboring state and was a familiar politician; Clinton was an unknown quantity. Now, with the field narrowed, political observers began speculating for the first time that Clinton might defeat Tsongas and capture the nomination.

"If [Clinton] wins New Hampshire, it will be as close as it will ever get to being over," said Brian Lunde, former executive director of the Democratic National Committee. "You'll be able to see the fat lady getting ready to sing at that point."

Clinton took no chances, and instead took advantage of his momentum. He also took advantage of the fact that Bush was getting clobbered in the polls over his handling of the recession. Pat Buchanan's candidacy was threatening a split in the Republican Party.

The governor capitalized on all of this by creating an advertisement that captured the Clinton television magic. The format was a direct talk from Clinton to the New Hampshire voter in which he said, "The people of New Hampshire know better than anyone: America's in trouble. In the '80s the rich got richer, the middle class declined, poverty exploded, politicians in Washington raised their pay and pointed fingers, but no one took responsibility....I'm Bill Clinton and I believe you deserve more than thirty-second ads or vague promises. That's why I've offered a comprehensive plan to get our economy moving again, to take care of our own people and regain our economic leadership...."

Days after the ad began running, Clinton took the top spot for the first time in a New Hampshire poll. He eked by Tsongas, 23 percent to 22.

Clinton's top-gun campaign team was providing the edge. By January, at which time he had been a candidate for less than three months, Clinton had raised $3.3 million, not counting federal matching money. About half of this had been donated by people from Arkansas, a state with only 2.3 million citizens. Clinton's fundraising machine held luncheons, dinners, and rallies and manned telephones to reach out across America for donations.

Clinton was way ahead of the others in campaign funds. Senator Tom Harkin of Iowa was second, with $2 million. Senator Bob Kerrey of Nebraska had gathered about $1.8 million, Tsongas had around $1 million and Jerry Brown had $500,000. None of the

Democratic candidates accepted money from political action committees and Jerry Brown refused donations larger than $100.

* * *

In Arkansas, the head of the AFL-CIO, who had long-standing disagreements with Clinton and who was dismayed to see Clinton gaining national labor support, sent reports on Clinton's labor record to federations in other states.

J. Bill Becker, the Arkansas AFL-CIO president, accused Clinton of hypocrisy for his stand on a tax break for the middle-class "when he's socked it to the middle class here with his tax programs."

Becker's main complaint was Clinton's support of right-to-work laws, which make union organizing difficult. Arkansas was a right-to-work state, and its law allows nonunion employees to work in a union shop without having to join the union or pay union dues, and requires unions to provide the same benefits for nonunion workers as for union members. The New Hampshire legislature was at that time debating right-to-work laws. Becker accused Clinton of advertising Arkansas to potential industry as a low-wage state.

Clinton responded that workers in Arkansas supported him because he had "saved" their jobs during the recession of the early 1980s by bringing in more industry and by creating tax breaks to allow industries to expand. He said he had told industry recruiters to stop advertising Arkansas as a low-wage state.

"As soon as I was aware of it, I told them not to do it anymore. I wanted Arkansas to never get jobs based on being a low-wage state. I wanted us to get jobs based on our being a smart-work, hard-work state."

Tommy McFalls, the vice president of the state AFL-CIO, then joined the fight on Clinton's side, saying labor leaders were "solidly behind" the governor and that Becker was not speaking for "the rank-and-file members."

The attacks continued. The League of Conservation voters issued a report that rated Clinton as having the worst record of all the candidates on environmental issues. They reported:

"According to many Arkansas environmentalists, Governor Clinton has a record of poor appointments to important commissions.

His restructuring of Arkansas's Pollution Control and Ecology Commission has been viewed as particularly bad," the report said.

All of this occurred as Clinton was preparing for another televised debate on January 19. The five candidates behaved themselves this time and focused on attacking President Bush. Each detailed his proposals, with Clinton stressing his tax cut for the middle class. Harkin and Tsongas sniped at Clinton over the tax cut proposal, but Clinton defended his position by saying it was an "essential" tool to restore the economy.

Clinton was asked whether the persistent reports of extramarital affairs would hurt him.

"I think it is highly unlikely, given the competitive environment I've been in, that you have anything to worry about on that score," Clinton replied.

Polls coming out in the days after the debate put Clinton at the top again. One poll even put Clinton ahead of George Bush.

On January 20, Clinton appeared on the cover of *Time* magazine for the first time. The magazine said Clinton had problems, calling him "a bold planner but a poor manager," but said "many Democrats believe he's electable, and that's what they want."

Against all odds, as January was coming to a close, Bill Clinton was on the verge of winning the New Hampshire primary on February 18.

* * *

On March 22, 1981, Rickey Ray Rector tried to enter a private party being held at a restaurant in Conway, a city about thirty miles north of Little Rock. When he was not allowed in the door, he pulled a pistol and shot three men, killing one, Arthur Criswell.

Two days later, Conway police officer Bob Martin went to the home of Rector's mother in search of the suspect. The policeman was sitting on a sofa, talking to her when Rector walked into the room, greeted Martin and fired two shots, killing him. Rector ran outside and shot himself in the head.

He survived the shooting, but the bullet wound and subsequent surgery resulted in a prefrontal lobotomy. Two months after the shooting, he was examined by doctors at the Arkansas State Hospital, the state's mental health institution, and was found competent to stand trial. A Conway circuit judge held hearings on

Rector's mental capacity, and two experts said Rector recognized the gravity of his situation, while two other experts said he had scant understanding of his surroundings and little memory of the shootings. The judge ruled him competent for trial.

On November 9, 1982, Rector was found guilt of first-degree murder in the death of Criswell and sentenced to life in prison. He was also found guilty of capital murder in the shooting of Martin and received the death sentence. According to press reports, Rector remained seated, stretched and yawned after the judge sentenced him to die.

Rector's case dragged through the court system for ten years before all appeals were exhausted. On December 27, 1991, Governor Bill Clinton set an execution time of 9 P.M. on January 24, 1992, for Rickey Ray Rector. Arkansas law allows a condemned person to choose electrocution or lethal injection. Rector chose the injection.

Arkansas had resumed executions in 1990 after a twenty-six year hiatus in which no person was put to death. The governor can grant clemency to condemned inmates, but Clinton has chosen not to grant clemency to any of the four men executed since 1990.

Two inmates were executed that year. The first was John Swindler. He had been a suspect in slayings in several states and was convicted for the 1976 killing of a Fort Smith police officer. The other inmate was Ronald Eugene Simmons, who had been convicted of killing fourteen members of his family. Both men died by lethal injection.

In the last days of January 1992, when the Clinton campaign was to be jolted by several shocks, the case of Rickey Ray Rector was overlooked by much of the national media, although two journalists, Jimmy Breslin of *Newsday* and Derrick Jackson of the *Boston Globe*, wrote scathing columns about the execution. "The killing of human vegetables" is "an exercise for brutes," Jackson wrote.

The week before Rector's execution date, the state parole board held clemency hearings. Rector's attorneys tried to prove that he was brain-damaged and unable to understand the concept of death. Several inmates on Arkansas's death row testified that Rector seemed to be unaware of his surroundings and that he sometimes howled and barked like a dog. There was testimony that Rector had undergone mental examinations in 1989 and 1991 and that he was found competent during both examinations. The parole board recommended that Clinton deny clemency.

Within days, a federal judge and the Arkansas Supreme Court had decided that there were no further grounds on which to contest the execution. Rector's attorneys asked Clinton for clemency. Clinton returned to Arkansas on January 24, the day of the scheduled execution, and he and Lieutenant Gov. Jim Guy Tucker both denied clemency for Rector. The United States Supreme Court then decided there was no reason to stay the execution.

Death penalty opponents accused Clinton of using Rector's execution as a cynical ploy for votes. Michael Dukakis had suffered severe criticism in 1987 for his staunch opposition to the death penalty. Clinton's critics said the governor was trying to prove that he was no run-of-the-mill liberal in the Dukakis mold. Clinton issued no statement on the execution, other than the denial of clemency.

Opponents of the death penalty began holding candlelight vigils outside the gates of Governor's Mansion. "I just hate it that somebody's death is going to be used as a platform for Governor Clinton's political career," said Carrie Rengers, a spokeswoman for Amnesty International, at one of the vigils.

On the afternoon of the execution, January 24, Rector's attorneys, Jeff Rosenzweig and John Jewell, visited the inmate to tell him that all of the appeals had been denied.

"I explained various aspects of the case he might not be familiar with. He thanked me. I got the impression he was listening," Rosenzweig told the *Democrat-Gazette*. But the attorney said he doubted Rector understood that he was about to die.

A prison spokesman, David White, who also saw Rector in those last hours, gave a different impression. White said, "He's still talkative. He is cognizant of the fact he is to be executed."

Rector was served his last meal of fried steak, baked chicken, beans, pecan pie and cherry Kool-Aid. One press report said he did not eat all of the pie; he was saving it for later.

Although the execution was to start at 9 P.M., it took medical technicians fifty minutes to find a vein in which to inject the lethal drugs.

Witnesses, who were not allowed to see the medical people at work, said they heard groans from behind the curtain that blocked their view of Rector. When asked about this later, prison spokesman John Byus said, "He was talkative. He was trying to help us find a vein." When the curtains were opened at 9:50 P.M., Rector was strapped to a hospital gurney. One witness said there was an intravenous needle inserted in Rector's hand. Rector was asked if he wanted to make a last statement. "Yes. I got baptized and saved," he said. Nineteen minutes later, forty-year-old Rickey Ray Rector was pronounced dead.

The next day, Clinton appeared before a meeting of Jesse Jackson's Rainbow Coalition and said, "Last night I thought of Mr. Rector, also of Robert Martin, the police officer who was killed in cold blood. I thought of them all and prayed that I had not made the wrong decision."

16

The Comeback Kid

IN 1988, LARRY NICHOLS WAS AN ARKANSAS STATE EMPLOYEE WHO had a keen interest in the contras, the right-wing group attempting to overthrow the leftist Sandinista ruling party in Nicaragua. Nichols also had a $21,500-a-year marketing job for the Arkansas Development Finance Agency, which helped issue bonds to finance low-interest mortgages.

He was an active member of the Freedom Feet Project, which was part of the New Orleans-based Caribbean Commission. Such groups feared the Sandinista government in Nicaragua would establish a Communist toehold in Central America that would sow the seeds of communism throughout nearby countries. Their biggest fear was that the Communists could become a dominant political force in Mexico.

Several Nicaraguan contra leaders lived in exile in the United States, including Adolfo and Mario Calero, two brothers who operated a contra fund-raising and publicity mill near New Orleans. The Associated Press reported in January 1988 that a check of Nichols's telephone calls from his state office showed that he had made more than 142 calls to contra leaders in the United States, including the Calero brothers. Nichols had also made 330 other telephone calls that AP reporter Bill Simmons found dubious. The total bill came to more than $800.

Nichols said the calls were legitimate because the contra leaders put him in touch with conservative congressmen to talk about mortgage revenue bonds. He also said his boss, Wooten Epes, authorized the calls. Epes denied it. Governor Bill Clinton issued a statement saying he doubted Nichols's calls had been about bonds.

Nichols resigned, saying Epes and Clinton had forced him to quit. He said he had "not used Arkansas taxpayers' dollars to assist the Nicaraguan revolutionary movement" and complained about "the knee-jerk liberal reaction from the governor's office."

The episode was forgotten for two years, until September 12, 1990, when Nichols filed a suit seeking more than $3 million in damages over the incident, charging that he had been unjustly fired. The suit, filed in circuit court in Little Rock, created a dilemma for reporters and editors. Among other things, it alleged that Governor Bill Clinton had engaged in extramarital affairs with five women.

Neither Little Rock newspaper wrote about the alleged affairs. Small stories about the lawsuit were buried in the *Arkansas Gazette* and the *Arkansas Democrat*. Both newspapers immediately sent out teams of reporters to investigate the charges. They came back with denials from all of the women named. Nothing was ever printed.

The only central Arkansas media outlet to report the sex allegations was a Little Rock radio station, KBIS-AM, which listed the women's names as given in the lawsuit. One of those women was Gennifer Flowers.

A few months later, Flowers's attorney wrote a letter to KBIS, saying the station had "wrongfully and untruthfully alleged an affair between my client, Gennifer Flowers, and Bill Clinton." The letter threatened a lawsuit, although none was filed.

When Bill Clinton hit his peak of popularity in New Hampshire, the mainstream media and the tabloids sent squads to Little Rock to investigate his background. All of them raced to the courthouse to dig out Larry Nichols's 1990 lawsuit and its sensational charges. The tabloid *Star* quickly printed the lawsuit's allegations.

On January 23, 1992, Little Rock media received advance copies of the February 4 issue of the *Star*. In a a followup on the *Star*'s previous story, Gennifer Flowers said she had carried on a twelve-year affair with Bill Clinton. This was the same Gennifer Flowers who, angered by a radio station's report, had threatened a lawsuit only a year before.

Flowers also said she had taped some phone conversations with Clinton. The article was written in such a scandalous manner, with such clinical sexual detail, that it was a true shocker, even for the hard-boiled political observers who had been hearing rumors for years and had long been expecting some such sexual revelation to derail Clinton's campaign.

Bill Clinton, who had been so lucky at dodging the lightning, was knocked for a loop by this report, even if it did come from a supermarket tabloid. Clinton had been in New Hampshire, riding the crest of his newfound popularity, when the story hit. Bad weather forced him to cancel some New Hampshire stops, so he headed to Little Rock to attempt damage control.

A campaign spokesman issued a statement saying the allegations "attributed to Gennifer Flowers in the *Star* tabloid are false." Hillary Clinton, campaigning in Atlanta, said of the *Star*'s story: "It's not true. I just don't believe any of that." She accused Clinton's political enemies of fomenting the trouble. "All of these people, including that woman, have denied this many, many times. I'm not going to speculate on her motive. We know she was paid."

ABC's "Nightline" devoted an entire program to the issue, and attempted to wrestle with how the media should handle it. The *Star* set off a great deal of hand-wringing in newsrooms across America, but in the end they all aired the allegations.

By the next day, the *Democrat-Gazette* had discovered some discrepancies in Gennifer Flowers's description of her work history, including:

- Flowers said she had performed on the "Hee Haw" television show. A spokesman for the country music program said Flowers had never appeared on it.
- She said she had received a nursing degree from the University of Arkansas School of Nursing in Little Rock and that she had attended both the University of Arkansas at Little Rock and the University of Arkansas at Fayetteville. No record could be found under her name at the nursing school or the university's two campuses.
- She claimed to have been an opening act for country music

star Roy Clark, but a spokesman for Clark said Flowers had worked for him as a backup singer for about six months but had never been a featured performer in his show.

Clinton headed back east, hitting the campaign trail, determined to overcome whatever damage had been done. In one Saturday, he would hit Washington, Boston, New Hampshire and Boston again for a series of speeches and fund-raisers.

"Nobody has to decide what this election is about but you—you, the people of New Hampshire, and you, the people of the United States," Clinton told a rally in Manchester.

Another tactic had been decided upon: Bill and Hillary Clinton would appear on the "60 Minutes" television show to discuss the allegations.

In Little Rock, Larry Nichols, whose lawsuit was the source of all this trouble, had changed his mind. He announced that he was withdrawing the lawsuit and that his allegations of Clinton's affairs were "based on rumors." Nichols had become an integral component of a raging national debate, and was finding the media pressure unbearable. He recounted an instance in which he had stepped out of his shower to discover a television crew in his living room, ready to pepper him with questions. There was speculation that the Clinton forces had applied some muscle to Nichols, but he denied that, as did the Clinton camp.

In a statement, Nichols said:

It is time to call the fight I have with Bill Clinton over. I want to tell everybody what I did to try to destroy Governor Clinton. I set out to destroy him for what I believed happened to me. I believe I was wrongfully fired from my job. Nobody has wanted to listen to me. All I wanted was a fair and honest hearing about what really happened. I want my family to know that I didn't do the things I've been accused of.

This has gone far enough. I never intended it to go this far. I hoped all along that the governor and I could sit down and talk it out. But it just kept getting bigger and bigger.

My family was hurt. And unfortunately no one can make an ass out of himself better than I can, so I've got to be the one that corrects it and stops it. There's a big difference between what I set out to do and what happened.

The media has made a circus out of this thing and now it's

gone way too far. When that *Star* article first came out, several women called asking if I was willing to pay them to say they had an affair with Bill Clinton.

This is crazy. One London newspaper is offering a half-million dollars for a story. There are people out there now who are going to try to cash in.

I apologize to the women who I named in the suit. I brought them into the public's eye and I shouldn't have done that. The least significant parts of my case were those concerning the rumors. I have allowed the media to use me and my case to attack Clinton's personal life.

There were rumors when I started this suit and I guess there will be rumors now that it is over. But it is over. I am dropping the suit.

In trying to destroy Clinton, I was only hurting myself. If the American people understand why I did this, that I went for the jugular in my lawsuit, and that was wrong, then they'll see that there's not a whole lot of difference between me and what the reporters are doing today.

Nichols again said he was not coerced into dropping the lawsuit, and Clinton spokesman said Nichols received no settlement.

In a New Hampshire poll, Clinton dropped 12 points to 27 percent, where he was tied with Tsongas. In a matter of days, Clinton's hard-won top position had vanished.

On Sunday morning, January 26, security guards sealed off the third floor of the Boston Ritz-Carlton, where the "60 Minutes" interview was to be taped. It was Super Bowl Sunday, and a short version of "60 Minutes" would fill whatever time was left after the football game ended. Although the interview lasted about ninety minutes, the "special edition" program was only about fifteen minutes long. There was a brief scare during the taping when a heavy photo light fell from a wall and struck Hillary Clinton on the shoulder, but she was uninjured.

CBS interviewer Steve Kroft pointedly asked Bill Clinton if he had had an affair with Gennifer Flowers. Clinton said he had not. Kroft then asked if he had had any extramarital affairs, and Clinton replied:

I have acknowledged wrongdoing. I have acknowledged causing pain in my marriage. I have said things to you and to the American people from the beginning, that no American politician ever has.

I think most Americans watching this tonight will know what we're saying. They'll get it and they'll feel that we have been more candid, and I think what the press has to decide is, are we going to engage in a game of "gotcha"?

As Kroft pressed the question, Clinton said, "I'm not prepared to say that any married couple should ever discuss that with anyone but themselves."

Kroft zeroed in on Gennifer Flowers:

Kroft: I want to go back and ask you the question again. Who is Gennifer Flowers? Do you know her?

Clinton: Oh, yeah.

Kroft: How do you know her? How would you describe your relationship with her?

Clinton: Very limited, but until this, friendly but limited. I met her in the late '70s when I was attorney general. She was one of a number of young people who were working in the television stations around Little Rock. And people in politics and people in the media knew each other then just as they do now. She left our state and for years I didn't really hear from her or know what she was doing. Then she came back sometime a few years ago and went to work again in the state, so that's...who she is.

Kroft: She was a friend and acquaintance? Does your wife know her?

Clinton: Yes, she was an acquaintance. I would say a friendly acquaintance....She would call from time to time when she was upset or thought she was really being hurt by the rumors and I would call her back. Either she would call the office or I would call her back there at the office, or I would call her at the house. And Hillary knew when I was calling her back. I think once I called her when we were together and so there's nothing out of the ordinary there.

Kroft: She is alleging and has described in some detail in a supermarket tabloid what she calls a twelve-year affair with you.

Clinton: That allegation is false.

Kroft: I am assuming from your answer that you're categorically denying that you ever had an affair with Gennifer Flowers.

Clinton: I've said that before, and so has she.

At one point, Kroft used the word "arrangement" in describing the Clintons' relationship. Bill Clinton interrupted by saying: "Wait a minute. You're looking at two people who love each other. This is not an arrangement or an understanding. This is a marriage."

Hillary Clinton added: "I'm not sitting here because I'm some little woman standing by my man, like Tammy Wynette. I'm sitting here because I love him and I respect him and I honor what he's been through and what we've been through together, and you know, if that's not enough for the people, then heck, don't vote for him."

Clinton said he and his wife were being put into the odd position that, at least in modern politics, divorce is better than reconciliation, meaning that if he and Hillary had obtained a divorce because of the problems, the scrutiny of his personal life would have lessened.

"Are we going to take the reverse position now that if people have problems in their marriage, that there are things in their past which they don't want to discuss, which are painful to them, that they can't run?" he asked.

Clinton reminded Kroft that in September, before he had announced his campaign, he had told a group of journalists in Washington that he and Hillary had endured "some problems." He added, "It hasn't always been easy, and...for me personally, if perfection was a standard, along with a lot of other people in life, I couldn't meet the standard."

The Clintons returned to New Hampshire immediately after the interview and resumed campaigning. "I have said all I have to say, and I'm not going to talk any more about it," Clinton told reporters in New Hampshire. "I'm going on with this campaign."

At a rally in Portsmouth, someone attempted to ask Clinton a personal question. People in the crowd shouted down the questioner. Clinton told them he wanted to return to a discussion of the issues, and he believed the voters wanted to do that too:

Your presence here today validates the point that I have been trying to make over and over again, all along. This election is far more about you than about me, and you should be hiring the person who can do the best job for you to turn this country around, to turn this state around, to put our people back to work, to save our jobs and our future.

A lot of you have told me to hang in there the last couple of days, and about how rough all this is. Yeah, it's rough. But it's nothing compared to somebody going home at night and sitting down over a table and looking at their children and wondering if they're ever going to have another job again, and feeling like they have failed their kids. You talk about rough— that's rough.

It got rougher for Bill Clinton. While he was heading to Louisiana for an appearance, Gennifer Flowers was making her debut in a conference room of New York's Waldorf-Astoria Hotel.

Reporters packed the room as Flowers, surrounded by security guards, entered and moved up to a stage. She was accompanied by her attorney, Blake Hendrix of Little Rock, and several *Star* employees.

She was angered by Clinton's denial that they had had an affair, she said, and that was why she was going public.

"When I heard the *Star* was going to run a story about Larry Nichols's lawsuit, when I heard Bill describe our relationship as an absolute, total lie, I knew what my decision should be—to tell my side of the story truthfully and as quickly as possible," Flowers said.

"Yes, I was Bill Clinton's lover for twelve years, and for the past two years I have lied about the relationship. The truth is, I loved him. Now he tells me to deny it. Well, I'm sick of all the deceit and I'm sick of all the lies."

Flowers said she had watched "60 Minutes" the night before and "felt disgusted...I saw a side of Bill I never knew before....The man on '60 Minutes' was not the man I fell in love with."

A ten-minute segment of audiotapes, which Flowers said were telephone conversations between her and Clinton, was played. In the tapes, Flowers is the only one who talks about sex in graphic terms. Clinton's replies at those points are garbled. Much of what he says is ambiguous.

On the tapes Clinton can be heard advising Flowers: "If they ever hit you with it, just say no and go on. There's nothing they can do."

The tapes have unexplained pauses and patches. At many points, it is difficult to determine the context of the conversation. Flowers and the *Star* refused to release all of the conversations, which Flowers said were taped in December and January.

At one point on the tapes, Flowers discusses the possibility of television programs such as *Inside Edition* and *Hard Copy* conducting interviews with Larry Nichols. Clinton replies that Larry Nichols alone is not enough to attract their attention.

> **Flowers:** Right. Well, he better not get on there and start naming names.
> **Clinton:** Well, that's what I mean. You know, if all the people who are named deny it, that's all, I mean, I expect them to come look into it and interview you and everything, but I just think if everybody's on record denying it, you've got no problem.
> **Flowers:** Well, I don't think, well, why should they waste their money and time coming down here unless someone showed them some interest? See? They weren't there tonight and they're not going to be there.
> **Clinton:** No, no. See, that's it. I mean, they're going to run the Larry Nichols thing down, they're going to try to goad people up, you know, but if everybody kind of hangs tough, they're just not going to do anything. They can't.
> **Flowers:** No, they can't.
> **Clinton:** They can't run a story like this unless somebody said, "Yeah, I did it with him."

At one point in the tapes, Clinton mentioned New York Mayor Mario Cuomo's showing in the polls and describes Cuomo as "aggressive." Flowers responded by saying she thought Cuomo might have "mafioso" links. Clinton said, "Well, he acts like one."

After the tapes were played, the press conference was opened to questions. Attorney Hendrix attempted to act as moderator but soon lost control as reporters yelled questions at Flowers. A shouting and shoving match ensued as television photographers tried to force print photographers to move from in front of the TV cameras. Hendrix threatened several times to stop the session when reporters asked what he believed to be inappropriate questions. He finally shut it down after someone yelled, "Did the governor use a condom?"

One of the more interesting revelations Flowers made was that she had been approached by a "local Republican candidate" who had asked her to go public with her claims. She refused to identify the "candidate," as did her attorney. It was an enigmatic little statement on which she never elaborated.

But it was a bit of vindication for Bill and Hillary Clinton, who were charging that their Republican enemies in Arkansas had masterminded this scandal. The Republicans in Arkansas were quick to deny it, with the exception of former Congressman Tommy Robinson, who said he had known during the 1990 gubernatorial election that prominent Arkansas Republicans were compiling a sex dossier to use against Clinton. Top state GOP officials denied that charge, too.

The "mafioso" reference to Cuomo caused Clinton some problems. On January 28, Clinton issued a statement apologizing to Cuomo and Italian-Americans. "I meant simply to imply that Governor Cuomo is a tough and worthy competitor."

Cuomo rejected the apology, saying, "This is part of an ugly syndrome that strikes Italian-Americans, Jewish people, blacks, women, all the different ethnic groups."

The local newspapers discovered that Flowers had worked for a Republican candidate in a local legislative campaign in 1990. It appeared that she had been working for the candidate during the time she claimed she had had an affair with Clinton.

Although Gennifer Flowers had been an entertainer on the Little Rock nightclub scene for a decade or more, few people knew much about her. *Spectrum Weekly* discovered that her real name was Eura Gean Flowers and that she was born in 1950 in Oklahoma City. When she was a child, her family moved to the small east Arkansas farming town of Brinkley, where her father, Gene Flowers, was a crop-duster pilot. She adopted the name "Geannie" while growing up and became "Gennifer" when she started her singing career. Her parents were divorced in 1968, the year she graduated from high school. Her mother remarried, and her father headed for Alaska, where he worked as a hunting and fishing guide on Prince William Sound. He was married three times before he was killed in 1973 in an airplane crash in Arkansas.

Gene Flowers was a boisterous man who lived life to the fullest. In a 1972 interview with an outdoors writer for the *Arkansas Gazette*, Gene Flowers described himself as "a fair pilot, a fair public relations man, and a helluva BS'er, and I just figured folks in Alaska would appreciate some good Arkansas hospitality."

There were reports that Gennifer Flowers did not get along with her father and, in fact, had developed a strong dislike for him. Friends of Gennifer Flowers said this feeling about her father transformed itself into a resentment of men in general. Acquaintances said she used men for her own benefit, keeping the relationships short. There were no records to indicate that she had been married. *Spectrum* quoted a local musician who had performed with Flowers several times as saying: "She seemed to thrive on that witty, vivacious Southern belle kind of personality, and she was good at it. Gennifer is a very shrewd person with a real cruel, canny intelligence. Her self-preservation instinct is strong, I always felt."

Spectrum discovered that Gennifer Flowers had, indeed, enrolled in the University of Arkansas at Fayetteville. Her records were found under her real name, Eura Gean Flowers. It appeared that she registered for her freshman year, 1968–69, but no record, under any of her names, could be found after that.

How much money was Gennifer Flowers paid for her story? Neither she nor her lawyer would say. The Clinton camp said she received $50,000. The *Wall Street Journal* said she got between $130,000 and $175,000. She was paid enough so that she didn't have to worry about her state job, from which she was fired a few days after the New York press conference because she didn't return to work.

Both Clintons began devoting their considerable energy to the campaign, and to stressing their belief that the Republicans were out to destroy it. Hillary Clinton, while campaigning in Colorado, said, "We now know that when Republicans first offered money to this woman to change her story she held out, apparently negotiating with the media, *Star* magazine, to change a story she had denied repeatedly."

That same day, Bill Clinton was in Texas, attempting to pull the discussion back into the arena of political issues. He attacked President Bush's State of the Union speech, saying its economic package was only "Band-Aids."

Still, reporters dogged him with "the question."

"I've taken my character test," he said in San Antonio. "Now the character test is what you do with 'cash for trash.'"

As January came to a close, Clinton's blitz across New Hampshire began paying off. He had gained his old place at the top of the polls, with 37 percent to Tsongas's 24. This resurgence caught the attention of the national news weekly magazines, which printed articles and essays on the tangled-up ball of questions concerning Clinton's personal life and the media's right to pry. Most of the pieces were sympathetic to Clinton—even those in arch-conservative magazines such as the *American Spectator*.

For better or worse, Clinton now had more name recognition than any other candidate.

* * *

The late-night talk show hosts had pretty much exhausted their supply of Clinton sex jokes by early February. Clinton had conceded the February 10 Iowa primary to native son Harkin. With only a few days remaining until the February 18 New Hampshire primary, Clinton had recaptured his momentum.

The morning of February 6, the *Wall Street Journal* published an article that described how Clinton had evaded the draft in 1969. The article made it appear that he had signed up for ROTC in order to receive a deferment, but had then withdrawn from the organization after he realized he could probably avoid the draft by receiving a high lottery number. The news didn't play well in New Hampshire and, to make matters worse, Clinton did not have a very good explanation of what occurred. He said he couldn't remember all of the events of those few weeks in 1969, but he insisted that he had put himself up for the draft and had never been called.

The anti-Clinton campaigns in New Hampshire sponsored by his political enemies in Arkansas had been making much of the "Slick Willie" image and of Clinton's method of giving elliptical answers to questions. The draft story raised the by-now-familiar doubts in the minds of New Hampshire voters. Was Clinton being less than honest? Why didn't he just tell the truth? If he's lied about this, will he lie to us if he's elected?

On February 11, ABC newsman Ted Koppel sent a message to

David Wilhelm, Clinton's campaign manager. Koppel said he had a letter Clinton had written in 1969 in which he stated in clear terms his opposition to the then-raging Vietnam War, his active participation in antiwar demonstrations and his strong feelings against the draft.

Since becoming a politician, Clinton had always done a delicate little dance around the antiwar issue. It was originally raised in 1974 in his first political campaign, and Clinton had given indirect answers over the years to questions about his positions on the Vietnam War and his draft status. He had said frequently, when asked about his position on the war, that he had "attended" some antiwar protests but had never participated.

His draft record after he graduated from Georgetown was a convoluted affair, partly because of Clinton's maneuverings and partly because the Nixon administration frequently changed the way the draft was set up.

Koppel said ABC News would use the letter in a broadcast. He also said he had received the letter from two sources who had obtained it from the Pentagon. Clinton tried to preempt the effect of the broadcast by hurriedly calling a news conference in Manchester to reveal the contents of the letter and to explain why it was written and the context of the times in which it was composed. Clinton also pointed to the Pentagon source as proof that the Republican administration was targeting him for personal attacks.

Clinton said, "It represents a pattern by people desperate to stay in power and willing to impugn the motives, the patriotism and the lives of anyone who stands in their way. It's me today; it could be Tsongas or Kerrey or Harkin or somebody else tomorrow."

As it turned out, Koppel had given some wrong information to Clinton. He had not received the letter from Pentagon sources. Koppel later learned that it had come from retired Colonel Clinton Jones, who had been with the Army ROTC at the University of Arkansas.

Jones said he took the letter from Clinton's ROTC file because he was angry that Clinton had backed out on a deal to join the corps. He declined to say why he had waited so long to release it or why he had released it to ABC in 1992, when the Arkansas press had been investigating Clinton's draft status since 1974. He also denied that he had done it for the Republican Party, describing himself as a Democrat.

All of this was bad news for the Clinton camp. At the very time that Clinton was beginning to reconnect with the voters on issues of substance, the question of his personal integrity was being raised again. Now all of his energy would be spent in explaining this draft and antiwar business. Once again, he was on the defensive. No one knew whether a candidate could survive two such blows against his personal life.

Clinton decided to publish the entire letter in a newspaper advertisement and to let the voters judge. He also bought two thirty-minute segments on local television stations to take telephone calls on questions about the direction of his campaign. Clinton needed the immediacy of television to send his message. He couldn't wait for the twelve-hour delay of the print media.

The letter was written to Colonel Eugene Holmes, head of ROTC at the University of Arkansas. At the time he wrote it Clinton was twenty-three years old. Here is the text, all of which Koppel read on his "Nightline" program:

University College
Oxford, England
December 3, 1969

Dear Col. Holmes,

I am sorry to be so long in writing. I know I promised to let you hear from me at least once a month, and from now on you will, but I have had to have some time to think about this first letter. Almost daily since my return to England I have thought about writing, about what I want to and ought to say.

First, I want to thank you, not just for saving me from the draft, but for being so kind and decent to me last summer, when I was as low as I have ever been. One thing which made the bond we struck in good faith somewhat palatable to me was my kind regard for you personally. In retrospect, it seems that the admiration might not have been mutual had you known a little more about me, about my political beliefs and activities. At least you might have thought me more fit for the draft than for ROTC.

Let me try to explain. As you know, I worked for two years in a very minor position on the Senate Foreign Relations

Committee. I did it for the experience and the salary but also for the opportunity, however small, of working every day against a war I opposed and despised with a depth of feeling I have reserved solely for racism in America before Vietnam. I did not take the matter lightly but studied it carefully, and there was a time when not many people had more information about Vietnam at hand than I did.

I have written and spoken and marched against the war. One of the national organizers of the Vietnam Moratorium is a close friend of mine. After I left Arkansas last summer, I went to Washington to work in the national headquarters of the Moratorium, then to England to organize the Americans here for demonstrations Oct. 15 and Nov. 16.

Interlocked with the war is the draft issue, which I did not begin to consider separately until early 1968. For a law seminar in Georgetown, I wrote a paper on the legal arguments for and against allowing, within the Selective Service System, the classification of selective conscientious objection for those opposed to participation in a particular war, not simply to "participation in war in any form." From my work I came to believe that the draft system itself is illegitimate. No government really rooted in limited, parliamentary democracy should have the power to make its citizens fight and kill and die in a war they may oppose, a war which even possibly may be wrong, a war which, in any case, does not involve immediately the peace and freedom of the nation. The draft was justified in World War II because the life of the people collectively was at stake. Individuals had to fight, if the nation was to survive, for the lives of their countrymen and their way of life. Vietnam is no such case. Nor was Korea, an example where, in my opinion, certain military action was justified but the draft was not, for the reason stated above.

Because of my opposition to the draft and the war, I am in great sympathy for those who are not willing to fight, kill and maybe die for their country (i.e., the particular policy of a particular government) right or wrong. Two of my friends at Oxford are conscientious objectors. I wrote a letter of recommendation for one of them to his Mississippi draft board, a letter which I am more proud of than anything else I wrote at Oxford last year. One of my roommates is a draft resister who is possibly under indictment and may never be able to go home again. He is one of the bravest, best men I know. His country needs men like him more than they know. That he is considered a criminal is an obscenity.

The decision not to be a resister and the related subsequent decisions were the most difficult of my life. I decided to accept the draft in spite of my beliefs for one reason: to maintain my political viability within the system. For years I have worked to prepare myself for a political life characterized by both practical political ability and concern for rapid social progress. It is a life I still feel compelled to lead. I do not think our system of government is by definition corrupt, however dangerous and inadequate it has been in recent years. (The society may be corrupt, but that is not the same thing, and if that is true we are all finished anyway.)

When the draft came, despite political convictions, I was having a hard time facing the prospect of fighting a war I had been fighting against, and that is why I contacted you. ROTC was the one way left in which I could possibly, but not positively, avoid both Vietnam and resistance. Going on with my education, even coming back to England, played no part in my decision to join ROTC. I am back here and would have been at Arkansas Law School, because there is nothing else I can do. In fact, I would like to have been able to take a year out perhaps to teach in a small college or work on some community action project and in the process to decide whether to attend law school or graduate school and how to begin putting what I have learned to use.

But the particulars of my personal life are not nearly as important to me as the principles involved. After I signed the ROTC letter of intent I began to wonder whether the compromise I had made with myself was not more objectionable than the draft would have been, because I had no interest in the ROTC program in itself and all I seemed to have done was to protect myself from physical harm. Also, I began to think I had deceived you, not by lies—there were none—but by failing to tell you all the things I'm writing now. I doubt that I had the mental coherence to articulate them then.

At that time, after we had made our agreement and you had sent my 1-D deferment to my draft board, the anguish and loss of self-regard and self-confidence really set in. I hardly slept for weeks and kept going by eating compulsively and reading until exhaustion brought sleep. Finally, on September 12, I stayed up all night writing a letter to the chairman of my draft board, saying basically what is in the preceding paragraph, thanking him for trying to help in a case where he really couldn't and stating that I couldn't do the ROTC after all and would he please draft me as soon as possible. I never mailed the letter, but I did carry it on me every day until I got on the plane to return to England. I didn't mail the letter because I didn't see, in the end, how my going in the army and maybe going to Vietnam would achieve anything except a feeling that I had punished myself and gotten what I deserved. So I came back to England to try to make something of this second year of my Rhodes Scholarship.

And that is where I am now, writing to you because you have been good to me and have a right to know what I think and feel. I am writing too in the hope that my telling this one story will help you to understand more clearly how so many fine people have come to find themselves still loving their country but loathing the military, to which you and other good men have devoted years, lifetimes, of the best service you could give. To many of us, it is no longer clear what is service and what is disservice, or if it is clear, the conclusion is likely to be illegal.

Forgive the length of this letter. There was much to say. There is still a lot to be said, but it can wait. Please say hello to Col. Jones for me.

> Merry Christmas,
> Sincerely,
> Bill Clinton

The letter, coupled with the details of Clinton's chesslike calculations on his draft status, outraged Vietnam veterans in New Hampshire and across the nation. It also created a sense of disappointment in Clinton's supporters, who admired his candor at releasing the letter, but wondered why he hadn't cleared the decks of this Vietnam debris years ago. Certainly, they reasoned, he had received enough chances with the Arkansas press to set the record straight. His supporters feared, and rightly so, that all of this would only magnify his Slick Willie persona.

This development, even more so than the Gennifer Flowers episode, struck fear in the Clinton camp. His trump card was the Super Tuesday primary in the Southern states, coming up on

March 10. The campaign leaders feared that Clinton's Vietnam record—specifically his lack of one and his less-than-honest answers about the draft—would not play well in super-patriotic Dixie.

The day the letter was published, another poll came out in New Hampshire. Clinton had dropped into second place, 7 points behind Tsongas. It was a 12-percentage point drop from his peak on January 29.

Harkin said the letter would be the end of the Clinton campaign. It "seals his fate," he said.

Clinton came back slugging, but he had dropped the harangue about Republican dirty tricks and "cash-for-trash" journalism. He told crowds that they were being shortchanged because the focus of the campaign had moved from political issues to personal questions.

"The character issue in this election is who is really willing to put it on the line to change your lives," he said at a rally in Manchester. "Only you can decide what this election is about. This belongs to you, not anybody else."

He also took a potshot at Harkin's statement about his fate being "sealed." "I don't think it makes him a bigger man to put other people down. That's been his whole strategy in this campaign."

Clinton's popularity began a precipitous drop. There was talk that he would withdraw. "All I've been asked about by the press are a woman I didn't sleep with and a draft I didn't dodge," he said.

In the last two days before the New Hampshire election, Bill and Hillary Clinton double-teamed the voters. In Manchester, they appeared at coffee shops where voters were having breakfast; they went door-to-door in several neighborhoods, handing out campaign videotapes of Clinton discussing the issues. More than a thousand volunteers spread out over the state, doling out the same videotapes. The work became frenzied, but it could not dispel the cloud of doubt that had gathered over the camp.

Two days before the election, another televised debate was held. It was different for Clinton this time. He was not the front-runner; Tsongas was to be the punching bag now. The Seabrook nuclear power plant in New Hampshire had recently been finished, after years of controversy, and the other candidates criticized Tsongas's support for nuclear energy.

Harkin had been attacking Clinton for days on several issues, including Clinton's views on abortion, but he dropped this tactic during the debate and appeared almost serene.

Clinton said he had been the most specific of the candidates in solving problems. He said he had a "radically different approach to government. I've got more than a plan—ten years of leadership. Embrace this challenge with me and we can change America again."

Much of the rest of the debate was a collective attack on Bush. Clinton escaped any questions about his personal life.

Then a glimmer of light burst through the storm. That day Clinton edged up a point in one of the polls. Other polls showed a wide variation, but all had Tsongas leading Clinton.

At 9 P.M. on election night, February 18, Bill Clinton threw himself a victory party. It was a peculiar move, because Clinton had come in second to Tsongas in the race. Tsongas had received 34 percent; Clinton, 26; Kerrey, 11; Harkin, 11; Brown, 9; and Cuomo, in a write-in, 3 percent. Cuomo, embarrassed, quickly asked the write-in supporters to call it off.

No doubt about it, Clinton had been on a roller coaster since the middle of January. He hadn't won the race, but he had made a majestic showing. Clinton had said time and time again that people "continue to underestimate me," and he had again proven himself right.

In the 1988 election, Gary Hart was forced to withdraw after a major sex scandal broke loose. Senator Joseph Biden withdrew from the same campaign after it was revealed that he had plagiarized a speech. Clinton had endured two knockout scandals that would have floored any other candidate. He had only finished in second place, but he was still a contender and he was still building a political base.

"New Hampshire, tonight, has made Bill Clinton the Comeback Kid," Clinton said, spreading his infectious enthusiasm as the results rolled in. "I just can't wait now to take this campaign across the country. I cannot wait to win the nomination."

Bill Clinton had pulled off a New Hampshire miracle. He had returned from the depths, but he had not done it alone. He had assembled an extremely adept campaign machine. Perhaps the most important cog in that machine, besides Bill Clinton, was Hillary Clinton. The personal attacks had brought her out front, and her name recognition was now almost as high as her husband's. She also projected a strong presence on television, just as Bill Clinton did. At times, she threatened to eclipse him.

In the next few months, Hillary Clinton would become a potent political force, one whose personality would both help and harm her husband's career.

17

The Woman
From Park Ridge

Suppose I'd sat down and tried to map out my life. Do
you suppose I would have said I'd be married to the
governor of Arkansas and practicing law in Little Rock?
No way.

—Hillary Clinton in an interview
with the *Arkansas Gazette*, July 22, 1990.

WHEN THE NATIONAL PRESS DISCOVERED HILLARY CLINTON, THE
adjectives came frothing from the word processors: "strong-
willed"; "determined"; "high-powered"; "forceful"; "feminist";
"independent."

But until 1983, by which point her husband had been in the
public eye for nearly ten years, most Arkansans didn't know much
about Hillary Clinton. They knew she was from somewhere else,
somewhere up north. They knew she was now a Little Rock lawyer.
They knew she showed up with Bill Clinton on the campaign trail,
wearing thick glasses, looking bookish and professional. Although
she was careful never to appear bored during these occasions, she
sometimes seemed detached, perhaps thinking of something
else—her legal work, her family, anything but this endless round of
fish fries and dinner speeches.

206

In private and professional circles she was another woman completely. She was ambitious and aggressive in her law practice and in her devotion to children's causes. She sat on the boards of several huge corporations, including the retailing phenomenon Wal-Mart. She was a dedicated ally and counselor to her multitude of close friends. She had an easy laugh, a quick wit and a sense of humor that quickly put strangers at ease. She was a devout Methodist, attending a church in downtown Little Rock with daughter Chelsea. (Bill Clinton was a Baptist. In the South, where religion is part of the psyche, it is not unusual for couples to attend separate churches and still maintain a religious accord.) Acquaintances say Hillary Clinton was the bedrock of her family when it endured emotional hardships that would have destroyed most other relationships.

In 1983 Hillary Clinton stepped firmly into the political realm and under the public microscope, as her husband appointed her head of the committee that would design new standards to bring Arkansas schools into the twenty-first century. Hillary Clinton was out front, appearing on the television news and in the newspapers. She shed the thick glasses for contact lenses and changed her general appearance to a more fashionable style.

Hillary Clinton expressed a *passion* that had been missing from Arkansas's plodding politics. This passion and determination took many people by surprise. In public, she had been the woman-behind-the-man for so long that she had almost faded into the wallpaper. Who would have guessed that the person to stoke the fires of education reform would be Hillary Clinton?

She attended public meetings in all of Arkansas's seventy-five counties, impressing crowds with her ability to grasp the problems and to listen to what people were saying. For most people in Arkansas, it was their first real exposure to her.

Most impressive of all, she said what many Arkansans wanted to hear: that it was imperative that the state's school system be improved and that she and the committee would come up with workable solutions. She explained that there was no magic cure to the problems. Arkansas had been down, impoverished, outcast for so long that there was a certain sense of defeat that was nearly indelible.

Hillary Clinton stated in the most forceful terms that the hard work would have to begin now and would have to continue for as long as two decades before measurable success could be achieved. Perseverance, she said, was the key. She articulated the problems, but more important, she articulated the solutions. Arkansans were impressed by someone who could get to the heart of a problem and was willing to skip the usual political palaver.

It was at this moment that Arkansans began wondering whether they had elected the wrong Clinton.

Columnist Starr gives much of the credit for the success of the 1983 school reform program to Hillary Clinton. "Nobody should underestimate the role of Hillary Clinton in all of this," he said in an interview. "As a matter of fact, I think [Bill Clinton's] success in 1983 and the failures that he had since then are due to the fact that in 1983—and indeed through 1987, when the standards were finally implemented and the teacher test was taken care of— Hillary stayed as active in education as he was. After that, after 1987, she went off to practicing law, and that's when we hit the plateau where nothing really much happened."

By 1992, Hillary Rodham Clinton was a familiar face in households across America. She had been profiled by the news magazines, the *Wall Street Journal*, the *New York Times*, and *Vanity Fair* and had appeared on "60 Minutes," "Prime Time Live" and other national news programs. In the old days, her name was Hillary Rodham. For political purposes, she became Hillary Clinton. Now the press had christened her as just "Hillary." The single name had become so familiar that millions of Americans who had never met her, who had never known her, were calling her "Hillary," as if a surname was superfluous for such a sweeping personality.

Hillary Rodham Clinton had taken a long, strange trip from Park Ridge, Illinois. In a 1991 interview, she described her early life, and the influence education had had on her direction:

I was born in Chicago and my parents moved to a suburb called Park Ridge when I was very young. Mostly because they wanted to be in a good school district. I mean that's what the motivation was for the ex-GIs after World War II was to try to find a good place to raise your kids and send them to school. And I've often kidded my father, who has never been a fan of taxes or government, about moving to a place that had such high property taxes to pay for school. But even though it was a very conservative, Republican community, there was just no griping during the '50s and '60s about paying for good education. I had two younger brothers. We all went to public schools, had a superb public school education. I really felt well prepared.

I went to Wellesley College, which is a women's college outside of Boston. I don't know why I chose that, other than during my senior year I had two young teachers—one had graduated from Wellesley and the other graduated from Smith. They'd been assigned to teach in my high school and they were so bright and smart and terrific teachers and they lobbied me hard to apply to those schools, which I had never thought of before. And then when I was accepted they lobbied me hard to go and be able to work out all of the financial and other issues associated with it.

So I went to Wellesley, and it was another educational experience for me. I always was interested in school. My parents impressed upon me that education was absolutely the key to personal growth, development, success.

My mother didn't go to college, so she was particularly anxious that her children would go to college. My father went to college on a football scholarship and was sure that if it hadn't been for the football scholarship in the '30s he might not have been able to go to college.

They expected us to do well and work as well as we knew how. And I felt very fortunate because as a girl growing up I never felt anything but support from my family. Whatever I thought I could do or be they supported. There was no distinction between me and my brothers or any barriers thrown up to me that I couldn't think about something because I was a girl. If you work hard enough and your really apply yourself then you should be able to do whatever you choose to do."

Hillary Rodham graduated from Maine Township High School-South in Park Ridge in June 1965. In high school, she was an outspoken conservative, supporting Republican Barry Goldwater in 1964 in his losing bid against President Lyndon Johnson. Her move to the other end of the political spectrum began about a year later, when a minister in her church, the Rev. Don Jones, opened her eyes to the poverty of inner-city Chicago. The girl from the comfortable suburbs was particularly struck by the plight of the children she saw.

The political transformation gathered speed at Wellesley. By 1967, she was supporting U.S. Senator Eugene McCarthy, probably the most liberal of the Democratic candidates seeking the presidential nomination. She received high honors on her graduation in June 1969 from Wellesley. Hillary Clinton felt she had an obligation to pay back some of what she had received:

> So when I was a senior at Wellesley I decided I wanted to go to law school and I applied to several law schools. I ended up going to Yale. All during my growing-up years I had a combined message of personal opportunity but also public responsibility—that there were obligations that people who were as lucky as I was owed society.

While at Yale Law School, she campaigned for another noted Democratic liberal, U.S. Senator George McGovern, who was trying to unseat President Richard Nixon. In June 1973 she received her law degree from Yale Law School, where she was an editor of the *Yale Law Journal*.

Soon after leaving Yale, she worked for about six months as staff attorney for the Children's Defense Fund, where she developed a still-burning interest in children's issues.

In 1974 she worked on the legal staff of the House Judiciary Committee, which was holding an inquiry into the possible impeachment of President Nixon over the Watergate scandal. She said that when Nixon suddenly stepped down in 1974, "We were all taken by surprise that he resigned, because we would have stayed on as the staff to prosecute the impeachment in the Senate."

Hillary Rodham was unsure about what she wanted to do next. She and Bill Clinton had been keeping up a long-distance relationship. About a year before the Nixon surprise, Hillary Rodham had come to Arkansas:

> "I first came to Arkansas to visit Bill in 1973, to visit his family and see the state. And I was very taken by how

beautiful it was. You know, he picked me up at the airport in Little Rock and we drove up Highway 7 [a scenic mountain highway], and it was just beautiful. And then in 1973, when we both graduated from Yale, he came right home to Arkansas to teach in a law school and I was very unsure about where I wanted to be. I certainly was not ready to move completely to Arkansas yet, because I just didn't know whether that would be a decision that Bill would stick to. I really didn't know what to expect."

After the stint on the Judiciary Committee, Hillary Clinton was ready for a change.

I really didn't know what I wanted to do, but I wanted to get out of Washington. I was exhausted—we'd been working eighteen-, twenty-hour days. And when I had visited Bill, I had met the dean of the law school at Fayetteville and he had said to me if you ever want to teach, let me know. So I figured, what the heck, it wouldn't hurt. So I picked up the phone. I called Wylie Davis, who was the dean at the law school. About August 20th or so I pulled into Fayetteville, Arkansas, found out I was going to teach criminal law, was going to run a legal aid clinic, run a project that sent students down to the prisons to work with prison inmates. [I] was just kind of thrown into teaching right off the bat.

Bill was, at that time, in the general election [for Congress]. So we had a very interesting first couple of months there, and I loved Fayetteville. I loved the university. I loved the law school. I loved my colleagues. I made some of the best friends I ever had in my life.

They were married in 1975. When Bill Clinton was elected attorney general in the late 1970s, he and Hillary moved to Little Rock, where she joined the Rose Law Firm, one of the most prestigious in the state. She quickly gained a reputation as an energetic, hard-charging lawyer. She was appointed chair of the American Bar Association's Commission on Women in Profession in 1987 and was listed among the country's top one hundred lawyers by the *National Law Journal* in 1988 and 1991.

In 1985, she helped start what is known as HIPPY—the Home

Instruction Program for Preschool Youngsters. Under the program, aides and tutors go into homes to teach impoverished mothers how to teach their four- and five-year-old children at home. Thus, underprivileged children who normally got little or no schooling at home were able to receive a head start. The HIPPY program became a passion with Hillary Clinton:

> It became clear to me that we could have the most astonishing schools in the world and we would still not be reaching the needs of all of our children, because half of all learning occurs by the time a person is five. And the way that our children are treated in the first five years—the way their health is attended to, to say nothing of intellectual stimulation and family support, will have a very big influence on how well they can do for the rest of their lives. Most people who have the kind of impoverished, often neglectful backgrounds that we see so often among many of our children today just come into school with so many problems that it's very difficult to deal with. I do not believe that there are very many parents who are deliberately harmful to their children. There are some and there will always be some....But there are countless numbers of adults who do not know what to do for their children and do not know how to be an effective parent. And they need help and they need support to be able to fulfill that most basic function. So a good preschool program, whether it's center-based or home-based, has to help the family understand how to fulfill its obligations to little children.
>
> I am just absolutely convinced that an investment in preschool is one of the smartest investments Arkansas can make. The single biggest determinant, based on the studies that I've seen, as to whether a child finished school and how well that child does, is the educational level of the mother. And a woman doesn't have to be, herself, well-educated to see that her child succeeds, but she has to understand the value of education.
>
> A lot of other programs are well-meaning, but they basically put too much responsibility on the mother. I mean, if the mother knew what she was supposed to do, she would go do it. But to be told, on television, or to come to a community meeting or even to a school meeting where someone stands

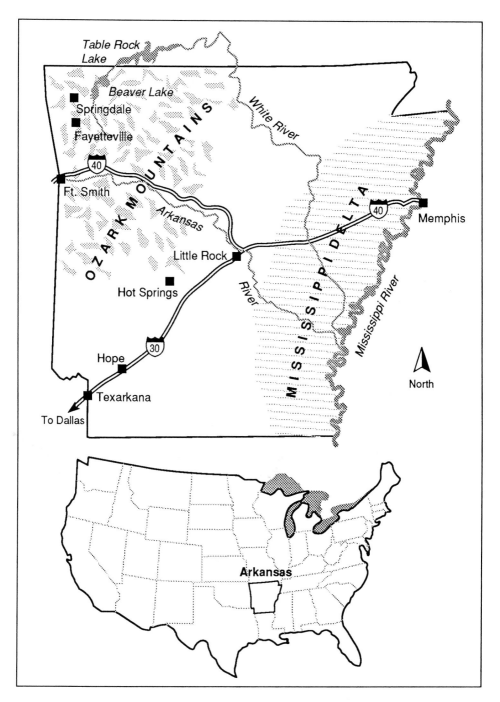

Map of Arkansas and the United States. (David Fike)

By 1992 northwest Arkansas was in the middle of an economic boom due largely to the enormous growth of the livestock industry there. The area was producing more than one billion farm animals a year, mostly chickens (as seen above in a house that holds twenty thousand), and creating as much waste as forty million people. As a result, Governor Clinton faced a serious environmental problem because the disposal of the waste began to pollute the White River (below), which runs through Arkansas. (Photo by Jonathan Portis)

Modern Arkansas: The Eastman Kodak plant (above), in Batesville, is one of Arkansas's largest manufacturers. The skyline of Little Rock (below) as viewed from across the Arkansas River. The Old State House can be seen in the lower right corner. (Kodak photo courtesy of *White River Journal*, Little Rock Skyline photo by Jonathan Portis)

The young governors: Clinton (left) with Mississippi Governor Ray Mabus (center) and Louisiana Governor Buddy Roemer in 1990. (Photo *Arkansas Democrat-Gazette*)

The Capitol of Arkansas, near downtown Little Rock. (Photo by Jonathan Portis)

The Old State House, Arkansas's first Capitol, where Clinton announced his candidacy for the Democratic nomination for president. (Photo by Jonathan Portis)

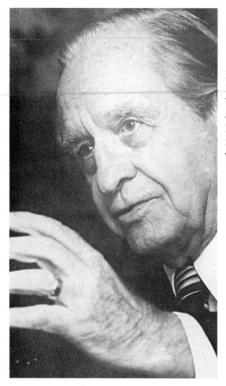

Former Governor Orval Faubus, who made Little Rock the site of a civil rights showdown in 1957. The state that gave the nation Orval Faubus, the arch segregationist, has now given the country Bill Clinton, a liberal Democrat and integrationist who has become very popular among black voters.

Arkansas's first Presidential candidate, Clinton, at age forty-five announces his candidacy in Little Rock on October 3, 1991.
(Photos courtesy *White River Journal*)

Clinton, Hillary, and Chelsea talk with a very tall Uncle Sam at a Little Rock parade. (Photo by Stephen Steed)

A hands-on politician, Clinton likes to interact with potential voters, as seen here greeting the people of Little Rock on the street. (Photo by Stephen Steed)

Clinton, Hillary, and Chelsea wave to the crowds as they march in a parade on the streets of Arkansas's capital, which vaulted the young Governor to national notoriety. (Photo by Stephen Steed)

up and lectures and says here's what you should do for your child, is like speaking a foreign language to many of these people. They have to be shown how to do it. They have to be, in a sense, "re-parented" to be able to be a good parent. And HIPPY has a structure to try to do that, which is very simplistic in many ways, but which is within the grasp of even illiterate parents.

Such activism by Hillary Clinton and others angers the conservative "pro-family" groups who believe the government, or agents of the government such as teachers and social workers, should not go into the home and "interfere" with parental care of children.

Hillary Clinton is a feminist, although she is wary of the extremist baggage the term carries. She has written and spoken extensively on her views as to the rights of children. There is no doubt that these views are, and will continue to be, impressed upon her husband.

One example of her stated feminism can be found in a speech she delivered in 1988 in Atlanta:

One thing which I think would improve the quality of education about 100 percent in five years is to increase by one-hundred-fold the number of women superintendents and principals. I think if you go into schools and talk with the people who understand children and are sensitive to their needs, many of them are women who have absolutely no chance of exerting leadership in the present system. What I find after going from school to school is that the good teachers, many of whom are women, have adapted a strategy of defensiveness toward the outside administration. They basically close their doors and say, "I'm not going to let those people get to me and my students; and I'm going to do the best I can this year." The principal, who is often a fellow who took the night courses and wrote the thesis at the school of education about basketball theory, and is working his way up to superintendent, doesn't have a clue about how to get the most out of his teachers, how to encourage that development, that spark, that enthusiasm. He's not a bad guy, he's a good guy. But he is not a leader in education.

Hillary Clinton's most controversial views are those on children's rights. At the core is a dispute over the legal "competence" of children. As the law stands now, children are legally incompetent—their rights are controlled by their parents or other designated adults—until they reach age eighteen. Hillary Clinton argues that it is nonsensical to believe that a person is incompetent one day and fully competent the next, upon achieving the age of majority.

Children's rights advocates also cite instances where parents are neglectful, indifferent, absent—or worse, abusive. Children have no rights of recourse in which they can demand proper care and education or even protection from dangerous parents. Being legally incompetent, children have no access to the rights granted all other American citizens.

In "Children's Rights: Contemporary Perspectives," a study written in 1979, when she was thirty-two, Hillary Clinton said: "The first thing to be done is to reverse the presumption of incompetency and instead assume all individuals are competent until proven otherwise."

She also wrote in the study: "Decisions about motherhood and abortion, schooling, cosmetic surgery, treatment of venereal disease, or employment and others where the decision or lack of one will significantly affect the child's future should not be made unilaterally by parents."

Critics have said the idea of all children being declared competent conjures up images of kids suing their parents over their allowance or bedtime. Hillary Clinton's emphasis is on giving children a legal basis to protect themselves in court. As it stands now, they have none. (Infants, under her proposal, would still be presumed incompetent.)

Under Hillary Clinton's proposals, and the proposals of the Children's Defense League, the government would be responsible for the care and nurturing of children even outside the home.

The Children's Defense Fund was founded in 1973 by Marian Wright Edelman, who is still its president. Hillary Clinton has been a leader of the group since 1976 and became chair in 1986.

The group's goal has been to provide better child care for underprivileged and working families. It has called for publicly funded health care and day care facilities for children and for child care subsidies to poor parents and child care providers. These proposals have met strong resistance in Congress.

Hillary Clinton has pointed to France as a model of child care. Under the French system, child care is "a coordinated, comprehensive system, supported across the political spectrum that links day care, early education and health care."

In February 1992, Hillary Clinton took a leave of absence as chair of the Children's Defense Fund, citing the time-consuming effort of the presidential campaign. Observers believe she also separated herself from the Children's Defense Fund to prevent the perception that the group was aligned with one candidate or one political party.

In the early stages of the 1992 campaign, few members of the national press bothered to take much notice of the potential controversy of some of Hillary Clinton's statements. Garry Wills wrote a long explication of her positions for the *New York Review of Books*. One of the few who challenged her policies was Paul A. Gigot, who, in a March 13, 1992, article in the *Wall Street Journal*, said:

> This mentality informs her politics. She believes in—no, swears by—the virtues of government social work. [She believes] schools that can't even teach English are somehow supposed to become surrogate parents, too....It shouldn't surprise that Ms. Clinton also endorses expensive, publicly run day care. In 1990, even many liberals in Congress abandoned this sort of Great Society notion in favor of vouchers. But Ms. Clinton, as chair of the Children's Defense Fund, lobbied hard for the nanny state. It's a safe bet that CDF's founder, Marian Wright Edelman, would end up in a Clinton cabinet. This doesn't sound like "reinventing government," a favorite Clinton theme.

Marian Edelman said in April 1992 that she would accept no cabinet position. In the media, Paul Gigot was almost alone in focusing on Hillary Clinton's political positions, but the Bush administration is sure to take much notice of them during the general election.

Most of the reportage of Hillary Clinton concerned itself with her personal life—the admitted troubles in her marriage—and with her personal appearance—her hair, her clothes and, for some reason, the fact that she sometimes wore a headband.

There is no doubt, for Arkansans at least, that Hillary's new personal image is a calculated one, merely because it is so different from the image of previous years. Arkansas viewers who watched her appearance with her husband on "60 Minutes" were struck by what was the most obvious change: Her voice carried the definite inflections of an Arkansas accent. This woman from a Chicago suburb who was educated at Wellesley and Yale had, until recently, spoken in the neutral tones of the Midwest.

A profile in the May 1992 issue of *Vanity Fair* portrayed her as a dominant force who had to harangue her reluctant husband and his campaign staff into publicly confronting the Gennifer Flowers scandal. The magazine depicted her as a decisive woman who had the ability to separate the "Hillary" of the tabloids from the personal "Hillary" who had to deal with the deep pain the attacks were causing her and her family.

Most Arkansans were not surprised that Hillary Clinton got into trouble when she spoke her mind, such as when she made the "Tammy Wynette" remark about "standing by her man," or when she said "I suppose I could have stayed home and baked cookies and had teas" instead of pursuing a professional career, or when she suggested that reporters should be scrutinizing rumors about George Bush's love life.

Some supporters of Hillary Clinton were a bit disappointed when she was quick to apologize for the perceived transgressions. They saw apologies as too reminiscent of her husband's tactic of a quick reversal in the face of controversy. There is a large contingent that believes the political handlers should "let Hillary be Hillary," that she should be allowed to stake out her territory and defend it, without apology.

Some pundits perceive her as a loose cannon. She is anything but. Hillary Clinton is a controlled rationalist with the unusual skill of being able to inject intensity into a flagging, cynical debate. There has been talk of her becoming a cabinet member if her husband is elected president, perhaps attorney general or secretary of education. The Clintons have tried to deflect such speculation.

Even one of Bill Clinton's harshest critics, columnist Starr, admits that Hillary Clinton contributed to his changing attitudes on the governor. After he got to know her at a function in March 1982, Starr said, "She and I talked for a while and I decided that any guy that she would marry could not be all bad."

Probably the toughest challenge of the 1992 campaign for Bill and Hillary Clinton was the separation from daughter Chelsea, who was born in 1980, toward the end of Clinton's first term as governor. During the presidential campaign, Chelsea was in the sixth grade in a Little Rock public school. Her parents tried to stay in touch as often as possible, which meant several phone calls a day. One or both parents tried to return to Little Rock at least once a week to be with Chelsea.

The couple has tried to give Chelsea a normal upbringing. Bill Clinton, who never had a real father, had been determined to provide Chelsea with two strong parental figures.

Longtime friend Patty Criner said Bill Clinton has made a point of impressing on Chelsea the necessity of caring for unfortunate people. Criner said, "He has taken Chelsea to the Union Rescue Mission [a facility for the homeless] and soup kitchens every Christmas and Thanksgiving ever since she was old enough to go. He and Hillary have been trying to have Chelsea maintain a normal kid's life. It's hard when you live in the Governor's Mansion and you're the only child. They want Chelsea to understand that not all people live in a governor's mansion."

Like her parents, Chelsea Clinton has a multitude of friends who surround her and support her. Hillary Clinton has said those friends bolstered Chelsea during the dark days of the 1992 campaign, when the personal allegations against her father became commonplace on television and in the print media. Hillary Clinton insisted that Chelsea should not be insulated from such difficulties and that they have frequent frank talks about the problems.

In an interview, Bill Clinton praised his wife for raising what he called a "remarkable child."

"I have to give more credit to her mother than to me. She has her mother's character and intelligence, and she looks like she's going to have my energy level. And if she gets that, she'll have the best of both worlds. She'll have a massive constitution to endure long years of effort. She'll have Hillary's character and intelligence. She'll be in good shape."

18

Pressing On

BILL CLINTON HAD ESCAPED FROM NEW HAMPSHIRE WITH HIS campaign intact, but was still in deep trouble. The Georgia primary was coming March 3 and Clinton's fumbled draft record was expected to be a big sore point in that conservative Southern state. The Georgia primary was a week before Super Tuesday, when most of the other Southern states held their primaries. Clinton's success or failure in Georgia would be a bellwether for the South, where most of his real strength lay.

First, he had to deal with a serious legislative issue in Arkansas. In 1991 the Center for Youth Law in San Francisco had sued the state of Arkansas, contending it did not provide adequate care for abused and neglected children. The lawsuit said that children who had been placed in the care of the state were being monitored by underqualified social workers. The suit also claimed that the state did not have enough social workers and that children were shuttled too frequently from foster home to foster home and were separated from siblings. It also questioned the quality of health care provided for the youngsters. In an attempt at settling the lawsuit, Clinton had called a special session of the legislature for the week of February 24 to approve a two-year, $15 million proposal for improving the child welfare system.

The blame for the child welfare problem lay squarely on the

218

shoulders of Bill Clinton. He had spent much of the last two years preparing for a run for the presidency and had neglected the nuts-and-bolts management that a governor should perform to maintain control of the state agencies. It would be in Clinton's best interest to clear the air of this issue once and for all, before it became a distraction in the campaign.

Unfortunately, the legislative session occurred at the time when he needed to be campaigning hardest to fire up his come-from-behind attack on the February 23 Maine caucuses, the March 3 primaries in Georgia, Maryland and Colorado and later caucuses in Utah and Idaho.

Maine was a disaster. Clinton had campaigned there two days before the election, but on Tuesday he finished an embarrassing fourth, trailing Tsongas, Brown and a slate of uncommitted delegates. Lagging even further behind were Harkin and Kerrey. (Tsongas, being a regional candidate, had long ago acquired an edge.) South Dakota was no better. Clinton finished third, with Kerrey taking the top spot and Harkin snagging second. Tsongas dropped to the bottom.

Clinton shrugged it off, hoped it wasn't an omen and headed for Little Rock to deal with the lawmakers. Fortunately for Clinton, most of them supported his presidential bid, and, for once, the normally slow-moving Arkansas legislature went into fast-forward and approved a $15 million program within four days.

The money, taken from a pool set aside to settle federal litigation, would be spent over two years to hire 230 new staff members to handle child welfare cases, provide mental health care for needy children, increase cash assistance grants for poor families and raise the pay for foster parents. The package was rushed to the federal courts and a hoped-for settlement of the lawsuit.

Clinton was free again to focus on the presidency.

Those who know Clinton well say he has a temper. It's hard to detect in his public appearances, where he always manages to keep a pleasantly amused smile, even during the roughest times. But an open microphone during an event in Phoenix on January 26 caught Clinton in high dudgeon.

A reporter had erroneously told Clinton that Jesse Jackson was supporting Tom Harkin. "It's an outrage, it's a dirty, double-crossing, back-stabbing thing to do," Clinton had responded. He was talking to his staffers, but the microphone was still open at the Phoenix television station. "For him to do this to me, for me to hear it on a television program, is an act of dishonor. It's a back-stabbing thing to do. Everything he has bragged about, he has gushed to me about trust and trust and trust, and it's a back-stabbing thing to do."

But it blew over like a summer storm. Jackson assured Clinton that he was campaigning with Harkin in South Carolina, but had not endorsed him. Jackson had offered to campaign with each of the candidates. Clinton and Jackson made up. The episode offered a rare glimpse of an emotional Bill Clinton, although he downplayed his actions by saying, "I didn't fly off the handle. I just used strong words to describe how I felt at the moment."

Meanwhile, the Democrats had received a bit of good fortune. Pat Buchanan was slashing away at President Bush, and had managed to pull off an impressive showing in New Hampshire. As long as the Republicans were embroiled in their own civil war, the Democrats could expect little interference in their endeavors. But this left the gates open for the candidates to become careless about their attacks on each other. The epithets they used now would be sure to be picked up by the Republicans in the general election. The Democrats, with their selfish infighting, may have opened the door to their own defeat in November.

One such incident occurred shortly before the Georgia primary, when Tsongas accused Clinton of attacking his Greek heritage. Tsongas had been campaigning as a pro-business candidate and Clinton had said Tsongas put the interests of corporate America before the needs of the middle class.

"We lost our economic leadership as we became unfair," Clinton said. "We can't put off fairness under the guise of promoting growth. It won't work; it's not American." Tsongas somehow decided that statement was a "code" meaning that "real Americans" were not being given a fair shake by "foreigners."

Though neither candidate had said anything of much substance—Clinton's statement was a hollow campaign speech and Tsongas's perceived "code" was indecipherable to most observers—the exchange became heated.

Clinton, in his defense policy, had been calling for a scaling-down of nuclear weapons. Now that the March 24 Connecticut primary was nearing, he took a stand in defense of the multi-billion-dollar Seawolf submarine program, which President Bush wanted to scrap. It was an important economic issue in Connecticut.

Tsongas, in Florida on Clinton's turf, called Clinton a "pander-bear" for his two-way stand on nuclear weapons and the Seawolf.

"It was a cynical attempt to get votes from Connecticut," Tsongas said. "The American people are just hearing how cynical and unprincipled Bill Clinton is." Tsongas used the "pander-bear" theme in several speeches. He put an advertisement on Florida television that said, "Some people will say anything to be elected president."

Clinton said Tsongas's economic plan was "cold-blooded" and resembled Reagan's "tax-the-poor, protect-the-rich" program. Tsongas had proposed a tax on gasoline to wean Americans from dependence on foreign oil.

The fighting continued in another televised debate on March 2. The candidates attacked each other for "negative ads," and each denied that he had engaged in such activity. Clinton took it on the chin for his weak environmental record. Later, Democratic Chairman Ron Brown tried to shake the candidates back to reality by pointing out that George Bush was the real target.

March 3, Junior Tuesday, rolled around and Clinton received mixed results. His worries about Georgia were over: He received 256,135 votes and fifty-five delegates, swamping the other candidates, the closest being Tsongas, with 105,589 votes and twenty-one delegates. But Tsongas won Maryland with 218,339 votes, Clinton placing second with 180,868. Brown, the Western environmentalist, won Colorado. In the end, Clinton had 104 delegates, Tsongas 89 and Brown 27. Harkin gathered two delegates and Kerrey got none.

Clinton was elated over Georgia. It had practically cemented his sweep of Super Tuesday. He blamed the loss in Maryland on Tsongas's support among Washington insiders. "I'm not the favorite candidate of the Beltway," he said.

And then there were four. Two days after Junior Tuesday, Senator

Bob Kerrey, who had finished at the bottom in nearly every primary or caucus, withdrew after running out of money and votes. The immediate speculation was that Kerrey, with his war-hero status, would make a perfect running mate for whoever the nominee was.

"I'm not enthusiastic about the notion," Kerrey said.

Now it was a Clinton-Tsongas fight. The "character issue" was on the back burner and economics were out front. In televised debates and on the campaign trail through the South, Clinton attacked Tsongas's capital gains tax cut proposal and painted Tsongas as a big-business candidate, a Republican in Democratic clothing. Clinton favored a capital gains tax cut for smaller firms.

This was too much for Little Rock columnist Brummett, a liberal, who wrote:

> Until Tuesday night, Clinton's entire thrust as a Democratic presidential candidate was that he wanted to pull the party away from its traditional liberalism.
>
> This is the man who headed the Republicans in disguise otherwise known as the Democratic Leadership Council, the group that snubbed Jesse Jackson and existed on business lobbyists' donations.
>
> This is the man who supported the Persian Gulf war, at least in some of his comments, and tried to come up with a law banning flag burning that would be constitutional, as if that would be possible.
>
> This is the man who recently carried out the death penalty against a brain-damaged black man.
>
> This is the man whose economic record in Arkansas encompasses regressive tax policies—tax breaks for businesses paying low wages, sales taxes on food and used cars for the middle class and poor people.

Clinton swamped Tsongas in the South Carolina and Arizona primaries on March 7 and captured the Wyoming caucus, where Brown came in a close second.

The already strange campaign took another odd twist that day, when Texas billionaire H. Ross Perot began a petition drive as an independent candidate. Perot promised to spend as much as $100 million of his own money to get his name on the ballot in all fifty states. He supported abortion rights and gun control (Democratic planks) and the line-item veto (a Republican idea); he said he would end deficit spending and replace the current federal budget-making law with one "that cuts out all the tricks, loopholes and improper accounting procedures." To add to the irony, Perot was born and raised in Texarkana, Texas, just across the border from Hope, Arkansas, where Bill Clinton was born and lived his early years.

By March 9, Senator Tom Harkin was finished. His traditional liberal message had been rejected in nearly every primary and caucus. His much-hoped-for support from organized labor had moved toward Clinton. Labor leaders liked Clinton's "industrial policy" ideas of training for all workers, limits on credit card interest rates and apprenticeship programs for youths who don't go to college—an attempt at reversing the trend of falling wages for high school graduates. Harkin declined to endorse a candidate but vowed to "bear any burden" to defeat George Bush.

In Arkansas, the tabloid press was still fanning out across the state, offering wads of cash to anyone who would say anything the least bit scurrilous about Bill Clinton. Easy money is tempting in a cash-poor state, but most of the targets seemed to be resisting the temptation, remembering the embarrassment the Gennifer Flowers episode had caused Clinton. Arkansans who had been ambivalent about him were now flocking to his side, feeling that he was being trashed unfairly.

A second wave of reporters descended on Little Rock in March, when it became clear that Clinton was inching toward the nomination. This squadron consisted of individual teams of reporters from the *Los Angeles Times*, the *Washington Post*, the *New York Times*, the national magazines and several other publications. The reporters set up camp for an extended stay—perhaps weeks or months—while they scrutinized Clinton's legislative background, as well as the character issues. They hung out in the bars where the local politicos went to kibitz. They dined at the coffee shops and breakfast nooks, fishing for the offhand comment that might provide some new information.

Reporter Jeff Gerth of the *New York Times* got a jump on his colleagues with his revelation that Bill and Hillary Clinton had been business partners with a man who later became head of a savings and loan association, an institution that is regulated by the state.

The article revealed that the Clintons and James B. McDougal had invested in an Ozarks real estate venture called Whitewater Development Company, designed to sell lots for vacation homes. The business arrangement took place in 1978, when Clinton was serving as attorney general. McDougal was a longtime Clinton friend and a real estate developer.

They were still partners when Clinton became governor. During that time McDougal became majority owner of Madison Guaranty Savings and Loan. Hillary Clinton was a partner in the Rose Law Firm, which represented Madison Guaranty.

In the early 1980s, soon after federal regulators discovered that Madison was insolvent and in danger of closing, Clinton appointed a new state securities commissioner, Beverly Bassett Schaeffer, who oversaw the regulation of financial institutions. Gerth said Schaeffer offered "two novel proposals" for saving Madison.

The two proposals, not described in the *Times* but later explained in the *Arkansas Democrat-Gazette*, would have allowed Madison to sell preferred stock and form a brokerage service subsidiary. State officials said they were not "novel," but rather "standard" methods. The *Democrat-Gazette* reporters also found a letter from the commissioner to Hillary Clinton explaining the stock option. Independent audits in 1985 and 1986 found the S&L solvent, but in 1987 a new audit found it insolvent and state officials asked federal regulators to shut it down.

The crux of the issue was whether Clinton had used his influence to try to save a business partner's failing institution. Clinton has said he had no hand in the affair, and Hillary Clinton has said another lawyer in the firm handled business with Madison Guaranty, although the letter seemed to belie that statement. They insisted they had nothing to do with Jim McDougal's business affairs except for their partnership with him in the Whitewater land development. And they lost $69,000 on that venture, they said.

The *Times* article raised the question of whether the governor should be doing business with people who were regulated by his appointees. It also raised the possibility of several conflicts of interest that Hillary Clinton might encounter by working for the state's most influential law firm, which conducted a lot of business with the state. Bill Clinton's response was: "There was no impropriety."

Columnist Starr raised several questions about the complex affair:

> Clinton is correct when he says that he was not governor and McDougal was not a savings and loan president when the partnership was formed.
>
> However, there are indications that the efforts to keep the land development partnership alive were made long *after* Clinton was governor and *after* McDougal had become the wheeling-and-dealing head of a statewide financial institution.
>
> Did Clinton appoint a securities commissioner who understood that McDougal's failing savings and loan was to be given special treatment?
>
> Did Hillary Clinton offer what the *Times* described as "novel proposals" to help McDougal's S&L that were accepted without a whimper by Clinton's Securities Commission and the newly appointed commissioner who served at the will of the governor?

Now carrying this unwanted baggage, Clinton headed for an intense campaign in Florida, where Tsongas was moving up in the polls. Clinton needed to sweep all of the Southern states in the March 10 Super Tuesday primaries, only six days away, if he was to gather an unstoppable momentum. Tsongas was appealing to the "condo vote" in Florida—Northerners who had retired to the Sunbelt, carrying their political preferences with them.

Tsongas was still attacking Clinton's tax cut for the middle-class, calling it "kinder, gentler voodoo economics." Jerry Brown, citing the S&L episode, said, "You can't elect a candidate with a scandal a week, I'll tell you that."

Clinton achieved his dream on Super Tuesday. He won Florida, Louisiana, Mississippi, Oklahoma, Tennessee and Texas—a clean sweep of the South. So far, he had garnered 429 of the 2,145 delegates he needed to clinch the nomination. Tsongas captured his home state of Massachusetts and Rhode Island. Even Jerry Brown made a strong showing, adding some credibility to his renegade campaign.

Clinton was elated. "The people in the South heard the worst about me, but saw the best," he said. "It is only tonight that I fully understand why they call this Super Tuesday."

Clinton, Tsongas and Brown departed the tropical warmth of Florida for the arctic atmosphere of Chicago. The Illinois and Michigan primaries would be the winnowing process for the two front-runners.

Tsongas placed television ads in both states, saying "Paul Tsongas is no Bill Clinton...he tells the truth." Tsongas also told the *New York Times* that if Clinton won the nomination, "We're going to put up our most vulnerable candidate, whom Republicans will have no hesitancy in investigating in great detail...Whatever vulnerabilities I have on the issues, they're not vulnerabilities of character and judgment."

Clinton said that these remarks were a measure of Tsongas's desperation, showing that he had turned away from the issues.

"If there was some great flaw in character, I would not have been governor all this time," Clinton said. "I have no control over what [reporters] write or what others say. I know what my character is by living it."

The roller coaster was headed up again for Clinton. Two polls shortly before the Illinois and Michigan primaries showed him ahead of not only Tsongas, but President Bush as well.

* * *

Northwest Arkansas, with its mountains and lakes, is probably the most scenic area of the state. In 1992 it was in the middle of an economic boom. The headquarters of the retail giant Wal-Mart Stores were located there, as were a number of nationwide trucking companies. The state's biggest employer, the $2.7-billion-a-year poultry industry, was also well represented there.

The largest poultry products company in the nation, Tyson Foods, had its headquarters in the area. A number of other lesser-known poultry companies, such as Hudson Foods and Conagra Inc., had several plants there. Bill Clinton had for years enjoyed the political support of the poultry industry. Don Tyson, the head of Tyson Foods, was a particularly strong supporter. Tyson Foods was represented by the Rose Law Firm.

Don Tyson's father, the late John Tyson, is credited with establishing the poultry empire in Arkansas. John Tyson began a small chicken-processing operation in Springdale in the 1950s. At the time, northwest Arkansas was as poor as the rest of the state. The ground was rocky and practically useless for raising crops or larger farm animals, such as cattle.

The poultry companies established a pattern of business that changed the economic, as well as the environmental, landscape of the area. Owners of small farms were encouraged to build giant chicken houses, which resemble oversized military barracks and hold as many as twenty thousand chickens each. The poultry processors, such as Tyson, provided young chickens to the growers, who raised them and sold them back to the processors. This proved so profitable for small farmers that thousands entered into contracts with processors, building more chicken houses.

The farmers periodically cleaned out the chicken houses, scraping up the manure—or "chicken litter" as it is called—from the floors and disposing of it on barren pastureland. When the land produced lush green grass, the farmers realized that chicken litter was a natural, and abundant, fertilizer. It was spread over thousands of acres of land.

As the land became more fertile, other farmers moved in and began raising larger animals, such as cattle and hogs, which in turn created more waste material. By 1990, the area was producing one billion farm animals a year, mostly chickens, and creating as much waste as forty million people would have. The disposal of the waste created a storm of environmental concern.

Researchers learned that disease-causing pollutants, such as fecal coliform bacteria, from the chicken litter were washing from the land into nearby streams. The processing companies, which butcher the chickens and prepare them as food products for marketing, created another source of waste material during the processing. This material was treated by the processors' sewage disposal units, then sent to municipal sewage conduits, which treated it again before releasing it into rivers and streams.

In 1990, the state Department of Pollution Control and Ecology, which is in charge of environmental protection in Arkansas, tested the streams of northwest Arkansas and found that 94 percent of them were so infested with animal waste that it was dangerous to swim or fish in them.

In 1992, tests were again conducted, and the department reported that nearly 53 percent of the streams met the qualifications for their designated use as recreational water.

Environmentalists found it peculiar that the pollution levels should drop so drastically in the very year that Clinton was running for president. They charged that there had been a coverup. Steve Halterman, who owned a fly fishing school on the White River in the area, told the *Arkansas Democrat-Gazette* that the 1990 tests were conducted at 120 sites, while the new report had used only 70 sites for samples.

"Clinton's guys in Little Rock say they have the situation under control," Halterman told the *New York Times*. "It's not true. Not a one of them has walked these streams, floated these rivers or seen the pollution up close. What they're doing is all a show to keep what's happening to our water from becoming Bill Clinton's Boston Harbor." (George Bush had used the polluted Boston Harbor as a weapon against Michael Dukakis in the 1988 campaign.)

The largest stream in the area is the White River, which originates in Arkansas, flows north into Missouri, heads back south into Arkansas and eventually goes into the Mississippi River. It has a number of dams on it that create huge lakes for water supplies and recreation. The river and its tributaries are major tourist attractions.

Environmentalists charged that animal wastes were polluting the White River to the extent that fish were dying and water supplies were contaminated. The fight over water quality pitted the area's tourist industry against its poultry industry.

Because the national Clean Water Act exempted farmers from federal regulations, Arkansas's poultry industry was now encouraged to use its "best management practices" on a voluntary basis.

Teams from the *Washington Post* and the *New York Times* began reporting on the animal waste disposal problem in a series of articles.

The *Post* chronicled Bill Clinton's friendship with Don Tyson of Tyson Foods. The article detailed the tax breaks the poultry industry had received under the Clinton administration and pointed out that it had extraordinary clout with the Arkansas legislature.

"Poultry," said Don Allen, director of the Arkansas Poultry Federation, "is to Arkansas what steel was to Pittsburgh."

Clinton appointed a task force in 1990 to look into poultry pollution. The newspaper said the task force was "weighted with industry members and has spent two years studying the problem without recommending a single remedy."

Jim Lingle, an environmental lawyer from northwest Arkansas, told the *New York Times* that Clinton had taken on Georgia-Pacific, the big timber products company, over the issue of clear-cutting during his first term as governor. "It was a big factor in why he lost after one term," Lingle said. "You can fight that big industrial windmill like the paper companies and the chicken processors, or you can be governor of this state. When he was reelected in 1982, Bill Clinton decided he wanted to be governor."

Clinton press spokesman Mike Gauldin told the *Arkansas Democrat-Gazette* that the state had spent more than $3.3 million dealing with animal waste because "it has the potential to become a serious problem if not dealt with soon. We're nowhere near having the kind of problems alleged in recent press stories, but it's a growing concern that Arkansas is addressing before most other states."

John Tyson, son of Don Tyson and vice chairman of operations for Tyson Foods, defended the voluntary pollution control measures and said the poultry industry was working to contain the problem. "We're all responsible for northwestern Arkansas. We've got to get out of finger-pointing and get down to what really needs to be done here. I live here. Our employees live here. It's a beautiful area, and we mean to keep it that way," Tyson told the *New York Times*.

Brownie Ledbetter, an Arkansas activist, told the *Washington Post* that the problem lay in Clinton's business-as-usual politics. "The corporate folks have dominated this state economically and politically since it was a territory. That is not [Clinton's] fault," Ledbetter said. "He's just following the great Southern economic development plan: Come to us—we have cheap wages, few unions, all the tax breaks you could want and lousy environmental regulations."

* * *

Later in March, the *Washington Post* delivered another article containing more questions about the propriety of connections between Hillary Clinton's law work and state business. Reporters Michael Weisskopf and David Maraniss wrote:

> Rarely in American politics have married partners played such interconnected public roles, and the convergence of legal and political power in the Clinton family poses several problems for them as they seek to move on from a small-town, politically inbred capital to the White House.
>
> The Clintons have faced questions about potential favoritism for business clients of the prestigious Rose Law Firm, and conflicts of interest for a governor whose appointees regulate many of the business and financial institutions Rose represents, since they rose to power more than a decade ago.
>
> Clinton rivals say that the very listing of the governor's wife as a partner gives Rose's clients undue leverage in their dealings with state government. "If you want something special in this state, you go to the Rose firm," Sheffield Nelson, a Little Rock lawyer who lost to Clinton in the 1990 governor's race, said.
>
> ...The Rose firm offers the full range of representation before the government, from getting environmental approvals from the state Pollution Control and Ecology Commission, to lobbying to protect the poultry industry from strict regulations on animal waste, to writing the rules by which corporations treat their shareholders.

Once again, the inevitable conflicts between Hillary Clinton's professional life and her husband's political career were on the front pages of America's newspapers.

This became the focus of a heated exchange between Clinton and Brown during a debate on March 16. The Rose Law Firm represented Arkansas-based Tyson Foods, the poultry products giant. Brown tied it all together and attacked Clinton over the subjects of his wife's law firm and the poultry pollution problem.

"It's not only corruption," Brown said. "It's an environmental disaster, and it's the kind of conflict of interest that is incompatible with the kind of public servant we expect in a president."

An angry Clinton, pointing at Brown and stepping out from his lectern, shouted, "I don't care what you say about me...but you ought to be ashamed of yourself for jumping on my wife. You're not worthy of being on the same platform with my wife."

"Wait a minute, Bill," Brown interjected. "You're always trying to attack. You never answer the question."

"I'm saying that I never funneled any money to my wife's law firm, ever," Clinton said.

The next day, while campaigning in Chicago, Hillary Clinton defended her professional life. "I've done everything I knew how to do to be as careful as possible..." She said she had performed no state business for a fee as a lawyer, and that she accepted no partnership fees that were tied to state business. "I didn't think that anyone would presume anything, other than that I was trying to do the right thing all the way down the line. Right now, I'm a little confused about what the rules are."

Then she made what was to become one of the pivotal statements of the campaign:

"I suppose I could have stayed at home and baked cookies and had teas." A few minutes later, she added, "The work that I've done as a professional, as a public advocate, has been aimed in part at making sure that women can make the choices that they should make...I still think that is difficult for people to understand right now. This is a generational change."

While walking in a St. Patrick's Day parade in Chicago on the Monday before the primary, Bill and Hillary Clinton were the targets of several obscene comments. Some shouted "Adulterer!" Others yelled "Where's Gennifer Flowers?" But the Clintons walked on, smiling, ignoring the taunts.

The smiles were genuine the next day, as Bill Clinton won decisive victories in both Michigan and Illinois. He received 46 percent of the vote in Michigan. Jerry Brown made a surprisingly strong showing, finishing second with 28 percent. But the primary was a shocker for Tsongas, who received only 18 percent.

In Illinois, Clinton got 51 percent, with Tsongas coming in second and Brown third. Clinton now had a total of 949 delegates, with 2,145 the magic number.

Political observers believed it would be difficult for Clinton to lose the nomination. The *Arkansas Democrat-Gazette* asked Tom Mann of the Brookings Institution to assess the situation. "Clinton is now running against himself for the rest of the primary season," Mann said.

John White, former Democratic National Committee chairman,

agreed: "Short of something astounding happening, he's going to be the nominee." By this time, Larry Agran, who had announced his candidacy before Clinton joined the race, had retreated to his home state of California. The former mayor of Irvine did not withdraw from the race but limited his campaigning to a few appearances. Lacking money and delegates, Agran focused on the California primary on June 2.

The next battle would be Connecticut. But Clinton took a day off to relax. A friend invited him to play a round of golf at the Little Rock Country Club. The press, following his every move, noted that the club had an all-white membership, that although it had no rules against admitting nonwhites, and blacks frequently played there as guests, it had never admitted any as members.

Again, it was time to apologize. It was a thoughtless oversight, Clinton explained. He pointed out that he was not a member of the club and had only been a guest. "I'm a candidate for president now, and I shouldn't have done that, and I won't play golf there again until they integrate," Clinton said.

By the end of the week, Paul Tsongas had halted his candidacy, saying he lacked the money to fight the "expensive media war" in the upcoming New York primary. He suspended his campaign rather than formally ending it, in order to allow his pledged delegates to attend the convention. (Formally ending his campaign would have resulted in a redistribution of the delegates.)

Tsongas deflected questions as to whether he would consider accepting a vice presidential nomination, saying only that he would remain "a player" in the campaign. (Tsongas said on May 13 that he would not be a running mate for the nominee.)

Clinton tried to keep from sounding overconfident. "There are a lot of important states coming up, and the last thing I want these good people to think is that I'm taking them for granted," Clinton said. "There's a long way to go. I've got to get the delegates and I've got to unite this party."

He quickly added: "And I've got to defeat Governor Brown."

Brown, for his part, said the race was now a clear choice "between business-as-usual or a real change for the future."

Next to join the scoop-of-the-week bandwagon was the *Los*

Angeles Times, with a report that in 1985 Clinton had steered a big bond deal to a political ally. The ally, Dan R. Lasater, later served more than two years in federal prison on several cocaine charges. The implication was that Lasater got the deal because he had been a big political supporter of Clinton's.

The Clinton camp dismissed the charge as fabrication. Staffers explained that at the time the State Police needed a new statewide radio system, but there was no money for it. Several legislators balked at the idea of a bond issue to fund the radio system, because bond issues were usually used only for "bricks-and-mortar" projects. Clinton urged the legislators to approve the bond issue because it was an emergency, and wanted it done quickly. The legislators awarded it to the Lasater firm.

These newspaper articles were wearing away at the Clinton campaign. Most of the stories were complex and few readers could be bothered to explore every nuance, and so were left with the impression that "something wrong" had occurred. The effect on Clinton was that he was being besieged, day after day, by investigative reports of one kind or another.

The storm of bad news, however, did lead to one positive development: the entry of Betsey Wright into the campaign. She had been Clinton's iron fist during most of his campaigns, but had dropped out two years back to take a breather from the kind of head-banging crusades that Clinton engendered.

Wright quickly left Harvard, where she had been teaching political science courses, and headed to Little Rock to add muscle to the campaign's battle with the media. She took up her fighter's stance, facing down the *Los Angeles Times* reporters with accusations of sloppy, inaccurate and willfully misleading reporting. She even hinted that darker forces might be controlling the media: It seemed odd, she said, that these blockbusters always appeared on the eve of a primary, in this case the Connecticut primary. Betsey Wright was back, with a vengeance.

But the relentless pounding had taken its toll on the Clinton campaign. When the Connecticut primary rolled around on March 24, Jerry Brown was the winner, getting 37 percent of the vote to Clinton's 36. It was one more twist in a screwball election year, and came as a surprise even to Brown. Clinton called it a "small setback," although his camp was deeply worried that the recent barrage of press reports would continue to take their toll.

Brown called it a "shocking upset" and said that he had won because "people want change. I'm a vehicle for that."

He added, prophetically, "This thing is now coming to New York and this will be the battle where the party's going."

* * *

In the 1978 documentary film *The Last Waltz*, director Martin Scorsese asked rock star Levon Helm to describe the experience a Southern boy undergoes when he comes to New York to break into the big time.

Helm, a native Arkansan with a career in film as well as music, told Scorsese: "You just go in the first time and you get your ass kicked and you take off. Soon as it heals up, you come back and you try it again. Eventually, you fall right in love with it."

Bill Clinton didn't know it yet, but he was about to receive the kind of New York welcome Helm had described.

Clinton was in New York the day after the Connecticut primary, and he was running against Jerry Brown, not George Bush. His internal polls showed that he was virtually tied with Brown in New York.

He stood on a New York sidewalk and warned voters that Brown's proposed 13 percent flat tax would hurt them deeply.

"It triples taxes on the poor, dramatically increases taxes on the middle class and lowers taxes only on the wealthiest Americans," Clinton said. "...It's a war on New York tax, and we need to reject it in this primary."

Under Brown's plan, the income, corporate, Social Security and other federal taxes would be replaced with a simple 13 percent tax on all income and a 13 percent "value added tax" that would be similar to a national sales tax.

Clinton charged that the tax would put the heaviest burdens on the poorest taxpayers and give a windfall to the rich.

Brown made the round of morning talk shows. He was asked about his choice for vice president and he mentioned the Rev. Jesse

Jackson, saying the civil rights leader could bring the two races together.

Bill Clinton had one thing going for him—his face was staring out of every newsstand in New York City. The major news magazines had finally convinced themselves that Bill Clinton was a real candidate, only a breath away from capturing the nomination. *U.S. News & World Report, Newsweek,* the *New York Times Magazine* and even the *National Review* put glowing color portraits of Bill Clinton on their covers.

Jeff Gerth of the *New York Times* was back on the front page on March 27 with an article reporting that Clinton had excised a portion of a state ethics law that would have required him and his wife to report any potential conflicts of interest.

The article was both right and wrong. The original legislation proposed by Clinton would have required all "public servants," including legislators and the governor, to file a report every time they took a specific action or decision that might affect their family's personal finances. But the proposal never made it through the legislature after it became ensnared in parliamentary procedure. Clinton had been pushing for the ethics law and was angered that the legislature refused to pass it.

Clinton was determined to get an ethics law on the books. He decided to take the issue before the voters in a general initiative election. The writers of the original twenty-four-page proposal whittled it down to twelve pages. Because it would be put to the vote of the people, they deleted provisions for local and county officials, knowing that the proposal would never gain approval from the state's voters without support from local officials. Also left out by the writers was the phrase "constitutional officers," the top officers such as governor and secretary of state. The act was approved by the voters.

The writers of the law, such as state Senator Jay Bradford, said that it was done in a hurry to get it before the voters and that this haste contributed to the oversight.

"We made some errors, innocently," Bradford told the *Democrat-Gazette.* "It was not done with the intent to protect them [the top officials]." Also participating in the process were activists Brownie

Ledbetter and Scott Trotter, two of Clinton's most outspoken critics. Neither could remember how the exception to the law was made. No one who had a hand in drawing up the legislation said Clinton took a role in excising the portion that would have pertained to him and his wife.

But the damage was done. Jerry Brown's description of the "scandal-a-week" candidate was becoming all too accurate. And once again, the connection between Hillary Clinton's law work and state business was made.

"It's a total misrepresentation of Hillary," a Little Rock political observer said. "Most of the senior partners at the Rose Law Firm make more than $500,000 a year, but Hillary Clinton only made a little more than $100,000 last year. It's clear she could have made a lot more money by taking on state projects, or by devoting less time to pro bono work such as the Children's Defense Fund, but she chose not to do that and took the economic loss. Now, for all of her good intentions, all she receives is bad press."

(The Clintons' tax return for 1991 showed that Hillary Clinton had made $109,719 from her law practice and $70,200 in directors fees and honoraria—fees for making speeches. Bill Clinton made $35,000, the salary of an Arkansas governor, $3,166 from a "public relations" fund that state officers receive as an augmentation to their salary, and $5,500 in honoraria. The Clintons reported an additional $10,843 income from other sources, for a total of $234,428. They paid $48,608 in federal income taxes.)

Jerry Brown used the media scrutiny of Clinton to gain momentum. He placed an advertisement on New York television that said he had received no pay raise as governor of California, had cut taxes, had created new jobs and had appointed "unprecedented numbers of women and minorities."

The TV ad proclaimed: "Governor Clinton's Arkansas? A right-to-work state—ranks dead last in worker safety, its wages among the lowest in the country. And while Bill Clinton plays golf at a restricted all-white club, Arkansas remains one of only two states with no civil rights act. Now that's slick, but we want real change."

Clinton was still stumbling. On March 28, he started the day with a speech at Harlem Hospital but was interrupted by New Alliance Party presidential candidate Lenora Fulani and her followers.

"I want to talk about democracy," she shouted, while standing on a chair.

"Dr. Fulani, we are not here for you. The world doesn't revolve around you," Clinton said. He ended his speech and walked away. He had not yet been inoculated against the epidemic of New York hecklers.

But he did get a boost when he received the endorsement of Senator Tom Harkin and two big labor organizations—the Communications Workers of America and the International Ladies' Garment Workers Union. He also received some help from New York Senator Daniel Patrick Moynihan and Governor Mario Cuomo when they derided Brown's proposed 13 percent flat tax.

Brown tossed off the Harkin endorsement. "When you run a frontal assault on what you call a decrepit and corrupt status quo...you can't be surprised when people in that neighborhood band together in a mutual protection defense," he said.

An old ghost came back to haunt Clinton during a May 29 debate with Jerry Brown on WCBS-TV in New York. Reporter Marcia Kramer asked him if he had ever smoked marijuana while at Oxford.

"When I was in England, I experimented with marijuana a time or two and I didn't like it. I didn't inhale and I never tried it again," Clinton said.

It was another bombshell. Clinton had been asked this question countless times, and he had always given elliptical answers, such as saying he had never broken any state law. Why did he answer it this time? His explanation was that nobody had ever directly asked him if he had smoked marijuana while at Oxford. This was not entirely true. An *Arkansas Gazette* reporter had asked Clinton in 1990 if he had used drugs "as a college student." Clinton's response had been, "No."

In another CBS interview on May 29, Clinton said he didn't think the revelation would harm him. He cited similar confessions by U.S. Senator Albert Gore when he was running for president in 1988.

"Clarence Thomas, in his Supreme Court hearings, confessed that he had tried marijuana when he was a student. In the '60s, a lot of people tried it," Clinton said. "The only thing I can say is that I hope it doesn't do anything to encourage people to do the same thing today, at a time when instead of that you've got crack, you've got cocaine, you've got destruction."

Brown was asked the same question by WCBS. He responded: "No. Why don't you lay off this stuff? What you did twenty years ago is not relevant."

The New York tabloids, particularly the *New York Post*, went for blood. The *Post*'s headline on the marijuana story proclaimed "Clinton on the S-Pot." The *Daily News* said, "Weed Asked Him That."

Post columnist Mike McAlary, a society buddy of Governor Mario Cuomo's son Andrew, slashed at Clinton in column after column. "I think he's a complete bag of [excrement]," McAlary told the *Wall Street Journal*. "I've thought that from day one."

The *Post* ran a seminude picture of Elizabeth Ward Gracen next to a story about Clinton. Gracen, a former Miss America, had been one of the names included in the infamous Larry Nichols lawsuit, along with Gennifer Flowers and several others. Gracen, who had recently posed nude for *Playboy*, denied that she had ever had an affair with Clinton.

On and on it went. A morning radio shock-jock said he wanted to ask Clinton, "Aren't you sorry you didn't kill the other girls you slept with?"

Clinton became a kind of cartoon candidate, the dumb Southern hayseed who had the temerity to travel to the Capital of the World to beg for a few votes to become the president of the United States. Commentators began discussing whether there was a cultural bias in the press against Clinton. Even the respected magazine *U.S. News & World Report* published a caricature of Clinton with a piece of straw in his mouth, a mason jar at his elbow and cattle and goats in the background.

Clinton's damage-control unit went into overdrive. This sudden turn around, no-yes dance on the marijuana question raised the Slick Willie specter again, and coupled with the damaging news reports coming in daily, could only spell doom.

His operatives besieged the mainstream press, storming them with phone calls and reports and documents in an attempt at preempting further media strikes. Every criticism was countered with a detailed explanation. Betsey Wright, back in Little Rock, kept a close watch on the investigative reporters. When she detected them looking into a specific area, she would call them and start filling them in on the background of the situation— before they had a chance to write anything or even call her for a reaction. The reporters termed this "Betsey's radar." Clinton began calling quick news conferences to answer every charge.

Clinton had been hesitant to debate Brown, fearing it would only add to Brown's exposure. Now, Clinton called for more debates with his last surviving Democratic rival, saying he needed man-to-man showdowns to get his message across directly, without going through the media filter. His internal polls showed him tied with Brown, and time was running out.

"I'm willing to debate Jerry Brown anytime, anywhere, because I believe that when the voters hear what he has to say, they'll know that he has nothing to offer but platitudes and gimmicks."

An outside poll showed Clinton with 40 percent of the vote to Brown's 30, with much of Clinton's support coming from minorities.

Clinton attempted a bold move. Six days before the primary, he held a news conference to outline his foreign policy proposals, specifically for dealing with Eastern Europe. This time he went on the offensive against President Bush, charging that Bush had no vision of America's role in a constantly changing global situation.

Clinton's plan included contributing $1 billion to a $6 billion Western account to help stabilize the ruble so Russia could better import and export goods, but only after Russia implemented its own serious economic reforms. He also called for temporarily suspending Russia's servicing of its external debts and $1.2 billion in new U.S. loans to help the former Soviet states import manufacturing materials, food and medicine.

But President George Bush had his own "radar" tracking the Clinton campaign. Only a few minutes before Clinton made his announcement, Bush called a hurried press conference at the White House to announce his own multibillion-dollar aid program for Eastern Europe. It was almost a carbon copy of Clinton's plan.

Bush's press conference received top play in the newspapers and on the nightly news, while Clinton's speech was shunted off into the daily campaign roundups. Clinton had hoped to display once and for all his credentials for dealing with complex foreign policy matters.

It was the first real campaign battle between the Clinton and Bush teams, and Clinton's team had lost.

That same day, Clinton made an appearance on "Donahue" during which, dispensing with his small, quiet smile, he became quite angry. Host Phil Donahue questioned him for twenty minutes about allegations of marital infidelity.

"Believe it or not, Phil, there are people out there with futures that are worth fighting for, but it's very difficult, because people like you don't want me to," Clinton said. "I don't believe that I or any other decent human being should have to put up with the kind of questioning you're putting me through now. I think this is debasing our politics."

As Donahue persisted, Clinton replied:

"I've told you the only facts I think you're entitled to know. Have I had any problems with my marriage? Yes. Are we in good shape now? Yes. If I had been divorced, would you even be bringing this up? No. Should people be punished for keeping their marriage together? No."

The audience was clearly with Clinton. They cheered him frequently and nearly drowned Donahue with boos when he insisted on asking the personal questions.

Finally, Clinton said: "I am not going to discuss the details of this any further."

Donahue persisted.

"We're going to sit here a long time in silence, Phil," Clinton said. "I'm not going to answer any more of these questions. I've answered them until I'm blue in the face."

Clinton remained silent while Donahue attempted to regain control of the show. Donahue asked Clinton if he and his wife had ever been separated.

"No," Clinton replied. "And it's none of your business if we did."

Clinton needed some good news, and he got it on March 31. He swamped Jerry Brown in the Vermont caucus, receiving 46 percent to Brown's 16. But Clinton was still running scared. The tabloids were unrelenting in their ridicule and the mainstream press was still in Little Rock, poring over his record as governor.

The week before the primary, the *New York Times* began publishing a series of five background articles on Bill Clinton's years in Arkansas. Jeff Gerth's articles focused on tax breaks that Clinton's administration had given to industries to move to Arkansas, while at the same time raising the sales tax that the average citizen had to pay.

Reporter Steven A. Holmes looked into Clinton's black support and noted his appointment of several blacks to high government offices. But Holmes also pointed out that the poorest of Arkansas's citizens, the black residents of eastern Arkansas, had long been stuck in despair, with little hope of rising from a troubled agricultural economy.

B. Drummond Ayres tackled Clinton's vaunted education reforms and found little progress in Arkansas. "By most accounts," he wrote, "Clinton's efforts seem to have simply kept Arkansas, one of the poorest states, from falling even farther behind."

A survey of environmental standards in Arkansas by Keith Schneider once again revealed Clinton's lax attitude toward the problem of poultry waste pollution. On a more positive note, the reporter wrote that Arkansas, like the Northwest United States, is embroiled in a fight over timber-harvesting methods, and noted that during Clinton's years the state had purchased hundreds of acres of wilderness and streams for preservation.

The articles were well-balanced, well-written and well-documented. The reader was left to judge Clinton's accomplishments, or lack of them, as a governor of a disadvantaged state. For the most part, the series did not reflect the smug, condescending attitude that the establishment press usually displays when it ventures into the heartland. It did illustrate Clinton's weakest points as governor, but he couldn't complain that the press was not discussing the important issues and merely focusing on personal questions.

However, Clinton did complain, and loudly, during a fundraising speech when an AIDS activist began to heckle him. Clinton stopped his speech, pointed at the activist and began a long lecture that ended with him ordering the heckler to leave the room. Clinton then regained his composure and went on with his speech.

Jerry Brown had his hands full with a controversy over his

consideration of Jesse Jackson as a running mate. While campaigning on April 1, he warmly embraced Jackson and promised again to choose him as his running mate. This outraged Jewish voters, who were still bristling over Jackson's 1988 reference to New York as "Hymietown." They also disliked Jackson's ties with Palestine Liberation Organization leader Yasir Arafat and Muslim leader Louis Farrakhan, who had made several disparaging remarks about Jews.

On April 2, Clinton held a rally on Wall Street in which he spelled out his economic plan of a tax cut for the middle class and used his now familiar phrase of bringing America together from "Wall Street to the mean streets." Not surprisingly, he met with jeers from the lunch time crowd as he called the 1980s a decade of greed and restated his opposition to a cut in the federal tax on capital gains.

But after the speech, he gave his Secret Service entourage a shock by jumping directly into the crowd and heading straight for the most visible hecklers, where he attempted one-on-one discussions with them. It was Clinton at his best, talking and shaking hands, connecting, getting his message across directly.

In the next few days, Clinton seemed to adjust to the haranguing of the New York press and began displaying his sense of humor. He appeared on a television talk show and performed his Elvis imitation. He conducted an on-the-air exchange with radio personality Don Imus, who had led the pack in ridiculing Clinton as a "redneck bozo."

Imus, who had gotten a lot of mileage out of the Clinton sex rumors, didn't bring up that issue but did ask him if he had ever finished the infamous nominating speech for Dukakis in 1988.

"That's why I want to be the nominee for president, Clinton said. "If I come to New York [for the Democratic National Convention], then I can talk as long as I want. I've got about thirty more minutes to finish that speech in Atlanta."

Imus asked him about his musicianship and Clinton said he had chosen the saxophone because "you don't have to inhale. You blow out."

Clinton was also getting a break in the tabloids. Columnist Jimmy Breslin of *New York Newsday*, wrote: "Say what you want, but do not say that he quits."

Daily News columnist Pete Hamill wrote: "In spite of my own terminal skepticism, I've come to respect Bill Clinton. It's the late rounds and he's still there."

In perhaps the oddest twist, the *New York Post*, the tabloid that had bashed Clinton the hardest and most frequently, endorsed his candidacy for president.

"It speaks strongly to his strength of character that he has already survived a battering by the press on personal questions unprecedented in the history of American politics," the editorial said. "He has continued to campaign with remarkable tenacity, even as the ugly effort to pick apart his private life continued to gather steam. In our view, he has manifested extraordinary grace under pressure."

Jerry Brown wasn't having nearly as much fun. He went to speak to the Jewish Community Relations Council of New York, where he received a chilly response and many questions about his avowed choice of Jesse Jackson as his running mate. At one point, Assemblyman Dov Hikind approached Brown and began shouting at him. The candidate remained silent as members of the crowd escorted Hikind outside. When Brown resumed his speech, others challenged his remarks, and boos and hisses were heard until he finished.

The Clinton machine was in full operation at this point. A busload of black supporters from Arkansas headed for New York to fan out through the city to drum up minority support. Among them was Carol Willis, a longtime aide to Clinton.

Columnist Brummett later explained how the black contingent worked once it got to New York: "With help from New York City blacks, they covered sixty leading black churches. [Lottie] Shackelford [a Little Rock city director] alone spoke from five pulpits Sunday morning. She and others extolled Clinton's commitment to blacks and his record of appointments to boards and commissions, and dismissed the significance of his golf outing.

"Whenever a minister would balk at giving time to a Clinton campaigner, [Carol] Willis would telephone a black preacher in Arkansas, who would call and give Clinton a strong reference."

Two more stumbling blocks appeared only days before the primary. The May issue of *Vanity Fair* contained a quote from Hillary Clinton suggesting that the press should look into rumors of extramarital affairs involving George Bush. She quickly issued an apology, saying, "Nobody knows better than I the pain that can be caused by even discussing rumors in private conversations, and I did not mean to be hurtful to anyone."

On the same day, Cliff Jackson, the old Oxford friend who had become a bitter enemy of Clinton, released a letter from 1969 in which the candidate mentioned that he had received a draft induction notice. This only served to further muddle the Clinton draft question.

Clinton responded by saying he did get the induction notice, but had received it in Oxford after the date on which he was supposed to have reported for induction. He had asked his draft board for instructions, he said, and it had given him another six-month deferment. He said he had never mentioned the induction notice before because he didn't think it was important.

But the *Arkansas Democrat-Gazette* asked Opal Ellis, the former secretary of the Hot Springs draft board, to clear up the matter, and Ellis flatly denied that Clinton had ever received a notice.

"I did not send him an induction notice, Ellis said. "I would have been the one to send it out."

At that point, Clinton backtracked, saying he was confused over whether such a notice existed or whether it was a letter ordering him to report for an armed forces physical, which he did in 1969. Clinton said he would have to review his files to clear up the matter.

The last days before the April 7 primary were mostly quiet, with Clinton campaigning in black churches and among black groups in the city and Brown campaigning around the state. There was little fire left in either of them. Clinton was hoarse, barely able to speak. Brown displayed a weariness that few had seen in him.

The *New York Times* said of those final days: "If there is one sound that rose up from New York over the weekend, it wasn't a shout, but a giant collective sigh."

But there were plenty of shouts at the Ritz on the night of April 7, 1992. That was the club where Bill Clinton was throwing his victory party. He had won the New York primary, with 41 percent of the vote. Jerry Brown, with 26 percent, had placed third behind a quasi-candidate, Paul Tsongas, who had received 29 percent without even campaigning.

Clinton had been the victor in the three other primaries as well, taking 51 percent in Kansas, 33 percent in Minnesota and 38 percent in Wisconsin. He now had 1,267 delegates out of the 2,145 needed to win the nomination.

The press attempted to mute the victory by playing up the low turnout and murmurs of voter discontent. Bill Clinton, however, was having none of that. He had been viciously attacked and had not only survived, but had won, hands down.

That night, a television commentator asked him how he felt after having been bloodied day after day for two weeks. A jubilant Clinton dismissed it as a learning process: "The darker the night, the sweeter the victory," he said.

* * *

Clinton escaped from New York with his victory and his delegates, but not with his voice. The combination of chronic allergies and nonstop campaigning had wrecked his vocal cords. His Little Rock physician ordered a complete rest for at least a week. Nevertheless, on the Wednesday after the New York primary Clinton headed to Peoria, Illinois, to talk to United Auto Worker strikers and management at the Caterpillar tractor company. Nearly 13,000 workers were on strike, and the company was threatening to replace them permanently. A bill that would ban permanent replacement of strikers was pending in Congress, and Clinton said he would sign such a bill if he were elected president.

Clinton said after the meetings, "Remember going back to the Kennedy years there was always an attempt by government to avoid prolonged strikes and keep people working to settle. If I were president, I would have the Labor Department aggressively involved."

UAW officials in Arkansas were irritated by the pictures of Clinton shaking hands with the strikers. The officials charged that Clinton had done little to end a UAW strike at Champion Auto Parts in Hope, Arkansas, where Clinton was born.

James Baker, international representative for the UAW local in Hope, asked, "Has Clinton been to Hope? Not that I know of. Has he had any conversations with anybody? Not as far as I know." About three hundred union workers had been on strike at Hope since September 1991.

Clinton's voice was gone when he arrived in Little Rock on Thursday, April 8, the day Paul Tsongas announced that he would not reenter the race. Tsongas said Clinton's wins in New York, Kansas, Minnesota and Wisconsin convinced him to stay out. "We did very well, but so did Bill Clinton. He won those states. That winning removed the argument that my reentry would rescue this party. Indeed, his winning took me back to the option that I rejected three weeks ago, the role of spoiler. I reject that role." But Tsongas said he would keep his 539 delegates.

That same day Jerry Brown's fading campaign received some more bad press. ABC News reported that members of Brown's security detail during his tenure as governor of California in the 1970s had said marijuana and cocaine were used at parties at his Los Angeles home. One officer said, "Throughout the house were ashtrays with seeds or leftovers of burnt marijuana. After these parties were over and we cleared the residence we could smell the odor of marijuana and we found traces of a white powdery substance which we later identified as cocaine." The officers said they did not make arrests because their primary task was "the protection of the governor."

Brown denied the allegations. "I never saw it. It's not true," he told reporters while campaigning in Pittsburgh.

By Friday, Clinton was jogging through the streets of downtown Little Rock again, this time amid a flock of Secret Service agents and reporters. He had gained twenty-three pounds, most of it from junk food eaten on the campaign trail. His doctor had forbidden him to speak, so his vocal cords could heal. In meetings he communicated in writing. Rumors had arisen during the last week of the New York campaign that he would soon resign as governor. Clinton, in his fifth term as governor and his second four-year term, said in a statement, "I am not going to resign as governor of Arkansas—whether I am the Democratic nominee for president or not."

Clinton gradually began picking up support from the "super-delegates," current and former elected officials, including Democratic members of Congress, who would vote in the party convention July 13–15 in New York. Officially, they were uncommitted, but ten House members, including House Majority Leader Richard Gephardt, backed Clinton. In the Senate, Jay Rockefeller of

West Virginia also joined the Clinton side, saying, "It's time for us to change course. It is time to get something done. It is time to put an end to George Bush's obstructions. Only one person still in this race can do that."

President Bush, who had won overwhelmingly in every Republican primary since New Hampshire, had vanquished Pat Buchanan. As he focused on a race against Clinton, Bush said he had ordered his campaign managers to "stay out of the sleaze business."

These reports should have been heartening to the Clinton campaign, but there were glum faces in the Little Rock headquarters over the persistence of Clinton's negative ratings in the polls. This problem was starkly illuminated on the cover of the April 20 issue of *Time*, which used a reversed black-and-white photographic negative of Clinton on its cover.

"Rarely if ever have party voters approached their choice with so many misgivings," the magazine said, citing exit polls that showed only 20 percent of New York Democrats thought Clinton had the honesty to be president, while 46 percent thought he did not. The article quoted Democratic National Chairman John White as saying, "Clinton is going to have to find some forum in which he confronts these character questions directly."

The magazine expected Bush to "be the soul of propriety" in the campaign while the "truly rough stuff will rise, virgin-like, from the same 'independent expenditure' group that produced the Willie Horton ad in 1988."

Clinton picked up 41 of Virginia's 78 pledged delegates in caucuses on April 13, but the gain was diminished by the lowest voter turnout in twenty years. The showings set off some alarms in the Clinton camp, which expected better returns in a Southern state. Clinton was further hobbled by his doctor's orders to remain silent for another day. He was forced to cancel a major economic address in Philadelphia. Clinton needed to be barnstorming through Pennsylvania in order to reverse his negative image in time for that state's primary on April 28. On Saturday, April 18, he made a quick trip to Philadelphia and then to Pittsburgh, where he strolled through an outdoor market, talking to voters, and then attended at Phillies-Pirates game. He headed back to Little Rock for the Easter weekend.

Pennsylvania Governor Robert Casey was no fan of Clinton's. Casey, a Democrat, opposed abortion rights and supported a restrictive Pennsylvania abortion law that was being considered by the United States Supreme Court. Casey said he could not endorse Clinton while polls showed many Democrats wanted other choices. "We have to recognize reality. The primary process is not producing someone who has a good crack at winning in November," Casey said.

Clinton used a Little Rock fundraising dinner on April 20 to lash out at his critics, especially those who were saddling him with the Slick Willie image. "I have proved one thing—I'm not very slick. I often say something I shouldn't. It makes the evening news just a little bit off-kilter so that characterization they like to make of me can be reinforced one more time."

He also took on the critics of his close relationships with business interests. "A lot of people criticize me because I get along with people. I thought the object of politics was to get things done. The object of politics in Washington for too long has been to ignore getting anything done but always make sure you're postured right on the evening news."

By April 22, "Earth Day," less than a week from the primary, Clinton was back in Pennsylvania and treading on thin ice. He excoriated Bush's environmental record. "Too often, on the environment, as on so many other issues, the Bush administration has been reactive, rudderless and expedient," Clinton said. He proposed a national bottle-refund bill, more fuel-efficient cars and a ban on new offshore oil drilling. He said he would seek protection of old-growth forests in the Pacific Northwest.

Clinton had ignored Jerry Brown during the Pennsylvania campaign, focusing on Bush, but Brown immediately jumped into the fight by saying Clinton had a "miserable" record in Arkansas and the Democratic Party could expect "an environmental backlash of no small dimension" if Clinton became the nominee. Bush spokesman Marlin Fitzwater said Clinton "does know pollution. He's got it, he's caused it, he's nurtured it and he's done nothing to clean it up."

Clinton made a quick side trip to a Florida fund-raiser and again ran into trouble, this time with students at Florida A&M University at Tallahassee. Clinton tried to focus his criticism on Bush, but students kept pressing him about the character questions. One student, who said he agreed with Clinton on most of the issues, wondered about Clinton's honesty in answering the marijuana question, especially the "didn't inhale" statement.

"I answered the question honestly. If you never inhaled a cigarette it's hard to [inhale] anything else. It's silly, but it's not morally relevant. I just said it as a nervous afterthought because it happened to be true."

Another student raised the question, "Can I trust you to be honest when it comes to keeping promises."

An exasperated Clinton shook his head and said, "This is crazy. How do you think I got elected five times?"

As the audience applauded, Clinton said, "I think I've done a pretty good job, being an imperfect person, in trying to follow the real moral obligation in life, which is trying to do better tomorrow than you did today. What you're seeing is what you get. If you don't want it, vote for Bush. Send me back to the house. I've got a great life, but [if Bush is elected] it's going to be a bad, cold four years for America."

As the April 28 primary neared, polls in Pennsylvania worried the Clinton camp. He was doing no better than 38 percent, reflecting a distrust over the character issue. The Pennsylvania governor, Robert Casey, still caused trouble. Casey, who had major differences with all of the Democratic candidates over the abortion issue, said Clinton's accumulation of delegates was worthless because Clinton could not defeat Bush. "Governor Clinton keeps winning and nobody's cheering," Casey said.

On the day before the election, Jesse Jackson caused a small stir. Jackson had been uncharacteristically invisible in the campaign except for a brief moment before the New York primary when Jerry Brown said Jackson would be his vice presidential running mate. In an interview with the New York *Daily News* and in comments to the Associated Press, Jackson said Clinton should offer him the vice presidential position. "It must not be seen as a threat, just a normal deliberation," Jackson said. He was asked if he would support the ticket if he were not selected, and Jackson responded, "Well, I have supported it all of these years, not being on the ticket, but things do change."

When the press reports appeared, Jackson retreated, saying,

"The eventual nominee of the party has the option of whom he will recommend to be on the ticket. Let me be clear. At no time did I threaten the candidate or the party over the vice presidency or anything else."

On the morning of the Pennsylvania primary, April 28, 1992, Bill Clinton put on a red Arkansas Razorbacks T-shirt and green jogging shorts and trotted through the maze of downtown Philadelphia, sticking to his vow to stay fit and healthy. Later that night, the persistent gloom over the Clinton camp evaporated when Clinton captured 56 percent of the vote in the Pennsylvania primary, for a total of 1,554 delegates. He needed only 591 more delegates to seal a first-ballot nomination. Fourteen primaries, including big ones in California, New Jersey, Ohio, Alabama, New Mexico and Montana—all on June 2—were still to come. Jerry Brown received 26 percent in Pennsylvania, and Tsongas mopped up the remainder. Clinton saw the primary as a victory over the character questions.

Exit polls showed 61 percent of the voting Democrats interviewed said they believed he had the integrity to serve as president. That was an eleven-percentage-point jump from the 50 percent of New York voters who were doubtful about his character. The Comeback Kid had come back one more time, saying, "We were able to run the most positive, issue-oriented, change-oriented campaign that I've had the honor of running. I was able to talk about my life. I was able to talk about my record as governor."

But Clinton wasn't finished. The next day he was in Washington, courting the "superdelegates" in Congress. The Democratic Party created the superdelegates in 1984 to neutralize the influence of liberal activists on the nomination. The superdelegates can support anyone for the party's nominee, regardless of how their home states vote. In 1992 there were 772 superdelegates, composed of 260 congressional Democrats, all thirty-two Democratic governors, 400 members of the Democratic National Committee and eighty state and party officials chosen by state parties. They represented about 18 percent of the convention.

All through his campaign Clinton had tarred Congress as one of the "problems" that prevented "change" in America. But on this day he got along famously with the group. Late in afternoon, after several meetings, he had lined up thirty-two previously uncommitted Democrats, including Senate Majority Leader George Mitchell of Maine, who said, "There is broad and enthusiastic support for Governor Clinton's candidacy. We are convinced he will be the nominee of the party and that he will be the president of the United States."

*   *   *

As Clinton emerged as the top Democratic candidate for president, party operatives began worrying that the Republicans would soon play their trump card—the racial issue.

Since the days of Richard Nixon, the American electorate had been split along racial lines, with white voters, who carry the most clout at the polls, supporting Republican presidential candidates. The Democrats usually won the smaller, and less effective, black vote. At this point in the campaign, Bush and Clinton had participated in what the *Wall Street Journal* called "a conspiracy of silence" to avoid specific discussions of racial problems. Bush was hesitant to discuss his record on domestic issues, especially programs for low-income citizens, nor did he want to bring up reminders of the Reagan Administration, which black Americans believed had been antagonistic toward them. Clinton, for his part, did not want to appear to be another typical liberal Democrat offering government handouts to black Americans, thereby driving the white voters into the GOP camp.

But Democratic Party operatives knew Bush was fearful of Clinton and that Republicans were ready to polarize the electorate and start rounding up the white vote. Any day, the Democrats expected Bush to begin using such code words as *welfare*, *quotas* and *family values*, which would force Clinton to defend the Democratic ideals on the racial issues and unveil himself as a true liberal.

Elections can turn on a dime, and that's what happened on April 29, 1992, when south-central Los Angeles exploded in riots over the Rodney King verdict.

King was a black man who had been beaten by four white policemen during his arrest on March 3, 1991. The beating was recorded on videotape by an amateur photographer and was shown across the nation on television. The four officers were indicted later in March on several charges, including the use of excessive force. Because of publicity, the trial was moved from Los Angeles to neighboring Ventura County. The officers' trial began on February 5.

On April 29, the all-white jury, which included an Asian and a Hispanic, found the officers not guilty on ten of eleven counts, and a mistrial was declared on the eleventh count.

South-central Los Angeles, a mostly black neighborhood, became the focal point of the rioting as blacks expressed anger at the verdict. After two days of violence, fifty-one people were dead, 2,383 were injured and more than 16,000 had been arrested. Thousands of buildings had been looted or burned, resulting in more than $700 million in damages. The National Guard was sent to the neighborhood to protect firefighters and to restore order.

The rioting spread to other cities, notably San Francisco, Las Vegas and Atlanta, where violence erupted from peaceful demonstrations, ending in scuffles, window-smashing and looting. In New York, on May 1, workers left offices early because of rumors, later proven to be exaggerated, of protesters fanning through the city.

Clinton was still in Washington on Thursday, the second day of the riots, when he blamed the violence on President Bush, accusing him of ignoring racial division and fostering "more than a decade of urban decay."

Bush appeared on nationwide television on Friday to announce that he was sending federal law officers, army troops and marines to patrol sections of the Los Angeles. He also asked the Justice Department to investigate possible civil rights violations.

Clinton softened his line that day during a news conference in Little Rock, saying, "I don't think today is the day for us to be casting stones and placing blame." He praised Bush for his actions. "I think that is the appropriate thing to do," Clinton said.

By Saturday, Clinton was in New Orleans to speak to the Democratic Leadership Council, where he blamed both Democrats and Republicans for the racial trouble. "Thomas Jefferson once said that the crisis of slavery is a fire bell in the night. The crisis in Los Angeles in now our fire bell in the night," he said. He was careful not to condemn the jury's verdict or to criticize the rioters, and said the trouble arose from a divided America. Clinton talked about his daughter, who attends public school in Little Rock, which have experienced a measure of violence.

"She tells me stories that sometimes cause me to fear, but I believe we must face our fears and not run from them because, basically, she has gotten a good education and revels in the biracial life she lives and there's been more hope than fear in her experience," he said.

Clinton talked of "the profound divisions in our community" and said the "hard truth" is that race is at the "root of much of this." Many of the council members welcomed Clinton's speech, but some murmured that the governor, who had originally captivated the Democratic Leadership Council by portraying himself as a moderate who could stop the party's liberal drift, was being too conciliatory toward the people who had created anarchy in Los Angeles.

In contrast, Bush positioned himself as a leader, dispatching troops and establishing law and order. "Let me assure you, I will use whatever force is necessary to restore order. I guarantee you, this violence will end," Bush said. As for the four acquitted policemen, Bush added, "The verdict Wednesday was not the end of the process."

By Sunday, Los Angeles was quiet, as residents and volunteers worked to clean up the damage while soldiers stood guard. The political fight, however, was starting to heat up.

Clinton, speaking in a church in Washington, said, "I want the American people to know that in cities like Los Angeles and Washington...there are community leaders who have struggled against all the odds, and in the face of massive neglect, have reinvested the values of American life in the toughest circumstances imaginable."

Jack Kemp, secretary of Housing and Urban Development, issued a statement saying Clinton's campaign had "reached a new low when he attempted to politicize the tragic situation in Los Angeles and turn it to his self-perceived political advantage."

Hillary Clinton, speaking in Columbia, Missouri, to a state Democratic convention, said Bush had contributed to "a spiritual crisis in this country" because he lacked vision. "It is very difficult to lead a life, let alone lead a great country, without a vision of what that country should be."

Throughout the week, black leaders like Jesse Jackson and Congresswoman Maxine Waters of California had been blaming the Bush and Reagan administrations for the riots, insisting that

Republicans had neglected racial problems and had failed to provide jobs for the growing numbers of unemployed blacks, which fueled the frustrations in the inner cities.

Bush spokesman Marlin Fitzwater fired back on Monday, blaming the Great Society programs of the 1960s and 1970s for the unrest. "We have seen a breakdown of leadership structures and families and no commitment to communities," Fitzwater said. He did not cite specific programs, but said "handouts" offered by Democratic presidents had created the problems.

On the same day, Bush proposed $600 million in emergency aid for south-central Los Angeles, including $300 million in low-interest Small Business Administration loans to burned-out businesses and $300 million in emergency grants. He called this proposal a short-range plan and vowed to "help get to the core of the problem." Fitzwater added that the administration would push for "enterprise zones," which give special tax advantages to businesses that locate in low-income areas.

Clinton, who was in Los Angeles touring the devastated area, called Fitzwater's attack "the last refuge of a desperate person" and said Bush and Reagan had destroyed much of the Great Society programs. As for Jack Kemp, Clinton said the HUD secretary "has been the most critical member of the Cabinet, of President Bush's inaction, and my guess is he got a little heat for it and was just trying to make up some political ground on the home court."

Steering away from Democratic giveaways, Clinton returned to his oft-repeated campaign belief that citizens must solve their own problems through cooperation. He said the people he talked to in south-central Los Angeles were "not asking to return to what we tried in the sixties...more direct aid through top-down government bureaucracies. But they don't want any more neglect." He proposed community banks in inner-city neighborhoods that would make loans to low- and middle-income residents and businesses. "They want to be empowered to control their own destiny," Clinton declared.

By Tuesday, the Los Angeles curfew had been lifted and Mayor Tom Bradley said the city was "back to normal." Bush, contending he wasn't playing the "blame game," headed for Los Angeles to tour the area and meet with community leaders. Clinton headed for North Carolina, which was holding a primary that day, as were the

District of Columbia and Indiana. He was rewarded with a sweep of all three, garnering 74 percent of the votes in the District of Columbia, 63 percent in Indiana and 64 percent in North Carolina. Jerry Brown made a poor showing, but Paul Tsongas captured a respectable percentage, indicating that some Democrats still favored his probusiness theme. Clinton added 144 delegates to his total, which was more than 80 percent of the delegates needed to acquire the Democratic nomination.

One week and a day after the riots started, Bush toured the burned-out areas of south-central Los Angeles, expressing "horror and dismay" at what he saw. Reporters said Bush seemed genuinely shocked at the destruction. Speaking at a church in the community, Bush said, "We are embarrassed by interracial violence and prejudice. We're ashamed. We should take nothing but sorrow out of all of that and do our level best to see that it's eliminated from the American dream."

Bill Clinton was back in Little Rock on May 7 for the fourth execution in two years. Steven Douglas Hill, twenty-five, the youngest of the thirty-five men on Death Row, was to be executed at 9 P.M. for the October, 15, 1984, shooting of Arkansas state trooper Robert Klein. Hill was seventeen when he was convicted of killing the trooper. He and another inmate had escaped from a state prison facility and broken into a house to hide. As Klein approached the house, Hill fired a 20-gauge shotgun, killing him. Hill confessed to firing the gun, but said during his trial that his confession had been coerced.

In the last days before the execution, Hill's companion during the escape, Michael Anthony Cox, who had pled guilty in exchange for the dropping of capital murder charges, said he had fired the gun. The state parole board did not believe Cox, citing evidence that only Hill's fingerprints were found on the weapon. The board recommended that Clinton deny clemency to Hill.

During the day of the execution, Hill's lawyer appealed to the United States Eighth Circuit Court of Appeals, which rejected a stay of execution by an eight-to-one vote. Clinton then denied clemency. The lawyer appealed to the United States Supreme Court, which unanimously and without comment denied a stay. A request for reconsideration was rejected by the Supreme Court without dissent.

About sixty protesters of the death penalty gathered outside the gates of the Governor's Mansion that night. They yelled for Clinton to come outside and talk to them, but Clinton did not appear.

Hill died at 9:09 P.M., about eight minutes after the lethal drugs were injected into his body. Unlike the final minutes of Rickey Ray Rector, Hill's execution encountered no technical problems. Of the four men executed since 1990, three were white and one, Rector, was black.

The next day, Clinton talked to Noel Oman, a reporter for the *Arkansas Democrat-Gazette*, about Hill's execution. "The others were all multiple murderers," Clinton said. "I spent a lot of time going over the...videotape of the clemency hearing, a lot of written records.

"I even went back yesterday and called the State Police and got some information from the case file. I spent several hours personally going back over this case."

Clinton defended the jury system in making his decision. "I think the presumption should always be against overturning the verdict of a jury and the sentence of the court, but I think that when someone asks for clemency and a life hangs in the balance, particularly when it was not a multiple murder case, you have to really get fixed in your mind about intent, consequences, circumstances."

As for making the decision, Clinton said, "Those are very, very tough days and tough nights. When it's done, it's out of my hands...but these are very difficult times." He added, "I have no guilt. The law of the state is clear. I support the law."

* * *

Bush concluded his thirty-eight-hour inspection of Los Angeles on Friday vowing not to allow conditions in the inner city to "return to the status quo." He proposed another package of aid for the city, this one costing $19 million, which would provide more money for housing for about 175 low-income people, police officers to fight drug dealers, Head Start programs and health and drug treatment clinics.

The president's speech was broadcast live on CNN, which interviewed Clinton after Bush finished. "What struck me about this is that this speech could've been given three years ago,"

Clinton said. "I remember when he was nominated for president how he said he was haunted by those children in the inner cities. But for over three years, he ignored their interests until this riot in Los Angeles brought them back onto the from pages."

Clinton added that Bush "rediscovered Jack Kemp today, which must be rewarding for Jack Kemp, since he's been out there all alone, advocating these empowerment and enterprise strategies. But the American people have to wonder whether this is like it was back in '88: the right rhetoric but there'll be no action following it."

On Sunday, May 10, Clinton headed for California again, this time campaigning for the June 2 primary in that state. Since his win in Connecticut, Clinton had avoided mentioning Jerry Brown, the former California governor, but focused on Bush. In speeches at two San Francisco churches, Clinton never mentioned Brown's name, but tackled the racial code words of "welfare" and "family values" in attempt to frame the argument before Bush could set the issues agenda.

He said the inner-city turmoil revealed that the nation was "in the grip of a selfishness that would kill any nation" as a result of Republican policies for twenty years.

"Oh, to be sure, it was heartbreaking to see some little children going into the stores in Los Angeles and stealing from their neighbors. But they live in a country where the top one percent of Americans have more wealth than the bottom ninety percent."

Clinton said he believed Bush had neglected public education and citizens without health insurance. "We are wasting people in America by the millions."

John Sasso, a Democratic strategist, told the Associated Press that Clinton was aggressively defining the issues. "He's running an offensive campaign on the values issues. In 1988, George Bush filled in our values for us—unpatriotic, soft on crime, permissive, liberal elitists and so forth."

Both Clinton and Bush were feeling the pressure from H. Ross Perot's "undeclared candidacy." Perot needed 54,275 signatures from voters to gain a spot on the Texas ballot, and by May 11 he had turned in more than four times that number. "They said this couldn't be done. Political experts said ordinary people couldn't get this job done. Well, you showed 'em," Perot told a crowd of three thousand supporters at the state Capitol in Austin.

Perot made a reference to Los Angeles in his remarks: "We are a melting pot. The other parties are trying to split the melting pot into different pieces....We will not be a part of that. In blunt Texas talk, if you hate other people don't vote for me."

But Perot encountered trouble. Former aides to President Richard Nixon described Perot as "the ultimate insider." Charles Colson, Nixon's former special counsel, said, "The guy was an amazing operator. I don't know anybody in the whole four years I was at the White House who was able to muscle himself in quicker into the President's own confidence."

White House memos showed that in 1969 Perot offered $50 million for a public relations effort that included buying a major newspaper and the ABC television network. He also proposed spending $10 million of his own money to create a "Nixon think tank." The memos showed Nixon accepted the offers, but Perot never delivered.

Colson, who worked on the think tank with Perot, said the offer was "one of the most effective con jobs I ever saw in the White House. He never put up a nickel. He parlayed that offer...into access, which ended up costing him nothing."

Peter Flanagin, a Nixon economic adviser, said Perot's characterization of himself as an outsider was "nonsense."

"He knows how to play every instrument in that band. He was the ultimate insider," Flanagin declared.

Perot denied the he ever offered money, saying Nixon aides would solicit money from him with "beautiful and strange ideas. And I always made it very clear to them I wasn't interested."

The documents showed that Nixon talked Perot into investing $55 million in a troubled Wall Street stock brokerage, duPont Glore Forgan. The firm eventually went bankrupt and closed. Perot said he only made the investment after Nixon aides "got down on their hands and knees" and said that saving the firm would avoid a financial crash on Wall Street. Perot said he lost $60 million on the venture.

As the media pressured Perot for specifics on his platform, he insisted that Americans were not interested in a platform—that they knew what he stood for—but that he would offer something for the media to chew on.

Clinton dismissed a *Time* magazine poll that showed Perot as the favorite of 33 percent of the people surveyed. Bush received 28 percent, and Clinton garnered 24 percent. Clinton said it was one of a "thousand polls between now" and November, adding, "It's the American people disgusted with the primary process, disgusted with politics as usual."

The governor continued to roll up support in the May 12 primaries winning 75 percent of the vote in West Virginia and 48 percent in Nebraska. With nearly two months left in the primary season, Clinton had received 85 percent of the vote needed for the nomination.

On Saturday, May 16, Clinton and Jerry Brown were both in Little Rock, although their paths never crossed. Clinton was in town to take care of some local business, while Brown came south to seek votes in the March 26 Arkansas primary and to dramatize what he decried as Clinton's defective record on environmental issues.

The old Vertac Chemical Corporation plant in Jacksonville, a suburb of Little Rock, had been a source of environmental problems for years. The plant had once manufactured herbicides, including, during the Vietnam War, the defoliant Agent Orange, but had long since closed, leaving behind thirty thousand barrels of toxic waste. Many of the barrels contained a highly poisonous by-product called dioxin.

The fight over disposal of the waste had continued for nearly a decade. The problem was complicated by the fact that the plant was situated in what is known as "tornado alley," a roughly southwest-to-northeast corridor stretching across Texas, Oklahoma and Arkansas where tornados formed on a frequent basis. It was feared that, sooner or later, a storm would hit the plant and scatter the barrels, which were stored in flimsy sheds, over a wide area.

State and federal regulators prevented the barrels from being moved, fearing the spread of contamination. The regulators eventually allowed on-site incineration of some of the chemicals, a plan that Clinton approved.

Local activists opposed the incineration, which was conducted in a thickly populated area. They feared that burning the chemicals would spread the toxic waste through the air. They wanted the barrels stabilized in special protective bunkers until a new technology could be perfected to transform the waste into harmless material.

Clinton's support for the incineration had infuriated the local activists. The burning of some of the chemicals had begun only a few months before Brown's visit.

Brown toured the Vertac site and was quick to criticize Clinton. "This state is an environmental disaster," he said. As Brown walked around the site, he told reporters: "Groups who study the environment know Clinton's been very deficient on environmental grounds. In order to facilitate his business friends, he's been lax on his environmental standards. Everybody knows that. I have the best record on the environment. I'm here to highlight that."

Previously, Clinton had accused Brown of belittling Arkansas by comparing it to Third World countries. Local reporters asked Brown about that characterization. Brown denied that he had disparaged Arkansas, saying Clinton had made a baseless accusation. "That's one of the little tricks of campaigns—to blame your opponent for something he did not do and then attack him," Brown said. "That's the kind of deception that people always complain about when talking to him."

Both Clinton and Brown headed to Oregon to campaign for that state's primary on May 19, which Clinton captured, adding a few more delegates to his total. On that same day, Vice President Dan Quayle established himself as Bush's lightening rod on the "family values" issue.

Quayle, speaking in San Francisco, lashed out at the television show *Murphy Brown*. The program's storyline depicted the main character, played by actress Candice Bergen, as being pregnant and choosing not to marry, but deciding to raise the child alone.

Quayle said, "It doesn't help matters when prime-time TV has Murphy Brown—a character who supposedly epitomizes today's intelligent, highly paid, professional woman—mocking the importance of fathers by bearing a child alone and calling it another 'lifestyle choice.'"

The vice president also addressed the Los Angeles riots, saying, "Instead of denouncing wrongdoing, some have shown tolerance for rioters. Some have enjoyed saying, 'I told you so.' Who is to blame for the riots? The killers are to blame. Yes, I can understand how people were shocked and outraged by the verdict in the Rodney King trial. But there is simply no excuse for the mayhem that followed."

The next day, a media storm broke over Quayle's *Murphy Brown* remarks, but his statement on the riots was mostly forgotten in the ensuing fray. President Bush's spokesman, Marlin Fitzwater, made a fumbling attempt at praising the show's "pro-life values" because the fictional character chose not to have an abortion. The Bush administration had been avoiding bringing up abortion because the Republican Party was in turmoil over the issue. Several polls showed a large percentage of Republicans who wanted a pro-choice plank in the party's platform. Bush feared these Republicans would move toward Perot, who supported the pro-choice position.

Bush tried to back away from both Fitzwater and Quayle by saying, "Children should have the benefit of being born into families with a mother and a father who will give them love and care and attention all their lives." But he added that this "is not always easy, not always possible." Quayle, for his part, stood his ground, saying, "My point is that this is typical Hollywood, glamorizing something that is wrong with society."

Clinton, attending a fundraiser in Miami, came close to siding with Quayle by saying, "I think [the *Murphy Brown* show's] impact on Los Angeles was marginal. There's a lot of violence on television that may have a bigger impact on what happened in Los Angeles than Murphy Brown's sitcom." But Clinton insisted that he did not approve of out-of-wedlock births. "I agree that that's not the example we want to set for our children."

Perot, in Frankfort, Kentucky, to file petitions to get his name on the state's ballot, found it all amusing. "Only in America would that be a front-page story," he said. "So, it must have been a very slow day in Washington....I just thought it was goofy."

A few days later, Hillary Clinton weighed in on the *Murphy Brown* debate. Speaking to students at Santa Clara University in California, Hillary Clinton said of Quayle, "I wonder if he lives in the same America we live in, if he sees the same things we see. Part

of what it means to believe in family values is to value every family."
She cited Clinton's mother, who was widowed three months before
he was born and was forced to leave the boy with his grandparents
while she attended nursing school. "I wish people in high office
understood the real problems people in this country face," she
said.

By late in the week, the "family values" debate was in full swing,
with both Clinton and Bush campaigning in Cleveland for the
Ohio primary, coming up on June 2. Bush, speaking at a fundraiser,
said, "I know that there are those who are deprived, who are born
into almost hopeless situations, but there are all kinds of ways that
we can help....We have got to find ways to strengthen the American family....This has nothing to do with *Murphy Brown*."

Clinton told Cleveland's City Club that "of course there's a values
crisis in America. But there's an action gap as well. Addressing one
without the other isn't a plan of action—it's posturing to distract
from inaction."

Bush tackled the critics who accused him of using code words
like "welfare," saying, "it's not a racist thing" to want to overhaul
the welfare system. "This isn't what we're talking about at all. It
isn't black versus white, or Hispanic versus anybody else. It's
what's fair and right. We've got to give some dignity to the family
and the way to do it is to reform the welfare system and we're
going to keep on trying."

The May 26 primary in Arkansas was approaching, and Clinton
made plans to return home for a Memorial Day weekend parade
and rally sponsored by his biggest supporters in Arkansas. The
sponsors insisted that the event was to honor Clinton's achievements in Arkansas, but it promised all the trappings of a national
political show.

Clinton had been dogged throughout his campaign by a group
known as ACT UP—the AIDS Coalition to Unleash Power. The
group's main purpose was to focus public awareness on what the
group believed was a lack of government action in dealing with the
rampant disease, acquired immune deficiency syndrome. The
organization insisted that it was not strictly composed of homosexuals although its most visible members were gay activists. ACT UP
was badgering Clinton because the Arkansas legislature had

passed a law in 1977 that made sexual relations between persons of the same sex a misdemeanor crime. At the time, Clinton served as Arkansas attorney general.

In 1991, a state legislator, Vic Snyder of Little Rock, tried to change the law, known as the sodomy stature, but his efforts were quashed by a legislative committee. Clinton was silent on the law in 1977 and 1991. On May 20, several gay activists met with members of his gubernatorial staff and later with his campaign staff. Shortly after the meeting, Clinton's campaign issued a statement saying, "Governor Clinton says he did not support the law at the time it was passed and he doesn't believe it should be on the books now."

After the statement was released, three groups—ACT UP, the Arkansas Gay and Lesbian Task Force and the Arkansas AIDS Brigade—held a news conference to commend Clinton's statement. The groups, however, asked Clinton to issue an executive order banning state discrimination on the basis of sexual orientation. Clinton had already pledged to issue a similar federal order if elected president. A spokesman for the governor's staff said such an order for Arkansas was being researched.

The parade and rally in downtown Little Rock on May 23 attracted a friendly crowd of about 3,500, although a few environmental activists and ACT UP protesters held signs and attempted, without much success, to attract attention. Clinton's Arkansas supporters weren't prepared for the crush of Secret Service agents, boom microphones and jostling photographers who forced much of the crowd away from the candidate.

Clinton, with his penchant for remembering faces, greeted many people by name as they pressed toward him. He had regained his health, lost weight and acquired a tan from his fitness routine. Hillary Clinton and Chelsea accompanied him in the parade, and they were joined by actress Mary Steenburgen, television producer Harry Thomason (both native Arkansans) and actress Markie Post of the popular *Night Court* television show.

At a rally after the parade, Clinton again went on the offensive on the "family values" theme, declaring, "There's been a lot a talk about family values lately, but I consider myself to be a pro-family, pro-growth, pro-job, pro-education, pro-choice Democrat."

The Arkansas primary was only three days away, and Clinton needed a strong showing to demonstrate to the rest of the nation that he had the support of the people he had governed for more than eleven years. Polls indicated Clinton would get his big win, but there were a few nagging doubts. The primary would be the first test for Clinton in Arkansas since the scandals broke over Gennifer Flowers, draft evasion and marijuana smoking. The Arkansas voter is unpredictable, and no one know that better than Clinton, who was still smarting from his defeat in 1980.

Jerry Brown made a last stand in Arkansas, flying in on Sunday, Memorial Day, and heading for the state's distressed Delta region to spend the night with an impoverished family. He slept in the family's ramshackle house, which had no running water, and rose the next morning to wash his face in a pan on the table outside. Still trying to showcase Clinton's neglect at home, Brown said, "I'm never going to stop this campaign. I don't care how I finish. There are just too many forgotten people....These are the places that are forgotten."

Brown created few ripples. In contrast to the media crush around Clinton during his parade, only three reporters—two from Arkansas and one from the Los Angeles Times—covered Brown's Delta visit.

Arkansans have come to expect a screwball ballot when they step into the voting booth. It was no different on May 26, when Democratic voters found that their choices were Clinton, Brown, "uncommitted" and Lyndon Larouche. The state Democratic Party had allowed Larouche on the ballot, even though he had been a fringe candidate in a previous presidential election and was now serving a fifteen-year sentence in a federal penitentiary for tax evasion and mail fraud.

Clinton took 68 percent of the vote, over 341,000, a bit lower than the predicted 70 percent. The uncommitted delegates received 18 percent. Jerry Brown garnered 11 percent and Larouche mopped up the rest.

Clinton picked up twenty-nine of Arkansas's thirty-six delegates to the Democratic National Convention. The rest went to the "uncommitted" category. Clinton also captured the Kentucky primary and the Idaho caucuses on the same day. George Bush easily won the Arkansas Republican primary with 45,729 votes to

Pat Buchanan's 6,648. Bush had long since acquired enough delegates to secure the nomination, but Clinton was still about one hundred delegates shy of the 2,145 needed for a smooth convention in New York.

The end of the primary season was a week away, with voting in six states—California, Ohio, New Jersey, Alabama, Montana and New Mexico—on June 2. California alone held 348 delegates, while the other states combined offered a total of 352 delegates. Jerry Brown, the former governor of California, was still immensely popular in that state. He and his father, Pat Brown, a retired politician, had never lost a primary in California.

Clinton had plenty of worries in California, but trouble was brewing elsewhere. Perot was gaining more media attention and had the potential to siphon voters from both Clinton and Bush. Several polls put Perot at the top, Bush second and Clinton finishing an embarrassing third. Clinton's tide seemed to be ebbing as Perot's surge of "plain Texas talk" splashed across the front pages and the television screens.

By the end of May, Perot had qualified for the ballot in eleven states, even though he still called himself an undeclared candidate. Perot had promised that if elected president he would hold "electronic town hall meetings" using satellite hookups across the nation. Under such a system, the public could have a direct back-and-forth dialogue with Perot.

On Friday, May 29, Perot held a satellite rally in Orlando, Florida, with two-way hookups in Ohio, Alabama, Kansas, Wyoming and Idaho. Perot and the Orlando crowd could hear the cheers from rallies in the other states, but there was no direct questioning of the candidate over the satellite connection.

Perot told the crowds, "If you don't have the stomach for [a hard-fought election], then let's not try it. But if we don't do it, we're not going to leave our children the kind of country our parents left us. It's that simple."

Reporters in Orlando asked Perot about a statement he had made earlier in the week on ABC's *20/20* news program, in which Perot said he would not appoint known homosexuals or adulterers to his cabinet.

Perot explained that he was talking about the nomination process, specifically the Senate hearings on Clarence Thomas's nomination to the Supreme Court. Those hearings exploded in controversy when a former employee, Anita Hill, accused Thomas of sexual harassment.

"I realized...the people in the confirmation process would destroy that person forever," Perot said. "But in terms of respect for individuals' rights, those are fundamental in our country....I don't feel it's the government's responsibility to get involved in people's lives."

He was also asked about his opposition to the Persian Gulf war, which Perot believed was unnecessary and merely a cynical effort at improving President Bush's ratings in the polls. "I want you to know I will not go to war to prove my manhood," Perot responded.

The next day, Perot attended a rally in Little Rock to get his name on the Arkansas ballot. State law required an independent party to hold a convention of at least six people, with four of them from each of the state's congressional districts. No petitions or signatures were necessary. "It's very simple. You can even have your convention in a small bathroom, I guess," a state election official told the *Democrat-Gazette.*

The rally was held in the Statehouse Convention Center, less than a block from where Clinton held his rally only a week before. It attracted a little more than three thousand people, about the same number that attended the Clinton function. For ballot purposes, Perot's party was called the Independent Party, and a retired navy vice admiral, James Stockdale, was listed as the vice presidential candidate. Stockdale had allowed his name to be used in Arkansas and other states until Perot formally selected a running mate.

Perot never specifically mentioned Clinton or Bush at the rally, but aimed his familiar Texas metaphors at the political establishment. "It's time to pick up a shovel and go clean out the barn," he told the cheering crowd.

Marilyn Quayle, wife of Vice President Dan Quayle, had recently accused Perot of trying to buy the presidency. Perot responded by saying, "That's right. I'm buying it for the people of the United States because they can't afford it."

The closest Perot came to mentioning Clinton was when he talked about growing up in Texarkana, Texas, which is near Clinton's birthplace. "Did you ever think you'd see a presidential campaign where you had one boy from Texarkana and another from Hope, Arkansas, in the same campaign?" he asked.

While Perot was stirring up the folks back home, Clinton was putting all of his energy into California. He had scrapped campaigning appearances in Ohio and New Jersey in order to focus on California and prevent an upset by Jerry Brown. Polls showed them essentially tied in that state. Clinton told reporters that Brown might win the primary.

Appearing on David Frost's television show on the Public Broadcasting System, Clinton said he had made a serious mistake by fumbling the marijuana question early in the campaign.

"I was dumb as a post the way I handled that," Clinton said, admitting he should have answered the question in full when first asked by Arkansas reporters. "That would have been that, and it would have been over," he said.

The day before the election, Brown said Clinton would receive enough delegates to secure the nomination, but he insisted Clinton could not be elected president, calling Clinton's campaign a "suicide mission."

On that same day, Clinton held rallies in the San Francisco Bay area, Fresno and the Westwood Plaza on the campus of the University of California at Los Angeles. The crowd of about three thousand at UCLA contained several supporters of Brown, Perot and Bush who attempted to shout down the candidate.

Clinton addressed them directly, saying, "I know there have been some hecklers in the audience today, but let me tell you something. There are some people from Arkansas here today who know the truth." Clinton pointed to several Arkansans who had come to California to campaign with him. "So, if you want to know what Hillary and I have tried to do at home, ask these legislators, ask these citizens, ask these people who live there, instead of these people who came here once again to divide the American people instead of listening and learning and unity."

On June 2, eight months after he had stood in front of the Old State House to declare his presidential campaign, Clinton had secured the Democratic nomination with a sweep of the final six states, including California. He had started late, vanquished six opponents, weathered numerous scandals and ill health to get to this point.

Clinton took 48 percent of the vote in California, compared to Jerry Brown's 40 percent, and had much larger margins in the other five states. Clinton's 189 delegates in California alone were more than enough needed for the nomination.

Yet Clinton was in trouble. He was still placing third behind Perot and Bush in several nationwide surveys. Exit polls in California showed Perot garnering enough strength to push Clinton to the bottom. There was talk of a three-way tie for the presidency, in which case the House of Representatives would make the selection.

It seemed that no matter how tough the battle or how convincing the victory, Clinton was always shadowed by defeat. Once again, he was having to come from behind.

"Winning this election is not what's at stake here," Clinton warned his supporters in California on the night of June 2. "Winning the fight for America's future is what's at stake here. And what I came here tonight to promise you is that I will stay up late and get up early and work hard as long as it takes to turn this country around and give it back to the American people."

During the bitter New Hampshire winter, Bill Clinton had christened himself the Comeback Kid. Now, as summer stretched out before him, he faced the unknown complexities of a challenge from a third-party candidate. Surely, Bill Clinton must have wondered if he had made his last comeback.

19

The Elusive Answers

When in doubt, tell the truth.
—Mark Twain

CAN BILL CLINTON BE A WORLD LEADER? HE TALKS AT GREAT LENGTH about the necessity of America playing a dominant role in a global economy. Does he have the courage to defend America's interests in whatever this global economy turns out to be? Does he have the leadership to face down the powerful medical and insurance industries, a huge business lobby *and* a dissipated Congress in order to get his national health care program installed? Does he really believe he can acquire a tax cut for the middle class without digging a deeper hole in the deficit?

George Bush, with the exception of the Persian Gulf war, has failed to demonstrate much leadership, or even much interest, in such important areas. Can Bill Clinton, untested by the fires of the presidency, do what Bush and his predecessors could not?

Is Bill Clinton a leader, or does he just want to be president?

There is no doubt that the 1992 campaign is the culmination of his ambitions. In his troublesome antidraft letter of 1969 he talked of worrying about his "political viability" and said, "For years I have worked to prepare myself for a political life characterized by both practical political ability and concern for rapid social progress."

269

The key to that statement lies in two words: "For years ..." When Clinton wrote that letter, he was only twenty-three. He had worked on a Senate committee and had established contacts with Washington's politicians, theorists and most influential writers, all before he had graduated from Georgetown University. He had soaked up Washington. He knew where all the power levers were and who operated them. It is arguable that in 1979, when Clinton was a thirty-two-year-old governor of an obscure state, he knew more about power-brokering in Washington than President Jimmy Carter.

Throughout his years as governor of Arkansas, Clinton spent an enormous amount of time in Washington, cultivating his contacts, cementing his alliances and perfecting his knowledge of the power structure. Clinton may know Washington as well or better than any politician in the United States, George Bush included.

The four most overused words in the campaign are "change," "anger" and "global economy." All of the Democratic candidates talked of a "global economy," both in the present and future tense. But none has defined this "global economy." Sometimes it appears to be a code phrase meaning "Japan" or "Germany" or "Eastern Europe." At other times it's just something ominous somewhere out there, like an asteroid about to hit the Earth.

They all talked of a nameless, faceless "anger" that they detected in the public, supposedly focused at America's leadership, or nonleadership. It's an expression of the public's exasperation with the power structure. But all of the candidates exempted themselves as targets of the "anger." They denied that they had any hand in creating this sorry mess that everybody is "angry" about, although all of the candidates except Ross Perot have been influential politicians for decades. It is strange that this "anger" is only detected every four years, when there is a presidential election.

As for "change," Clinton has used it in nearly every other paragraph. Even George Bush has taken to talking about "change," the very antithesis of conservatism.

But can Clinton really change anything? A better question is: Did he really change anything as governor? Arkansas has been destitute since it became a territory of the United States in 1819.

When it was admitted as a state in 1836, its population was around twenty thousand, but that number is unreliable because blacks and Indians may or may not have been counted. These few people were scattered over an area slightly larger than England. It was a frontier state, attracting land speculators, shysters, fugitives from justice and a few upstanding pioneer families. Its first years were marked by internecine fights among politicians who were more interested in land-grabbing than establishing a government.

The state took a disastrous course when it joined the Confederacy. Its treasury was emptied. After the war, worthless bonds were issued and the state became mired in debt and more factional fighting, some of it violent. National economic panics and depressions further sapped the state's strength. Poor land practices destroyed much of the farmable soil during the remainder of the nineteenth century.

At the beginning of the twentieth century there were few passable roads and little or no industry. There was one glimmer of hope: Engineers had learned how to drain the swamps and wetlands of eastern Arkansas into the Mississippi River, turning the bottomland into fertile ground for huge farms. The blacks and poor whites who lived in this area could survive by working as sharecroppers. Meanwhile, a few small industries were being established in the metropolitan area of Little Rock.

The Depression of the 1930s again robbed the state of what little money it had accumulated. Thousands of Arkansans joined their Oklahoma neighbors in the trek to California. In the 1940s, mechanized farming began to replace human labor in east Arkansas. This forced another migration as blacks moved north to Chicago and Detroit to find industrial jobs.

By 1950 the population patterns were established: The remaining blacks were in the flatlands of eastern and southeastern Arkansas, some finding jobs on the big, plantationlike farms, but most living on government subsistence. The mountainous western and northern sections were mostly white, the majority being poor farmers and a few middle-class merchants.

The huge forests of western and southern Arkansas attracted several timber and paper industries, which brought thousands of good jobs but created a legacy of questionable land management policy. The metropolitan areas around Little Rock and Fort Smith had acquired a number of industries, and these cities were experiencing an influx of white and black job-seekers from Arkansas's outlands.

Although Arkansas had been part of the Confederacy and had seen its share of violent racial strife, much of that seemed to be a thing of the past as whites and blacks struggled to make a living. Many Arkansans were taken by surprise when Governor Orval Faubus decided to make Little Rock the site of a civil rights showdown in 1957. The famous black composer, William Grant Still, who was born in Little Rock in 1893, said in his memoirs of his boyhood in Arkansas:

> I knew neither wealth nor poverty, for I lived in a comfortable middle-class home, with luxuries such as books, musical instruments and phonograph records. All of this was the result of my having had the good fortune to have been born to intelligent, forward-looking parents, as well as to the fact that Little Rock, where I grew up, was considered by many of us to be an enlightened community in the South. This was true to such an extent that in later years, when the city's name was splashed over headlines the length and breadth of the world, those of us who had lived there were incredulous. We could not believe that of Little Rock, because it was contrary to so much that we had known and experienced.
>
> It is true that there was segregation in Little Rock during my boyhood, but my family lived in a mixed neighborhood and our friends were both white and colored. So were my playmates. In many instances, their friendship lasted into adulthood.
>
> So, while I was aware of the fact that I was a Negro, and once in a while was reminded of it unpleasantly, I was generally conscious of it in a positive way, with a feeling of pride. At the same time, my association with people of both racial groups gave me the ability to conduct myself as a person among people instead of as an inferior among superiors. The fact that this could be done at all in the South represents, to me at least, an open-mindedness on the part of so many other residents of Little Rock.

But Little Rock and Arkansas were to be marked indelibly by the events of 1957. The state was yanked backward again, lumped with Mississippi and Alabama as a monument to inequality. It is still struggling to recover.

In the late 1960s and early 1970s the state enjoyed a succession of progressive governors. Winthrop Rockefeller, grandson of John D. Rockefeller, moved to Arkansas from New York after World War II to start a cattle ranch. He used his influence to entice New York bankers to invest in Arkansas industry and was soon drawn into politics, mostly in a futile effort to revitalize the state's Republican Party. In 1966, after Faubus had stepped down, Rockefeller was elected governor over Democrat Jim Johnson, who had run on a segregationist platform. Arkansans were fed up with hatred and divisiveness, and proclaimed their views by electing Rockefeller.

A liberal Democrat, Dale Bumpers, replaced Rockefeller after a couple of terms. Moderate Democrat David Pryor replaced Bumpers when Bumpers went to the U.S. Senate. Pryor joined the U.S. Senate soon after, leaving the governor's seat to the young idealist, Bill Clinton.

Clinton's ideals were put to the test. He was shouldering a hundred and fifty years of dismal state history. In his first year as governor, 1979, the state's per capita income was $6,183, the next-to-lowest figure in the United States (Mississippi was last). The national average was $7,820. In 1991, when Clinton had been governor for eleven years, the state's per capita income was $14,753, compared to the national average of $19,082. The state now ranked forty-seventh, above Utah, West Virginia and Mississippi. Its 4.1 percent gain over its 1990 ranking was the sixth largest in the United States—a modest advance, to say the least, but a significant one in a state as poor as Arkansas.

The gain can be attributed to a number of factors, but part of the credit should go to a 1985 law that gave manufacturers a tax break for new investments. That tax break created thousands of new jobs and preserved thousands more. The law was part of Clinton's industrial policy. The tax break is controversial, because sales and income taxes were raised to make up the difference. Still, it has kept a number of Arkansans employed, and thus able to pay taxes.

Clinton's philosophy in the last few years has been to attract and keep industry, almost at any cost. That philosophy has created a number of environmental problems. A study of the problems, the *1991–92 Green Index*, ranked Arkansas forty-eighth in overall environmental health. Clinton has formed advisory committees, urged "voluntary" guidelines and ordered stiffer fines for violators, yet the problems continue.

The environmental troubles illuminate a weakness in Clinton's economic policy of uniting government and private industry in solving problems: Almost always, industry has to be forced to spend money on environmental protection. Voluntary compliance is all but a failure in Arkansas, as evidenced by animal waste pollution in the northwest sector. Clinton has admitted that he has been too lax in some areas.

"I've made the choice from time to time for jobs in a poor state," he said in a speech in Philadelphia in April 1992. "But I've learned something that George Bush and his advisers don't understand: to reject the false choice between economic growth and environmental protection. Today, you can't have a healthy economy without a healthy environment."

Arkansans wonder why it took him so long to come to that realization.

Clinton has had a measure of success in education in Arkansas. Before he created the reforms of 1983, Arkansas schools were falling into chaos. There was little money. There were no real standards to measure achievement. Bill and Hillary Clinton worked feverishly to institute a controlled change of that situation. Today all schools in Arkansas offer courses in physics, chemistry, foreign languages and computer science; before 1983, many schools offered none of those courses.

The state now ranks third in the nation in the percentage of its total state and local budgets spent on schools. Almost 42 percent of its budget goes to education, compared to a national average of 35 percent. About 77 percent of all ninth-graders go on to finish high school; the national average is around 72 percent. Arkansas's improvement was a result of a law passed by Clinton that took driver's licenses away from students who did not stay in school. Clinton has been an adamant supporter of school health clinics, where birth control information is provided, in the face of virulent opposition from the state's conservative religious groups.

Clinton did not solve all of Arkansas's education problems, or even most of them. And if he merely halted the backward slide of education, he initiated an incremental change that, if perpetuated, promises to pay off in years to come. He instilled in Arkansans an awareness of the importance of education. That may prove to be his most valuable accomplishment.

He has appointed a number of blacks to high positions in state government. He has tried to get a civil rights bill passed that would bar discrimination in hiring and promotion, but the measure has been foiled by the legislature.

But what else did he change in Arkansas? Not much. The state's environment is in real trouble, and the policies to protect it are inadequate. Arkansas's inequitable tax code preys upon the people who can least afford to pay. Pervasive poverty keeps the state near the bottom of every comparison list. Health problems in the poor areas of eastern Arkansas resemble those of Third World countries.

What does Clinton say when these problems are raised? He points to Arkansas law, which requires a balanced budget and forbids deficit spending. All of these programs need money desperately, but there is only so much money available. When that's spent, the programs go begging. Bill Clinton, the thinker, the man of "change," the man who says the old-line Democrats must abandon their "tax-and-spend" approach, has come up with no ideas to solve that conundrum, except to raise the sales tax.

Bill Clinton has the knowledge and capability to effect "change." The question remains as to whether he has the courage to do it. In several recent legislative sessions, Clinton, the populist, had the opportunity to take on the state's corporate interests and bring a balance to the tax code. He chose not to fight.

It is, of course, unfair to believe one man can solve in eleven years what no one else was able to do in a hundred and fifty. As Donald R. Market, an economics researcher at the University of Arkansas, told the *New York Times*, "I don't know if a Bill Clinton or any other governor can turn a poor state into a rich one."

But, as Arkansas activist Brownie Ledbetter told the *Washington Post*, it is troubling that Clinton "has amassed so much political capital over the years that he could use to change things, but he hasn't used it."

What cannot be ignored is Clinton's huge base of support in

Arkansas. By April 1992, he had raised $11 million for his presidential bid. More than $2 million had come from Arkansas, a state with a population of 2.3 million. These people, who have been watching him for nearly two decades, apparently believe in his leadership ability.

* * *

Clinton's ideas and plans for America tumble out so fast, it is difficult to keep up with them. Several of his proposals would go a long way in restoring the average American's faith in government. His "play or pay" plan for national health care is one of his most attractive ideas. Under this proposal, employers would be forced to insure their workers or pay a special tax into a fund that would provide government coverage. Health care is a top concern in America today, and Clinton's plan seems to be the most equitable of those suggested so far.

On the education front, he offered two perceptive ideas: his "apprenticeship" program, which would provide vocational training for students who don't want to go to college, and his "domestic GI Bill," which would allow students to borrow money for college and pay it back through small incremental payments or through government service. The "GI" program was so attractive that President Bush borrowed it for his platform. Clinton is also stressing education—with a greater emphasis on science and mathematics—that would prepare Americans to compete in the "global economy." He wants full financing of Head Start, a prekindergarten program to prepare low-income children for school.

Clinton wants banks to cap their credit card interest rates, an idea that is sure to appeal to the average American. He would limit tax deductions for companies paying excessive salaries. He has not defined "excessive," but has hinted that it would be salaries of more than $1 million. More problematic is his "industrial policy" approach to furthering a partnership between business and the federal government. He favors "microenterprise" banks that would provide loans to small businesses or start-up businesses that can't find credit anywhere else. He would require companies to devote a percentage of their payroll to training workers.

Clinton has had a difficult time getting his policies across to the public. Much of the blame for this muted message lies with the press and television, which choose to serve up only small particles of information. The rest of the blame lies with the candidate himself. His tripartite New Covenant is brimming with ideas, but they seem to be spun from dreams. Some of his proposals are so complex, so bound by theory, that they are impossible to transmit to the average American. When Clinton talks of transcending the traditional distinctions of liberal and conservative and transcending the concepts of Democrat and Republican, he transcends the understanding of most Americans.

Many of Clinton's ideas, such as his health care plan, are firmly grounded in reality. When he uses plain talk, these ideas come alive. These plans are not mere dreams, but rather are a vivid blueprint for restoring self-confidence to America.

Some polls have shown that H. Ross Perot's maverick campaign is a bigger threat to the Democrats than to the Republicans. Perot is benefiting from what former President Richard Nixon calls "media steroids." The media were captivated by his swashbuckling business tactics and his curious platform of some liberal planks (pro-choice) and some conservative ones (the line-item veto). Perot has been the least specific of the candidates in his wild promises to control the deficit and reform the budget-making process. He has become irritable when television commentators tried to pin him down on his ideas.

If Perot succeeds in getting on the ballots of all fifty states, he will undergo the intense media scrutiny that Clinton endured. He is a hard-nosed businessman, accustomed to having his way, who will not suffer media questions gladly. Perot appeals to the disgruntled "none-of-the-above" voters, but is not likely to threaten either Clinton or Bush when the shallowness of his proposals is exposed and the media lose interest in him.

* * *

Paul Tsongas, writing in *Newsday* shortly after he halted his campaign, said there is a "general sense that Bush is controlled by his polling data and will never be mistaken for a man willing to suffer defeat in behalf of hard truths. Even in the business community there is growing frustration and anger about a leader who refuses to lead because he is the prisoner of his pollsters."

If the campaign becomes one of ideas and issues, Clinton will win. George Bush's few proposals have come only at the prodding of his campaign advisers, and his best ideas seem to have been appropriated from Bill Clinton. Most Americans want to vote for Bush because Clinton is an unknown quantity, but Bush refuses to give them a reason to vote for him.

If it becomes a campaign of personal attacks, in which the name "Willie Horton" is replaced by "Gennifer Flowers," Clinton will lose. He is vulnerable on the character question, because it is a no-win situation. If he gives a straight answer about the reputed indiscretions, he might lose the voters who disapprove of such behavior. If he keeps hedging, he might fail to win the votes of people who believe that he does not tell the truth when it is not in his best interest. The issue hangs over his head like a cloud; it follows him everywhere. And it is likely to become a thunderhead when the Republican campaign starts rolling. Why doesn't he address it once and for all, giving direct answers to direct questions? The unspoken answer: Because he does not want to lose.

If Bush is a "prisoner of his pollsters," Clinton is a captive to his fear of losing. Bill Clinton hates to lose. In his eighteen years in politics he has lost only two elections. And the first defeat, his congressional bid in 1974, was an admitted experiment, a sparring round against the champ.

But the second loss, in 1980, when he was tossed out of the governor's chair for two years, crushed Clinton's self-esteem and sent him into an emotional tailspin. He became withdrawn, muttering to his friends that Arkansas didn't deserve a man of his ability. He now professes to believe that he learns more from tough times than from easy experiences. What he learned in 1980 is that a political loss, especially one that threatens his career, hits him deep in the psyche. Losing made him terrified of losing.

Even the strongest Clinton supporters admit he will do almost anything to win. And they admit that this is his greatest weakness. The American public has picked up on this Clinton characteristic. In a *Time* magazine survey taken after the New York primary, 67 percent of the people polled said they believed Clinton would say anything to get elected president.

Clinton, of course, denies this charge. He blames this prevailing cynicism on the media. He says his message is distorted and filtered through the skeptical media, which passes this skepticism on to the public. He has a good argument; reporters and editors, like politicians, are bound by no creed other than their own. But even if sound, the argument is probably moot now. That skepticism is firmly planted in the public mind, and Clinton will have a devil of a time weeding it out. Besides, blaming the media is an exercise in futility. And Clinton, who has lived under the microscope for nearly two decades, knows this better than anyone.

Clinton must go after what Tsongas calls the "hard truths." The United States has a $3 trillion deficit that is multiplying every minute. Clinton, who talks of the future so frequently, must offer a concrete solution to the deficit problem, even if it is a painful solution for most Americans. Clinton "must be willing to suffer defeat," as Tsongas said.

The theme of Clinton's New Covenant is that real economic and social "change" must start with each individual, that every person must play a role in bringing America into a new understanding of itself, that every person must believe that he or she is participating in the shaping of a nation.

As an individual American, Bill Clinton should follow the course he has set out for others. He must examine himself—his strengths, his abilities, his faults, his weaknesses. And he must, above all, be honest about it. He must ask himself this question: Is he willing to expend his political capital to risk losing, in order to become a true leader? And he must answer it.

Only after he has answered that question in public, only after he has proven to himself and the country that he is willing to risk his political career to be a leader, will he be able to inspire Americans to believe that they can take risks, that they are not helpless, that they truly hold the power to change their lives and their nation.

Source Notes

Chapter 1. A Sense of Mortality

Much of the early information on Bill Clinton comes from an interview with Virginia Kelley by Charles Flynn Allen on March 10, 1991. Other sources are the *Current Biography Yearbook, 1991* (H. W. Wilson Company) and *Arkansas Gazette* articles from July 24, 1987 and July 31, 1987. The quotes from Bill Clinton are from an interview with Allen conducted on March 15, 1991. The quotes from Criner are from an interview with Allen conducted on February 5, 1991. Staley quotes are from a February 5, 1991, interview with Allen. Root quotes are from a February 18, 1991, interview with Allen. The quotes from Spurlin are from an interview with Allen on March 11, 1991.

Chapter 2. The Scholar Sees the World

The quotes from Senator David Pryor are from an interview conducted by Allen on February 15, 1991. The report on Clinton's Georgetown reunion is from an *Arkansas Gazette* article by Maria Henson published on June 5, 1988. The Staley, Kelley, Bill Clinton and Criner quotes are from the interviews cited above. The quotes from Strobe Talbott are from an interview conducted with Allen on March 14, 1991. Clinton's talk with columnist David Broder is from *Laboratories of Democracy* by David Osborne (Harvard Business School Press, 1988).

Chapter 3. An Experiment in Arkansas

Clinton, Criner, Kelley quotes are cited above. Quotes form state Senator Lu Hardin are from an interview conducted by Allen on February 5, 1991. Quotes from state Senator Morril Harriman Jr. are from an interview with Allen on February 6, 1991. The quotes of Clinton by Peter Applebome are from a March 8, 1992, article in the *New York Times Magazine*. David Pryor quotes are cited above. Quotes from Hillary Rodham Clinton are from an interview with Allen on February 15, 1991. The quote from Ernest Dumas is from Osborne's *Laboratories*, cited above. Gail Sheehy's article on Hillary Clinton appeared in the May 1992 issue of *Vanity Fair*. The quotes from Jim Guy Tucker are from an interview with Allen on February 6, 1991.

Chapter 4. The Born Politician

The Osborne quote is from *Laboratories*, cited above. The *Gazette* quote is from an editorial of November 7, 1974. The quotes from John Robert Starr are from his book *Yellow Dogs and Dark Horses* (August House, 1987). The quotes from the *Log Cabin Democrat*, the *Searcy Daily Citizen* and the *Helena World* appeared in a compilation of newspaper reactions printed in the *Gazette* on May 29, 1977. The Criner quotes are cited above.

Chapter 5. A Snowball of Political Misfortune

The quotes from Osborne are cited above. Starr's quote is from *Yellow Dogs*. Criner is cited above. *The Springdale News* quote appeared in a collection of newspaper reactions in the *Gazette* on November 16, 1980. Clinton's quotes are cited above. The *Gazette* editorial on Clinton's farewell appeared on January 14, 1981.

Chapter 6. The First Comeback

The quote from John Brummett is from a *Gazette* article on February 9, 1982. The quote from Starr is from an interview conducted by Allen on February 6, 1991. The quote from Ernest Dumas appeared in a *Gazette* column on November 5, 1982. The Robert Johnston quote is from a *Gazette* article of November 4, 1982.

Chapter 7. The Education Revolution

The quote from Dumas appeared in a column in the *Gazette* on September 7, 1983. The Kelley quotes are cited above. The quotes from Betsey Wright are from an interview conducted by Allen on February 16, 1991.

Chapter 8. Preserving the Standards

The quote from Starr is from the interview cited above. The quotes from Sid Johnson and Cora McHenry are from an interview with Allen on February 22, 1991. The quotes from Dr. Paul Root are from an interview with Allen on February 18, 1991. The quotes from Dr. Tommy Venters are from an interview with Allen on February 6, 1991.

Chapter 9. Fine-Tuning an Election Machine

Brummett's theories on Arkansans' attitudes toward a presidential election appeared in a *Gazette* column on February 24, 1987. James Powell's comments on possible presidential candidates appeared in a *Gazette* column on March 9, 1986. Brummett's comments on the "un-veto" appeared in the *Gazette* on April 22, 1987. The quotes from Billy Simpson are from an interview with Allen on March 14, 1991. The comments from consultant Raymond D. Strother were reported by Brummett in a *Gazette* column on July 19, 1987.

Chapter 10. "I Fell on My Sword"

The description of the Atlanta speech is from an interview with Hillary Clinton by Allen on February 15, 1991.

Chapter 11. The Fire of an Election

Brummett's comments on rumors of drug use appeared in a column in the *Gazette* on March 9, 1990.

Chapter 12. The Mud Hits the Fan

David Broder's description of the Nelson-Robinson political fight appeared in the *Washington Post* on May 27, 1990. Broder and several other Washington writers, notably Morton Kondracke of the *New Republic*, have kept a close eye on Clinton and Arkansas politics for more than ten years. The *Spectrum Weekly* article by Gordon Young appeared November 7–13, 1990.

Chapter 13. The Question and the Promise

The report on the Clinton presidential watch appeared in the *Gazette* on April 29, 1991. Max Brantley's quote from Clinton about the Persian Gulf war appeared in a *Gazette* article on January 15, 1991. The Sheffield Nelson quotes are from an interview with Allen on May 7, 1991.

Chapter 14. The New Covenant

The history of the Old State House in the Civil War is from *Our Arkansas* by John L. Ferguson and J. H. Atkinson (Arkansas History Commission). Excerpts from Clinton's speech are from the text in the special edition of the *Arkansas Democrat* printed on October 3, 1991. Brantley's comments appeared in a *Gazette* column on October 4, 1991. Meredith Oakley's and Starr's comments appeared in columns in the *Democrat* on October 3, 1991. Brummett's assessment of Clinton appeared in a column in the *Democrat* on November 3, 1991. The New Covenant excerpts are from "The New Covenant: Responsibility and Rebuilding the American Community" by Governor Bill Clinton, October 23, 1991. In the explanation of the theory of "new paradigms," the authors have oversimplified the definition for the sake of brevity. For a more complete, and more accurate, description of the theory, readers should examine David Osborne's *Laboratories of Democracy* (cited above), which expounds at length on the theory and how Bill Clinton fits into it.

Chapter 15. Up and Down in New Hampshire

James Carville was labeled "The Democrats' Lee Atwater" in the *National Review* on July 29, 1991, and in *Newsweek* on November 11, 1991. The Criner quotes are cited above. Hillary Clinton's quotes are cited above. The excerpts from part three of the New Covenant are from "A New Covenant for American Security" by Governor Bill Clinton, December 12, 1991. Randy Lilleston's comments on Harkin and Kerrey appeared in a commentary in the *Arkansas Democrat-Gazette* on December 15, 1991. Clinton's health care proposal appeared in "A Plan for America's Future" by Governor Bill Clinton, January 12, 1992.

Chapter 16. The Comeback Kid

The account of Larry Nichols's phone calls is taken from an article written by Bill Simmons of the Associated Press that appeared in the *Arkansas Gazette* on January 11, 1988. Clinton's letter to Col. Holmes is as it appeared in the *Arkansas Democrat-Gazette* on February 12, 1992.

Chapter 17. The Woman From Park Ridge

The comprehensive quotes of Hillary Clinton are from an interview conducted by Charles Flynn Allen on February 15, 1991. The speech on teachers v. principals is excerpted from "The Healthy Development of Our Youth," delivered in 1988 at the Atlanta Convention of Southeastern Council of Foundations. The study "Children's Rights: Contemporary Perspectives" was published by Teachers College Press, 1979. Readers interested in other works by Hillary Clinton on the topic of children's legal competence should examine "Children Under the Law (*Harvard Educational Review*, 1982) and "Children's Policies: Abandonment and Neglect" (*Yale Law Journal*, Vol. 86, No. 7, 1977). See also Garry Wills' article entitled

"H.R. Clinton's Case" in the *New York Review of Books*, March 5, 1992, for an extensive overview of Hillary Clinton's writings on children's rights and health care. The quotes of Starr are from a February 6, 1991, interview with Allen.

Chapter 18. Pressing On

The excerpt from Brummett's column is from the *Arkansas Democrat-Gazette* of March 15, 1992. Starr's column appeared in the *Democrat-Gazette* on March 10, 1992. The *Washington Post* article on the Rose Law Firm appeared March 15, 1992. The *Post* article on poultry politics appeared on March 23, 1992. The *New York Post* endorsement of Clinton appeared on April 3, 1992. The Brummett column on black campaigners in New York appeared in the *Democrat-Gazette* on April 12, 1992.

Chapter 19. The Elusive Answers

William Grant Stills's memoir, "My Boyhood in Arkansas," appeared in Volume XXVI, No. 3 of the *Arkansas Historical Quarterly*, Autumn 1967. Paul Tsongas's article appeared in *Newsday* and the *Arkansas Democrat-Gazette* on April 19, 1992. The quote from Brownie Ledbetter appeared in a *Washington Post* article on March 23, 1992. The quote from Donald Market is from a *New York Times* article on April 2, 1992.

Index